STUDIES IN THE NARRATIVE
METHOD OF DEFOE

BY

ARTHUR WELLESLEY SECORD

NEW YORK

RUSSELL & RUSSELL · INC

1963

UNIVERSITY OF ILLINOIS STUDIES
IN
LANGUAGE AND LITERATURE

FIRST PUBLISHED IN 1924
REISSUED, 1963, BY RUSSELL & RUSSELL, INC.
L. C. CATALOG CARD NO: 63—9507
PRINTED IN THE UNITED STATES OF AMERICA

95967

CONTENTS

PREFATORY NOTE

This study, begun in April, 1919, has been made at the suggestion and under the direction of Professor Ernest Bernbaum, to whose kind assistance I am under the deepest obligation. To other members of the University of Illinois Department of English, notably Professor Stuart P. Sherman, who has facilitated the investigation in various ways, and Professor Jacob Zeitlin, who has generously recommended the use of Library funds for the purchase of many expensive volumes, I am likewise indebted. Acknowledgment for assistance and encouragement should be made also to Professor T. C. Pease of the University of Illinois Department of History and to Professor W. P. Trent of Columbia University, who magnanimously offered his services in the course of the work. Professor W. A. Oldfather has helped materially in seeing the book through the press.

Others deserving mention as contributors to the completion of this study are Mrs. R. E. Kennedy and Miss Margaret Hutchins, both of the University of Illinois Library Staff, and Dr. Ruth Kelso, who read for me several otherwise inaccessible works in the British Museum. The Library of Congress, the John Crerar Library of Chicago, and the libraries of Harvard and Yale Universities have freely lent many valuable books which I needed.

Urbana, Illinois,   A. W. Secord.
June 1, 1923.

CHAPTER I

The Defoe Problem

The career of Daniel Defoe is, for a number of reasons, difficult to trace. Problems concerning his life, his character, and his writings have hitherto baffled every effort to solve them. For our meagre knowledge of the facts of his life we are largely dependent upon his own statements, which are not very precise and which too frequently are open to question. It was not till a quarter century ago that such elementary details as the approximate date of his birth, the name of his wife, and the fact that he was married but once (instead of twice, as tradition affirmed) were established.

Of his career, likewise, both as a government agent and as a writer, we are in much uncertainty. Defoe is at the heart of some of the most perplexing political questions of his day. As a lonely and persecuted tool first of Whig and then of Tory ministers, with his integrity suspected on all sides, his activities necessarily must have remained to a large extent secret. And his efforts to cover his tracks in journalistic encounters have further obscured his path. To arrive, therefore, at a fair estimate of his character is extremely difficult.

His earlier biographers, that is to say, those of the first half of the nineteenth century, unhesitatingly set him forth as a man of unimpeachable character—a patriot who stood for principle in the face of every adverse circumstance. But as the details of his governmental services became better known, opinion swung to the other extreme, until it became the fashion, as the late Mr. G. A. Aitken has remarked,[1] "to abuse Defoe as a spy, and to shake the head at the very powers which were formerly extolled. Instead of admiration at his skill in imparting verisimilitude, we are now told that he was a consummate liar." Mr. Aitken's remonstrance seems to have been directed particularly at Professor Minto, but it applies equally well to a number of other writers, among them Leslie Stephen,[2] who credited Defoe with the most amazing talent on record for telling lies. There is good reason to believe, however, that the more recent judgments of Mr. Aitken and Professor Trent are nearer the truth. Famous historical instances cited as evidence of his unparalleled ability to lie like truth prove to be true rather than fictitious records. In the light of this fact, Mr. Aitken pleads for a more lenient

[1] G. A. Aitken, *Romances and Narratives by Daniel Defoe*, I (1899), p. xiii.
[2] *Hours in a Library*, I, (ed. 1907), p. 4; first published 1871-9.

verdict. So, too, Professor Trent,[3] while unable to maintain his faith in Defoe's integrity, believes him not so much a liar as a casuist who, ruined by bitter persecution, thought himself justified in adopting any means of self-defense, but who never deserted a cause he believed to be for the best interest of the nation.

Concerning his writings a number of questions arise. Not ultimately the most important, but certainly the first one is that of his bibliography. What did he write? To understand the significance of this question one has to consider that for thirty or forty years he wrote copiously in both prose and verse on every sort of subject, made use of every medium of publication, and strove for anonymity by every possible subterfuge. Professor Trent's list of titles covers thirteen closely printed pages.[4] Not a few of the items have won their right to stand in the list after a century of hard fighting. The controversy over the "Memoirs of Captain Carleton," for example, dates back to 1830 when Walter Wilson first attributed that work to Defoe. Many still regard it as a genuine memoir. The "Memoirs of a Cavalier" was the subject of a similar dispute until Mr. Aitken stilled opposition, temporarily at least, by including it in his edition of Defoe, though he declined including the "Memoirs of Carleton."

A second question which has been asked with regard to nearly all of Defoe's narratives relates to their character: are they fact or fiction? Attention has already been called to the controversies over the "Memoirs of a Cavalier" and the 'Memoirs of Carleton"; those who opposed the attribution of them to Defoe did so on the ground that they were certainly genuine works of their purported authors. The "Journal of the Plague Year," long listed as history by many librarians, is declared by Professor Cross[5] to be fictitious throughout. A recent writer attempts to establish its historical character. "Captain Singleton," "Robinson Crusoe," and even "Moll Flanders" have at various times received credence. "The Apparition of Mrs. Veal," long confidently asserted to be fictitious, is now definitely established as fact.

Not the least of the problems concerning Defoe as a writer has to do with his methods and materials. We know little of his relation to his predecessors. A thorough examination of the sources of his inspiration and of his materials is needed. To talk of his ability to "lie like truth" is a manifest waste of time until we know something of the frequency of his false statements. To begin such a study is the primary purpose of this dissertation.

Before we enter upon an examination of Defoe's narratives, however, it will be of service to determine somewhat more fully the present

---

[3] *Cambridge History of English Literature,* IX (1913), p. 11.

[4] *Ibid.,* p. 467 ff.

[5] W. L. Cross, *Development of the English Novel* (1902), pp. 29, 30.

state of Defoe scholarship. By this means we shall clear the ground of the rubbish of opinions obviously out of accord with established facts. It is no less important to ascertain what is well grounded. We shall, moreover, get a better idea of those unsettled points upon which this study may throw some light.

Concerning Defoe's narrative skill critical opinion is in accord. From Charles Lamb to Professor Trent, he is proclaimed as a master of the art of telling a story, directly and plausibly, in terse, homely language. Another feature of his compositions which no writer fails to dwell upon is his genius for verisimilitude, secured by the judicious selection of details. It has even been argued that the source of his power and the key to his method is this "minute attention to detail."[6]

This unanimity of opinion does not, however, extend to larger elements of his narratives, such as character portrayal and the handling of plot. One writer finds his characters vividly drawn; a second more cautiously asserts them to be an improvement upon the achievements of previous narrators of prose fiction; a third sees in them only so many different aspects of Defoe himself; to a fourth his characters are mere types of human nature without individuality; others find them wooden or crude. His plots, likewise, are alternately praised for their excellence or censured for their shapelessness and lack of unity. This diversity of opinion arises in part from a natural difference of preferences and tastes, and in part from the fact that these opinions are not based upon the same books or portions of books. It is obvious, for instance, that a judgment founded upon the earlier part of "Colonel Jacque" with its vivid portrayal of the childhood of a young outcast and of his introduction to a life of crime, must differ from one founded upon the book as a whole, which later degenerates into a story of insipid and purposeless adventure with a consequent loss of interest on the part of both author and reader.

That Defoe occupies an important place in the development of English prose fiction no writer on the subject denies. With regard to that more complicated thing, the novel, his position is defined in various ways, according to the conceptions of individual critics of what constitutes a novel. There are those, Jusserand and Professor Saintsbury, for example, who find the novel in existence, if not exactly flourishing, long before Defoe began his longer narratives. Others find in "Robinson Crusoe" the first English novel. Still a third group reserves the term novel for nothing earlier than "Pamela." This diversity of opinion, concerned as it is with externals only, detracts little from the importance of Defoe in the development of the novel, whether he was a brilliant

[6] W. E. Simonds, *English Fiction* (1894), p. 42.

exponent of a form already in existence, the founder of that form, or its needful precursor.

A significant variation of the first view is that advocated by Professor Bernbaum, who has definitely shown two seventeenth century works to be fiction falsely pretending to be authentic biography.[7] Further research, he thinks, will uncover a whole school of such fiction "masquerading as fact." Not the least important point concerning one of these fictions, "The Counterfeit Lady," is that at nearly every point it anticipates the methods and materials of Defoe; that is to say, the methods employed by Defoe in "Moll Flanders," "Colonel Jacque," and "Roxana."

This brings us to one of the most important questions of Defoe's relation to the English novel, that of his literary development: his debt to his predecessors and his own literary growth. Four more or less clearly defined explanations for his definite advent into the field of long narrative, presumably fictitious, one finds in current histories of fiction. These four theories are, in brief, as follows: 1, that these narratives are a continuation of the picaresque tradition which goes back to "Lazarillo de Tormes"; 2, that they grow naturally out of Defoe's unscrupulous and mendacious methods of journalism; 3, that they are an expansion of the biographies, criminal and otherwise, of which the seventeenth and eighteenth centuries were so prolific; and, 4, that they grew out of such works as his moral treatise, "The Family Instructor," and "The Continuation of the Letters of the Turkish Spy."

If we set forth in greater detail these explanations of the amazing outburst of literary energy which "Robinson Crusoe" inaugurated in 1719, we shall better be able to evaluate them. The weakest assumption of the four is the first, which identifies Defoe's fictions with the picaresque tradition of which the adventures of that "witty extravagant," Meriton Latroon, was the chief seventeenth century example in English. Burton[8] dismisses "Robinson Crusoe" as a "picaresque tale" of the elder fiction of adventure. Harold Williams pronounces it a "splendid variation of the picaresque type."[9] For Holliday[10] it begins "along the picaresque lines" with "a few harum-scarum adventures." The Misses Hopkins[11] and Hughes declare it inferior as an example of picaresque fiction to "Singleton." Professor Cross, while allowing that "Robinson

[7] Ernest Bernbaum, *The Mary Carleton Narratives*, 1914; and *Mrs. Behn's Biography a Fiction* (in *Publications of the Modern Language Association*, XXVIII, 1913, p. 432 ff.).
[8] Richard Burton, *Masters of the English Novel*, p. 46.
[9] Harold Williams, *Two Centuries of the English Novel*, p. 22.
[10] Carl Holliday, *English Fiction*, p. 207.
[11] A. B. Hopkins and H. S. Hughes, *The English Novel before the Nineteenth Century*, p. X.

Crusoe" is "something different from the picaresque story to which it is akin," plainly asserts[12] Defoe's indebtedness to the picaresque type when, in his discussion of Head and Kirkman's "English Rogue," he remarks that "they sent their hero on a voyage to the East, and thus began the transformation of the rogue story into the story of adventure as it was soon to appear in Defoe."[13] The obvious inference (strengthened by his uncharitably calling Crusoe a rogue) is that a variation of the picaresque type produced the novel of adventure to which class "Robinson Crusoe" belongs, and that Defoe is indebted to Head and Kirkman (eventually if not directly) for the theme of adventure in foreign lands. In support of this last inference Professor Chandler cites a passage of Latroon's sea journal which he thinks may have influenced Defoe.[14]

That the picaresque story was the source neither of Defoe's inspiration nor of his material has been effectively argued by Professor Chandler, Miss Morgan, and Professor Bernbaum. In the words of the first named,[15] Defoe was the first to turn his back on the jests and tricks of the Italian *Novella* or Spanish romance of roguery for native material. Miss Morgan and Professor Bernbaum add to this the wide difference in tone between the cynical picaresque accounts and the narratives of Defoe.[16] And, finally, Professor Bernbaum points out that when Defoe turned to fiction the picaresque form had been dead for a half century; for, although the early years of the eighteenth century saw several translations of foreign examples, there were no native revivals of the form after the "English Rogue" (1665-1671).

The second theory, that Defoe's sensational journalism led him farther and farther into untruth until he turned wholly to fiction, would seem to identify his development as a novelist with his degeneracy as a citizen. Leslie Stephen[17] has argued that neither Defoe nor Richardson saw the difference between the art of fiction and the art of lying. Defoe had, said that critic,[18] the most amazing talent on record for telling lies. Professor Minto's opinion, identical with this, has already been quoted. Simonds[19] asserts that Defoe "concocted news unblushingly," citing the "Apparition of Mrs. Veal" and the account of the destruction of St. Vincent as examples, and fears that without such preliminary steps in

[12] W. L. Cross, pp. 27, 28.

[13] *Ibid.*, p. 20.

[14] F. W. Chandler, *The Literature of Roguery*, p. 217.

[15] Chandler, p. 286.

[16] Charlotte Morgan, *Rise of the Novel of Manners* (1911), p. 47; Ernest Bernbaum, *The Mary Carleton Narratives*, p. 97.

[17] *Hours in a Library*, I, p. 13.

[18] *Ibid.*, p. 4.

[19] Simonds, p. 41.

mendacity he might never have written his novels. It is assumed by another writer[20] that the persecution which followed the publication of "The Shortest Way," though bitter medicine for its author, taught him nevertheless where his genius lay—he could lie like truth; we are then led on to suppose that, having made this discovery, Defoe was continually on the lookout for opportunities of displaying it. The accounts of Mrs. Veal and of St. Vincent are again cited as instances of it before Defoe finally with his novels crowned all his achievements in the art of deception. Even so recently as 1918 a student of the English novel speaks of the "Storm," the "Apparition," and the "Destruction of St. Vincent" as instances of Defoe's invention of sensational news.[21]

It would be useless to maintain that Defoe was above reproach in the matter of concocting news; but so imperfect is our information that we should be very cautious not to allow a plausible assumption to lead us into untenable grounds. The scantiness of our knowledge should make us extraordinarily careful to read rightly those facts which are known. The amount of fictitious matter in any of Defoe's writings is not an easy thing to determine. Too much stress can not be laid upon the impossibility of telling from internal evidence alone whether a particular piece of Defoe's work is fact or fiction. As Professor Bernbaum has remarked of the seventeenth century criminal biographies, we must not judge a work fictitious "because it chances thus to impress us."[22] Years ago Mr. Aitken discovered that the "Apparition of Mrs. Veal" was an authentic account;[23] and more recently the patient researches of Professor Trent have robbed the other two instances of their value as evidence of Defoe's "creative mendacity"; for his release from Newgate, to which he had been committed for writing the "Shortest Way," preceded by several weeks the November storm of 1703. So that his account of that storm is not the invention of one unable to view its devastation; whether or not there is any invention at all in it we do not know. As for the news item relating to the destruction of the isle of St. Vincent, it likewise proves nothing as to Defoe's "unblushing" concoction of news. The facts are as follows. A rumor of the destruction of St. Vincent reached London, and Defoe, along with other journalists of the day, made use of it in Mist's periodical. There is no reason to suppose that he did so in other than good faith; on the contrary there is evidence to suppose that he continued to believe the rumor after his brother writers had been convinced of its lack of foundation.[24]

[20] W. J. Dawson, *The Makers of English Fiction*, pp. 9-11.
[21] Wilson Follett, *The Modern Novel*, p. 27.
[22] *The Mary Carleton Narratives*, p. 9.
[23] *The Nineteenth Century*, XXXVII (1895), p. 95 ff.
[24] W. P. Trent, *Daniel Defoe*, pp. 59, 156-7.

With discoveries of this nature to warn them, careful critics have become exceedingly wary of positive assertions of the truth or falsity of Defoe's narratives. In contrast with Professor Minto's sweeping dictum,[25] that we cannot accept any statement of Defoe in regard to himself unless it is corroborated by independent testimony is, Mr. Aitken's,[26] that we have no right to disbelieve his solemn protestations unless there is contradictory evidence. "Sometimes he lies, but sometimes he tells the truth," remarks Professor Bernbaum;[27] "the real difficulty is to ascertain his moments of veracity." Until we know more of the character of his narratives, that is, what parts are fact and what fiction, we cannot accurately generalize as to his methods of procedure.

These considerations, however, need not blind us to certain positive values which Defoe's journalistic career had upon his training for the work of novel writing. Beyond doubt it had given him excellent practice in the art of narration: a firmer grasp upon the methods of producing verisimilitude and upon the use of language, and skill in developing incidents. It had, moreover, made him alert to material for exploitation.

The view that Defoe's career as a novelist is to be understood in the light of the biographical productivity of the period is, as stated by its exponents, open to serious objection. There exists, moreover, much careless statement in regard to this development. Professor Minto speaks of Defoe's habit of issuing lives of celebrities upon their decease. "From writing biographies with real names attached to them," he continues, "it was but a short step to writing biographies with fictitious names."[28] Tuckerman likewise asserts that fiction entered his biography just as biography was later to enter his novels.[29] And finally Professor Chandler says that when Defoe "turned from composing criminal pamphlets upon Wild and Sheppard to write 'Moll Flanders' and 'Colonel Jacque,' he merely substituted imaginary for actual beings and enlarged the scale without altering the method of treatment."[30]

This sounds plausible enough, and would indeed be difficult to contradict had the pamphlets upon Sheppard and Wild actually preceded "Moll Flanders" and "Colonel Jacque," both of which were published in 1722. But the life of Sheppard did not appear until 1724, and that of Wild, until 1725. Strangely enough Chandler's careless statement has not only passed uncorrected, but it has since been quoted as an authorita-

[25] William Minto, *Defoe* (in English Men of Letters, VIII, 1895), p. 2.
[26] General Introduction to *Romances and Narratives by Defoe*, I, p. xxxii.
[27] *Mary Carleton Narratives*, p. 7.
[28] Minto, *Defoe*, pp. 134, 137.
[29] Bayard Tuckerman, *History of English Prose Fiction*, (ed. 1882), p. 184.
[30] *Literature of Roguery*, p. 186.

tive utterance by Dunn in his study of English biography.[31]   The chronology is of some importance here; for Defoe's period most prolific of biographies followed instead of preceding the opening of his career as a novelist.   It is indeed presumed that his attention was not drawn to the field of criminal biography until his association with Applebee, the publisher of confessions and speeches of dying criminals, in July, 1720, at which time "Robinson Crusoe" (Parts I and II), the "Memoirs of a Cavalier," and "Captain Singleton" were already in print.

As for the biographies known to have been written by Defoe previously to 1719 (the year in which "Robinson Crusoe" was published), they are neither very numerous nor very significant.   The life of Count Patkul proves to have been, as its title page asserted, written by L(ord) M(olesworth).   There remains, besides the memoirs, such as those of Shrewsbury, written for political purposes, the "Memoirs of Daniel Williams" only (1718).   Williams and Defoe, both dissenters and both vigorous opponents of the Occasional Conformity Bill, were friends; it is, therefore, no evidence that Defoe was in the habit of seizing every opportunity of bringing out a biography that Curll turned to him for a life of Williams. Some history he had written, such as the account of Charles XII of Sweden; but this points in the direction of the "Memoirs of a Cavalier" and the "Memoirs of Carleton," rather than toward "Robinson Crusoe."

The theory, then, that Defoe advanced step by step from authentic biography to biographical fiction is not borne out by the facts.   It is at best an assumption to be accepted with caution.   The resemblance, moreover, of "Robinson Crusoe" to biography is easy to exaggerate; for in spite of the title the story is almost wholly limited to an account of Crusoe's adventures at sea and on his island.   There is, to be sure, some attempt at setting forth his ancestry and the circumstances attending his home life, but not more than is necessary to explain how he came to go to sea.   All other matters of his boyhood and early manhood are passed over entirely; the story ends when, following their deliverance by pirates, he and Friday reach England.[32]

The fourth theory of Defoe's development in the field of fiction is that championed by Mr. Aitken and Professor Trent.   Both men are inclined to regard Defoe's debt to previous writers of fiction as slight, preferring to explain his narratives in terms of his own earlier writings.   For them, however, his journalistic and biographical labors, as steps by which he was led to write fiction, are not so significant as his moral treatises, such as the "Family Instructor," and his continuation of the "Letters of a

---

[31] W. H. Dunn, *English Biography*, p. 86.
[32] This of course considers Part I only.

Turkish Spy." From his moral treatises with their "dramatic setting" to the "novels" was a great step, believed Mr. Aitken, "but the change was one of degree rather than kind. The difference lay chiefly in the prominence now given the story, which took the leading place, hitherto occupied by the moral."[33] That is to say, the story, instead of existing for the moral, is told primarily for its own sake, and the moral is secondary. Professor Trent is more specific, naming the "Family Instructor" as illustrating Defoe's growing interest in fiction and suggesting that these semi-fictions, including the "Letters of the Turkish Spy" (not a moral treatise), may have stimulated him to write "pure fiction."[34]

It is impossible to pass lightly over a view given by these men, to whom every student of Defoe is immeasurably indebted. But one may seriously question its sufficiency. Certainly the "Family Instructor" and "Robinson Crusoe" differ in the extreme in subject matter, purpose, and form.

In summing up the discussion of the foregoing theories, we may dismiss the one asserting that Defoe in his fictions continued the old picaresque tradition as erroneous on the whole, though certain details of that theory are open to further investigation. The other three views emphasizing respectively the place of journalism, biography, and the moral treatises in Defoe's development as a novelist, are, within certain limits, of some positive value. They are not, moreover, mutually exclusive theories; they may, on the other hand, all be considered as different aspects of the same thing. Whether they are fully adequate, or whether some other elements are needed to round them out and complete them, is a question which can be answered only when we have a more thorough knowledge of the materials which Defoe utilized in composing his works.

The bibliography of Defoe has already been mentioned. That the status to which it has been brought is not permanent, Professor Trent would be the first to concede. According to his own statement[35] there are numerous works excluded which have almost as great right to be listed as many of those included. It is not known, moreover, whether certain of the works attributed to him are wholly the product of his pen, or whether he merely revised them or collaborated with others in their composition.

Of the sources of Defoe's narratives we know very little. It has so long been the custom of critics to speak of his genius for circumstantial lying that we are amused at Chatham's supposition that the "Memoirs of a Cavalier" is authentic; we smile tolerantly at the unsophisticated librarian who lists the "Journal of the Plague" as history, or the credulous student of African geography who proclaims Singleton as the discoveror of the

---

[33] General Introduction to *Romances and Narratives by Defoe*, p. xxix.
[34] *Defoe*, pp. 128, 155, 175.
[35] *Cambridge History of English Literature*, IX (1913), pp. 481, 2.

source of the Nile, or the newspaper reporter who wishes his employers to start a fund for purchasing the house in which Crusoe was lodged as a slave of Salee pirates. But the foundation for our superior wisdom is assumption—not fact,—an assumption that these narratives are fabrications, and that the more convincing they are, the more certain is their falsity. Critics have been ready to hazard off-hand opinions of Defoe's method of handling his material, but the patient investigation necessary to a sound understanding of what that material actually was has been, like the traveller to Jericho, passed by on the other side. There have been some serious efforts to throw light on Defoe's sources, chiefly by Mr. Aitken, but these have been limited to dogmatic mention of works by title with no attempt to set forth in detail his indebtedness to each.

An exception to this general statement is the case of the "Journal of the Plague," the sources of which have recently been studied with some thoroughness by Dr. Watson Nicholson.[36] It should be added, furthermore, that important work has been done with the sources of the "Memoirs of Captain Carleton."[37] But attempts to trace the source material of "Robinson Crusoe" have seldom extended beyond the island portion of the story.[38] There is a general agreement that the adventures of Selkirk form the basis of the story; beyond that a great deal has been suggested with no very satisfactory result.

To explain Defoe's art and to connect him with his predecessors there must be a thorough search for his ascertainable sources, to find out to what extent his narratives are based upon previously published works. That originals will ultimately be found for all of his longer narratives is the opinion of Professor Bernbaum,[39] who offers this assumption as an explanation of Defoe's remarkable productivity.

The confusion which arises from the lack of a better understanding of the sources used by Defoe is well illustrated in the case of the "Carleton Memoirs." When George Carleton, the hero and purported author of those memoirs, was discovered to have been a flesh and blood personage whose career approximately paralleled the account of him given in the memoirs, the book was promptly removed from the Defoe bibliography by Mr. Lee, and its hero enrolled in the Dictionary of National Biography by Leslie Stephen. It did not require, however, either a minute or an extended search[40] for possible source materials to demonstrate that the

[36] *The Historical Sources of Defoe's Journal of the Plague Year*, 1920.

[37] Colonel Arthur Parnell, in *English Historical Review*, VI (1891), pp. 97-151.

[38] Friedrich Wackwitz, *Entstehungsgeschichte von Defoes Robinson Crusoe*, 1909. A second work with precisely the same title and of the same year was written by Max Günther.

[39] *Mary Carleton Narratives*, p. 87.

[40] See Colonel Parnell's article mentioned *supra*.

book was of very questionable authenticity. A similar confusion concerning the nature of the "Journal of the Plague" could have been cleared away by comparing it closely with earlier accounts of the great plague.

It is upon just such questions as have arisen in this brief review that the present study undertakes to throw light. Three of the longer narratives of Defoe, namely, "Robinson Crusoe," "Captain Singleton," and the "Memoirs of Captain Carleton," have been studied closely. In general the purpose has been to discover the sources of those narratives in so far as they are discoverable, though for the "Carleton Memoirs" there is also the question of authorship to be considered. It is expected that a fuller knowledge of those sources will aid in the solution of a number of perplexing questions. It should, in the first place, help in determining something of the amount of fact in those supposedly fictitious accounts. We must, moreover, know approximately what his materials were before discussing his methods of workmanship. It may be that elements for which Defoe has received credit were already present in the borrowed materials with which he fashioned his structures. As we shall see, such a contention has been made in connection with the highly-praised "Journal of the Plague Year." The latter work, the sources of which are already sufficiently known, will be considered in the concluding chapter wherein I shall attempt to set forth Defoe's method of procedure as illustrated by the narratives studied. Having determined as far as possible what his materials were, we shall be able to point out more precisely how he set about utilizing and changing them. Of plausible assumptions in this regard there have been too many; we must now attempt patiently to get at the facts.

Such an enormous undertaking I cannot expect to dispose of with finality. I have no new theory of Defoe's art to substantiate. My studies are merely intended to get at such facts as are available. There is, consequently, no pretension to unity in the work as a whole other than that arising from the fact that each of the studies deals with one of Defoe's longer narratives, and that the purpose of the individual studies is much the same, namely, to discover how Defoe worked. My justification is the vastness of the field and the need of making a beginning somewhere.

Though it is generally acknowledged that the literature of travel exerted a strong influence upon Defoe's narratives, the nature and extent of that influence has not heretofore been sufficiently investigated. During the sixteenth and seventeenth centuries there accumulated a large body of such works, which I believe to be of the greatest importance to the student of Defoe's literary procedure. It is this field which I purpose to search for the sources of "Robinson Crusoe" and Captain Singleton." The ultimate goal is not the mere discovery of sources, but the ascertaining of Defoe's manner of working. Many of the voyages and travels investigated will, of course, yield no positive results. Negative results, however, are not without value, and, in so far as is possible, they will be given room.

In a search for sources uniform success cannot be expected. Many portions which appear to offer no clue as to their origin must, therefore, be eliminated from consideration. In countless other cases it is impossible to tell whether the suggested source was actually made use of by Defoe. But, on the whole, enough should be established to form a basis for tangible conclusions. Such conclusions will, of course, be tentative. Based upon four only of Defoe's works, they will be open to modification after similar investigation of his other narratives. They should, however, be necessary stepping stones to a better understanding of Defoe and of an important stage in the development of the English novel.

CHAPTER II

THE COMPOSITION OF "ROBINSON CRUSOE"

I. *Preliminary Statement*

"The Life and Strange Surprising Adventures of Robinson Crusoe of York, Mariner," one scarcely needs to be reminded, was published by "W. Taylor at the Ship in Pater-Noster-Row," April 25, 1719. On the 20th of August of the same year appeared "The Farther Adventures of Robinson Crusoe," and on the 6th of August of the following year appeared "The Serious Reflections of Robinson Crusoe." These three volumes, often referred to as parts I, II, and III, respectively, comprise the whole of Defoe's account of that famous mariner.

Part I, or "The Life and Adventures," contains the island story known to every one. It begins with a brief statement of the hero's birth at York in 1632. At nineteen years of age he ran away to London, taking ship at Hull and suffering shipwreck off Yarmouth on the way. Attempting to repeat a successful trading voyage to Guinea, he was captured by Turkish pirates and kept a slave for two years at Salee on the west coats of Morocco. Escaping in his master's boat, he and his comrade, a black boy named Xury, were, after a long and hazardous voyage to the vicinity of Cape Verde, rescued by a Portuguese vessel and carried to the Brazils where Crusoe set up as a planter. Four years later he embarked upon a voyage to Africa for slaves, but his ship was caught in a storm and blown northwest along the coast of South America, and at last was wrecked near the mouth of the Orinoco River. Crusoe alone of his eleven companions escaped to an island. His story of twenty-eight years of solitude on that island is too well known to need recounting. In 1686 his deliverance by pirates was effected, and he with his man Friday returned to England.

"The Farther Adventures" begins with the year 1694 when Crusoe returned to his island for a brief visit. Afterwards he spent several years trading in the East Indies, and at the last went home from Peking by way of Tartary, Siberia, and Russia. This closes the narrative; for Crusoe, reaching London in 1705, and being seventy-two years old, retired from active pursuits. "The Serious Reflections" is not narrative at all; instead it is a series of moral essays on various topics with Crusoe's name to give them interest.

"Robinson Crusoe," like many other books of popular interest, has given rise to a number of problems. Among the less important of these are the questions of authorship, and of the time and place of composition. It was once seriously argued that Defoe's patron, Robert Harley, Earl of Oxford, was the real author of part one;[1] and on this ground was explained its superiority over the succeeding portions composed by Defoe himself.   But that Defoe was the author of the whole story no one now doubts; and it is reasonably certain that it was composed in London not long before its publication.

More important are the problems of Defoe's art and method,— questions having to do with the amounts of truth and fiction in the narrative, and with the imaginative qualities displayed by its author.   Especially prolific have been speculations and surmises about the materials which form the groundwork of the story, and concerning Defoe's use of those materials.   It has been believed by many that Defoe went to see Selkirk at Bristol[2] shortly after the latter's return from Juan Fernandez, and that from him he procured oral and written information used in "Robinson Crusoe."   But, as Mr. Aitken has pointed out,[3] the evidence for this is not very substantial, and the opinion now held by the best Defoe scholars is that he knew no more of Selkirk than he had read in the published accounts of his island experiences.   Another theory, once held tenaciously by several writers on Defoe, but now accepted only in a very much modified form, is that "Robinson Crusoe" is an allegory of Defoe's own life.

Concerning Defoe's inventive faculty much is assumed; his genius for the creation of details is highly praised.   But there is no very precise knowledge of what parts of his narrative are his own invention and what are borrowed from other men's writings.   As has been said earlier, our information concerning the sources of "Robinson Crusoe" is slight indeed.

Of the attempts to trace the origin of the story in the English literature preceding it, the most elaborate is that of Dr. Friedrich Wackwitz,[4] who takes up successively the various traditions to which he thinks Defoe was indebted in composing Crusoe's adventures.   Among these he considers the treatments of desert island life, such as "The Isle of Pines," Peter Serrano's story in Rycaut's translation of "The Royal Commentaries of the Yncas," and "Ebn Jokdhan"; Selkirk he reserves for a special chapter.   Other traditions which he sets forth as having influenced the story are those of the voyages, of the "Abenteuerromans," and others of a political and religious nature.

[1] See, for instance, the article by W. L. Purves, *Athenæum*, 2 May, 1903.
[2] Wright, Thomas, *The Life of Daniel Defoe* (1894), pp. 164 ff., 230, 402.
[3] Introduction to *Robinson Crusoe*, I, p. lii.
[4] *Entstehungsgeschichte von D. Defoes "Robinson Crusoe,"* Berlin, 1909.

But in the way of discriminating among these suggested influences and sources Wackwitz does little for us. For instance, in the case of the studies of desert island life, he compares each individually with "Robinson Crusoe," but does not check them against each other to determine the extent, or the exact nature, of Defoe's debt to them. With the tradition of the rogue story, however, he is, as we shall see later, more specific.

Another study of the materials of "Robinson Crusoe," identical in title and date of publication with Wackwitz's dissertation, is that of Max Günther.[5] This treatise has the merit of introducing some important matters which Wackwitz either does not dwell upon sufficiently or passes over entirely. The latter limited his investigation to works in English, whereas Günther has considered a number of continental narratives pointing toward "Robinson Crusoe"; among them, Gabriel Foigny's "Les avantures de Jacques Sadeur," Denis Vairasse d'Alais's "Histoire des Séverambes,"[6] and Grimmelshausen's "Simplicissimus." He has, furthermore, shown something of the relationship between "Robinson Crusoe" and the accounts of voyages and travels in the collections of Hakluyt and Purchas and others.

Mr. Aitken, whose judgment on Defoe is always sane, has done little in the matter of sources beyond a dogmatic citation of certain works which he thinks Defoe may have used. He admits[7] the possibility suggested by Professor Arber that the idea of Will Atkins was taken from the account of John Whicker in Pitman's "Relation" (1689). He adds that Defoe "may also have used Villault's 'A Relation of the Coasts of Africa called Guinea' (1670), and Le Duc's Voyage à la Chine' (1700), besides Hakluyt and Purchas." Two other suggestions of sources, which as we shall see are unnecessary, Aitken cites in a footnote. One of these is from Henry Kingsley, who believed that in the "Farther Adventures" Defoe used Ramusio; the other is from the American author, E. E. Hale, who found a striking resemblance of the account of Crusoe's storm off Yarmouth to a Yarmouth storm described in Thomas Shepard's "Autobiography."[8]

Within our own century a number of Dutch and German investigators have strenuously championed as a most important source of "Robinson Crusoe" an episode of desert island life contained in a Dutch book, "The Mighty Kingdom of Krinke Kesmes." This work, written by Hendrik

[5] Max Günther, *Entstehungsgeschichte von Defoes Robinson Crusoe*, 1909.

[6] For a discussion of the authorship of this work see Geoffroy Atkinson's *The Extraordinary Voyage in French Literature before 1700*, (1920), p. 39. Herr Günther is uninformed as to who was the author.

[7] G. A. Aitken, Introduction to *Robinson Crusoe*, I, p. liv.

[8] *The Atlantic Monthly,* lvi (1885), p. 85 ff.

Smeeks and published at Amsterdam in 1708, has recently been brought more prominently before English readers by Mr. L. L. Hubbard, an American, who has translated into English the portion of the book which is said to have been used by Defoe, and compared it with "Robinson Crusoe."

But of all the many views as to the sources of the story Professor Trent[9] accepts none as well-founded save the one which credits Defoe with having been inspired by the published accounts of Selkirk's adventure. That Defoe may have read or heard the accounts of other castaways he thinks possible. He concludes, however, by asserting: "All that is certain is that Defoe's book speedily eclipsed whatever predecessors it may have had."

With so much uncertainty and speculation where we should have facts, the time is ripe to discover more precisely just what materials Defoe did make use of. With such facts at hand we shall then be able to test our present notions of Defoe's methods, correcting them where they are erroneous and supplementing them where they are inadequate. In the present study the special field of search will be the literature of travel and adventure extant in 1719. It will not, of course, be possible to cover minutely this vast territory, nor indeed is that necessary; sufficient will be done, however, to gain some specific facts to help us in the solution of the question of how Defoe worked, what his materials were, and how he changed them.

To throw light on the sources of "Robinson Crusoe" is no easy undertaking; and especially is this true of the island portion of the narrative. So well known is the story and so many have been the attempts to discover the materials with which it was fashioned that one must search closely indeed for further discoveries. The difficulty is increased, moreover, by the unlimited resources at Defoe's command. The imaginative splendor which burst upon England in the days of Raleigh, Drake, and Frobisher, and the keen interest in the wonders of foreign lands and in the prowess of British seamen, held their force scarcely diminished until the day of Defoe. The seventeenth century was distinctly an age of colonization. Empires of enormous proportions were being formed across the seas by the leading European nations. The bitterest rivalry existed between England, France, Holland, Spain, and Portugal over valuable seacoasts in North and South America, in Africa, and in the Far East. The squabble between Holland and Portugal over Brazil was barely settled when Crusoe is said to have become a planter there. The reports of the fabulous wealth to be obtained along the "coasts of

[9] W. P. Trent, Introduction to *Robinson Crusoe* (1916), p. xxv.

Africk called Guinee" were calculated to arouse the interest of traders of every nation.

So great was the international jealousy that throughout the century the Barbary pirates were allowed to flourish, each nation deploring their shameful practice of subjecting Christian captives to the galleys and to other cruel forms of slavery, but each secretly glad for the damage done to the commerce of competitors. Events of which Defoe must certainly have read were the expeditions fitted out by the English government against the pirates of Salee, among whom Crusoe was to spend two years of slavery. Lists of English seamen held at Salee were published, as well as numerous accounts of individual experiences of men who effected their escape.[10]

The stream of literature which all this maritime interest awakened is of the greatest importance to one who would understand Defoe's contributions to the art of fiction. Hakluyt and Purchas, the best known names in this field, are only the leaders in a movement whose force is not yet spent. Not only were there collections of voyages in England and on the continent all through the century, but with every turn of the breeze there were lengthy accounts of individual men being set forth. The Hakluyt Society has done excellent work in making many of the reports available to the general student; but many others are now lost entirely, or are at best represented by a few worn copies not readily accessible.

The influence of such a rich and varied body of narrative upon more artistic attempts at literary expression is not always sufficiently appreciated, though it has been considered with respect to individual men. The suitability of works of this character to inspire an imaginative mind is well illustrated in the case of Coleridge, two of whose poems are indebted to the literature of travel: the suggestion of the albatross in "The Ancient Mariner" is said to have come from Captain George Shelvocke's "Voyage" (1726); and "Kubla Khan" has recently been shown to owe more to Purchas than Coleridge acknowledged.[11] If, then, the accounts of travellers are qualified to inspire poetry, they should be no less of an inspiration to works of prose fiction, to which they are much more closely allied.

It is well known that Defoe's acquaintance with writings of this character was wide. A glance at the partial list of books in his library reveals the presence of a remarkable number of works of travel both

[10] See such titles as these listed under "Salee" in the British Museum catalogue: *A List of Sally Captives* (1637), and *Newes from Sally* (1642).

[11] Howard Parsons, in the literary supplement of *The London Times,* 9 March, 1922.

by land and by sea.[12]   One is amazed at his knowledge of distant places. Nothing that they had to offer was foreign to his interests.   Of the vast and little known domains of the Czar of Muscovy, and of Grand Tartary, he speaks with as much assurance as he might of Lincolnshire or of Kent.   A man may, he says,[13] "go round the world with Dampier and Rogers, and know a thousand times more in doing it than all those illiterate sailors. . . . He may measure the latitudes and distances of places by . . . . the charts of those that have surveyed them," and while they "know but every man his share . . . . he receives the idea of the whole at one view."

This we may be sure (as Mr. Aitken has remarked)[14] Defoe had done. The circumnavigation of the globe had been accomplished so frequently, he asserts,[15] that "the way is now a common road . . . . every ordinary sailor is able to do it . . . . and he that can carry a ship to Lisbon, may with the same ease carry it round the world"   When he makes Crusoe comment on the shortcomings of "our hydrographers" in regard to the geography of northeastern Asia, he but exemplifies his interest in the efforts to discover the northeast passage to America,—an interest to which he had given expression fifteen years earlier in the "Storm" (1704).

When, then, he sends his hero on a voyage to the East Indies by the conventional route, passing the Canary and the Cape Verde Islands, the Cape of Good Hope, and Madagascar on the way to Ormus, Goa, Achin, or any of the numerous points known to every man interested in East India matters, we need not expect any certain or definite source for that account, nor for any other brief and general account of voyages to well known parts of the world.   This is especially true where no incidents of the journey are related and the time and distances are not explicitly stated.

It must be understood that for two reasons the problem of sources for part one is not that for parts two and three.   In the first place, dealing with a single locality and working out a definite line of action, Defoe is compelled in the island story to go to greater lengths to disguise his materials borrowed from published sources so that those borrowings may not appear.   A little reflection will, I think, make this evident.   Studies of life on desert islands, plentiful as they undoubtedly were in the literature of the century preceding 1719, were, with few exceptions, neither long nor detailed.   Perhaps two or three covered more than a dozen pages; and many of them extended to no more than a few paragraphs.   To plunder from any one of these a story so abundantly stocked with detail as

[12] Aitken, *Defoe's Library* in the *Athenæum*, I June, 1895, p. 706.

[13] Daniel Defoe, *Compleat English Gentleman* (1890), p. 225.

[14] General Introduction to *Romances and Narratives by Daniel Defoe* (1899), I, p. xliv.

[15] Daniel Defoe, *New Voyage*, (1899), p. 1.

"Robinson Crusoe" is manifestly impossible; and had it been done the fact would have been evident to the first casual reader of the original. The best that any one of these predecessors could have done was to suggest a number of the more obvious difficulties facing a man left destitute to wrest a livelihood from the soil. And many of these solutions are so obvious that they would occur to any one independently, whether or not he had ever read of a like experience. No better testimony to the truth of this statement is needed than the fact that these previously written accounts of castaways agree in many details where it is certain that there could have been little exchange of ideas. For instance, Selkirk is credited with having secured a permanent food supply by the practice of taming kids and keeping them about his habitation. To whom was he indebted for the suggestion? Probably not to the experiences of Robert Knox on the island of Ceylon; and yet Knox had similarly insured his future supply of goatflesh. Tortoise flesh formed the sustenance of many of the castaways. In nearly every case the need of shelter soon led to the erection of huts or dwellings of some sort. Knox built two or three; Selkirk had two, George Pines had two, the Dutch boy of Smeeks had two. And so it goes. No especial foresight likewise suggested the need of clothing. This duplication of detail, though it allows Defoe to borrow with less certainty of detection, curtails greatly the number of ideas and devices which he may employ. So that had he drawn upon all of these narratives, he would still have much to work out, either through his own ingenuity or through suggestions gathered from works which did not deal primarily with desert island life. We have seen something of the unparalleled extent of Defoe's reading in the literature of travel and more or less authentic adventure. From his memory, richly stored with accounts of incidents which had befallen those adventurers and of the strategy by which they had extricated themselves, Defoe could draw many threads to weave into his fabric.

The second reason why the problem of port one differs from the succeeding portions is that with the island adventures of Crusoe Defoe undoubtedly took greater pains then with the sequel, as is evidenced by the testimony of thousands of readers. "Every now and then," to quote the words of Professor Trent, "someone discovers that it is an immortal story, and proceeds to announce his discovery to a wondering world." Evidently a book of such a character is no mere scissors-and-paste product taken in large sections from other accounts. Here if anywhere we shall find Defoe's creative imagination in operation.

If, then, we consider as possible sources only those accounts which deal with a solitary man upon a desert island, we shall not rightly understand the composition of "Robinson Crusoe." As the initial inspiration of the story they do very well, but go little further. In order to get the full quota of possible influences we must investigate every sort of experience under primitive conditions, that is to say, experiences dealing with nature at first hand without the ordinary equipment of civilized society. Had Defoe asked, can a man exist alone on an island for a long period of time? the accounts of Selkirk and the others would have replied, yes. Had he asked, how can he? they would have replied with all the details at their command. But how meagre they are when it comes to supplying Crusoe with his many devices! When Defoe became more specific and asked how a man makes canoes, tables, chairs, planks, earthenware, baskets, umbrellas, provides a supply of grain from which to make flour and bread, and does the many other things which his hero is to perform, they answered nothing at all; and Defoe had to turn to other records. Clearly any relation of how trees may be turned into planks without saws was welcome to him, and as we shall see he was familiar with one and possibly two directions for doing that very thing. When the question of boatmaking arises,. neither Selkirk nor the others have any suggestions to offer, and again Defoe turned to other sources.

Along with the six narratives of "Ein Mensch auf einsamer Insel" in English previously to 1719,[16] we must consider a number of other accounts of solitary and isolated life, though not in every case is the subject alone in his solitude. That is to say, he may have a few comrades, or he may be with a multitude of people among whom he is an alien. Some of these were more certainly known to Defoe than several considered by Wackwitz. Such, for instance, is the case with the very important account of nineteen years of island solitude experienced by Captain Robert Knox on Ceylon as a captive of the Sinhalese. The "Travels" of Mandelslo,[17] the influence of which upon "Captain Singleton" is unmistakable, contains three brief accounts of insular solitude. One[18] tells of a Frenchman who lived nearly two years alone on the island of Mauritius (near Madagascar). He was a member of a pirate crew whose ship was wrecked in the East Indies; all the men were lost except seven who managed to get to Mauritius where the Frenchman chose to stay rather than venture further in their small vessel. When rescued in 1601 he was naked, having torn his apparel to pieces in a fit of madness brought on by eating nothing but raw tortoises. He had been in a "burning feaver" which left him mentally

[16] Wackwitz considers (1) *The Isle of Pines;* (2) an account in Ringrose's *Bucaniers of America;* (3) Dampier's Mosquito Indian; (4) Peter de Serrano; (5) *Ebn Jokdhan;* (6) Selkirk.

[17] *Voyages and Travels of J. Albert de Mandelslo* in the *Voyages and Travels of Olearius* (1662). This work was in Defoe's library. (See Mr. Aitken's partial list in the *Athenæum,* 1 June, 1895, pp. 706-7.)

[18] Mandelslo, p. 246.

unbalanced, but was otherwise in good health. The other two relations appear on the same page.[19] One has to do with a Dutch seaman who in punishment was being left alone on the island of St. Helena. But "representing to himself the horrour of that solitude much beyond what it really was . . . . [he] fell into a despair" which made him disinter the body of a buried comrade and set out to sea in the coffin. His rash act aroused the compassion of his punitors; he was taken aboard and "came afterwards to Holland . . . . and related to many, how miraculously God had delivered him."

The third account is more significant. It deals with the experiences of a "Flemming named Picman" who having narrowly escaped being cast away on a rocky island along the coast of Scotland found another castaway already living there. The island was desolate and without shelter except for the ruins of a boat "wherewith he had made a kind of hut." Hardship had so emaciated his uncovered body that his discoverers doubted his materiality; but questioning him they found him to be an Englishman who had been wrecked upon the rocks. Only one companion escaped with him into the island where they suffered all manner of deprivations. Their sustenance was chiefly sea mews (seagulls) which they "set a drying in the wind and sun, and so eat them raw." Also they found eggs in the crevices of the rocks. The comrade disappeared a few weeks after, carrying with him the knife wherewith they had killed their food; whether in despair he committed suicide or whether he fell into the sea while climbing a hazardous precipice for eggs was unknown. Left alone, the other man found his afflictions doubled with no one to share them, though fortified with prayer against despondency. Another knife he made of a "great nail" from one of the boat's boards. Necessity, he reported, "put me upon another invention, which kept me during the last winter;" this was to bait a stick with sea-dog's fat and to capture the mews as they came to eat. His solitude had lasted about eleven months, and he was "resolved to end his days in it." His rescuers set him ashore in Ireland from whence he returned to England.

We have already noted one experience of insular solitude upon St. Helena. Hakluyt has two separate accounts[20] of a second recluse upon that same island, later to be famous as the scene of Napoleon's exile. This recluse was John Segar who after a year and a half was rescued by some fellow-Englishmen. The first report says that he was in good health, but that "whether he were put in fright of us . . . . or of sudden

[19] *Ibid.*, p. 280.
[20] Richard Hakluyt, *The Principal Navigations of the English Nation* (1904), VI, p. 402; X, p. 197. All references to Hakluyt are to this edition of Messrs. Maclehose. Günther, p. 50, quotes from Hakluyt one of these accounts.

joy when he understood we were his old consorts and countreymen, he became idle-headed," dying after eight days of sleeplessness. The second report says that between "excessive sudden fear & joy, he became distracted of his wits,"—a statement very similar to Crusoe's discussion of the disastrous effects of either sudden grief or sudden joy. This discussion, which accompanies his great happiness at having escaped unharmed to his island, closes with the verse, doubtless of Defoe's own composition:[21]

"For sudden joys like sudden griefs confound at first."

Segar's rescuers "found of his drying some 40 goats" and two suits of goatskin clothing "with the hairy side outward."

Further search would doubtless reveal a number more of such incidents available to Defoe, but I shall point out only one more desert island relation in English and two in foreign languages. The first is the "Voyage of François Leguat." Leguat, with seven comrades, was said to have spent several years of solitude upon the island of Rodriguez. This account, long regarded as authentic but recently demonstrated to be a compilation from earlier records,[22] appeared simultaneously in English and French versions in 1707. The two works in foreign languages are the "Simplicissimus" of Grimmelshausen in German, and the "Krinke Kesmes" of Smeeks, in Dutch, which appeared in 1669 and 1708, respectively; both books contain an episode of desert island life.

To discover such records of solitary life is, however, an easy matter compared with the more important task of showing which ones influenced the composition of "Robinson Crusoe." This problem Wackwitz has not attacked very strenuously, contenting himself with setting forth the claims of the six desert island relations noticed by him, and letting the reader decide for himself which, if any of them actually influenced Defoe. Other writers on Defoe, Professor Hastings,[23] for example, have remarked that Defoe used such details of Selkirk's experiences as had been published. But no one has made a serious effort to check these records by any means to determine which ones were known to and used by Defoe. The accounts noted above from Hakluyt and Mandelslo, being from important works which Defoe possessed and which upon several accounts he would be likely to have read, we may be fairly sure were known to him. Mandelslo's journal was, in fact, used by Defoe in composing "Cap-

[21] I, p.50. All references to Defoe's narratives are, unless accompanied by a statement to the contrary, to the Aitken edition of 1895. See the Oxford edition of *Robinson Crusoe* (1910), p. 297, for another explanation of the source of this verse.

[22] Geoffroy Atkinson in *Publications of the Modern Language Association*, XXXVI (1921), p. 509 ff.

[23] William T. Hastings, Introduction to *Robinson Crusoe* (1913), p. 24, note 1.

tain Singleton," as we shall see in the following chapter. Rogers's and the three other accounts of Selkirk it is impossible that he should be unacquainted with. It has not been remarked, moreover, that there is specific evidence of his having read the account of Peter de Serrano in Sir Paul Rycaut's translation of Garcilaso de la Vega's "Royal Commentaries of the Yncas" (1688); for he makes an obvious and suggestive allusion to that work when, in "Robinson Crusoe" itself,[24] he speaks of the accounts of religion among the "Uncas of Cusco in Peru,"—a certain reference to De la Vega (a native of Cusco) and his "Commentaries." The accounts in Dampier's "Voyage" were, as we shall see later, undoubtedly familiar to him. But we have no sort of evidence other than a general probability that he may have read "The Isle of Pines" or "Ebn Jokdhan." "The Voyage of Leguat," on the other hand, I shall show to have influenced the composition of "Captain Singleton."

It is not to be expected that any new or startling source for the island portion of "Robinson Crusoe" should be found at this late day. The tradition which affirms that Selkirk's adventures form the basis, or at least furnished the central idea, of the experiences of Crusoe is well founded. Just how soon that tradition began we do not know; but by 1744 an editor of Rogers's "Voyage" assumes[25] that fact to be common knowledge. A recent writer,[26] attempting to exalt the claims of a rival castaway suggests that Defoe may not even have been indebted to Selkirk for the idea of goats on Crusoe's Island, since the "Bucaniers of America" (1685) tells of bulls in the West Indies. "From bulls to goats," so his reasoning runs, "is not a far cry." The absurdity of this is obvious to one whose vision is not obscured by partisans opinions. He who forgets that Selkirk's experience was one of the outstanding events of Defoe's day, known to every Englishman, has lost the true historical perspective. When Londoners talked of desert island adventurers they naturally thought of Selkirk. Not only was his case the most recent one, but it had also been given much wider publicity than any of the others, through the interest aroused by his return. And though many travelers told of desert islands inhabited by goats (as St. Helena), we may be sure that Selkirk's island suggested Crusoe's island and that Selkirk's goats suggested Crusoe's goats. To attempt any such circuitous chain of reasoning as to arrive at goats from bulls is palpable nonsense. Selkirk undoubtedly furnished Defoe with the central theme of the story,—a fact upon which too much emphasis cannot be laid and which I shall assume as fundamental.

[24] III, p. 117.
[25] John Harris, *Navigantium atque Itinerantium Bibliotheca* (1744), I, p. 150.
[26] L. L. Hubbard, Introduction to the *Narrative of the El-Ho* (1921), p. xix.

This does not mean, however, that no other experiences than Selkirk's contributed to the account of Crusoe on his island. For, as Mr. Aitken and others have admitted, Defoe owed little to Selkirk for the great body of his material. The reappearance in 1718 of Selkirk's affairs in the second edition of Rogers's "Voyage" is generally thought to have led Defoe to the happy idea of composing his story; but for that story he may have turned to another account than Selkirk's,—one less known but more detailed, and more satisfactory to Defoe for both reasons.

I know of no narrative other than "Robinson Crusoe" of a man cast away by shipwreck and later delivered by pirates, with a long period intervening between the catastrophe and the deliverance. We have many accounts of men cast away and at least one of men delivered by pirates; but these are details which could easily be fitted into any skeleton outline. The first thing is to discover an account of a man whose isolation extends over a considerable number of years. To one who in his maturity rereads Crusoe's story, a very striking feature is the long period of time which elapses before deliverance came to the hero. When finally he and Friday reach London in 1687 thirty-five years have passed since the unhappy day which witnessed the departure, twenty-eight whereof were spent on the island. Obviously Defoe is attempting in the "Strange Surprising Adventures" of the York mariner ("the wonders of whose life exceed all that . . . . is to be found extant; the life of one man being scarce capable of a greater variety") to outdo anything to be found in print. To exceed the experiences of Selkirk and the others, which are set forth as possible sources of "Robinson Crusoe," Crusoe had no need of staying nearly a third of a century in solitude; for the hero of Juan Fernandez was rescued after but four years, and Peter de Serrano after seven; and no other castaway is known to have survived so long as that. As Professor Trent has observed, Selkirk's island is not Crusoe's island; and I may add that Selkirk is not Crusoe.

II. *Robert Knox's Contributions*

a. *The "Ceylon"*

There was another Englishman living in London in 1719 whose experiences, however much they might differ outwardly from those of Crusoe, resemble them inwardly quite as much as do Selkirk's. This was Robert Knox, whose nineteen years of loneliness on the island of Ceylon furnish a very real parallel to Crusoe's island life. It is true that Knox was a captive on a large and populous island, that he had a dozen or more fellow-Englishmen with him so that occasionally they might converse, and that part of the time they were allowed to live together; but these are the

external differences which perhaps have blinded investigators to the significance of Knox of a prototype of Crusoe. Both were on islands, both
were lonely, and both had their existence to maintain under similar
handicaps.

Who first called attention to the possibility of Defoe's indebtedness
to Knox for portions of Crusoe's story I do not know; but apparently it
was James Ryan, who, in the preface to his edition of Knox's collected
writings, asserts that Defoe knew Knox and got from him many suggestions for "Robinson Crusoe,"—an opinion to which Mr. John Masefield
has given wider publicity. Students of Defoe, however, have paid sing-
ularly little attention to the matter. The inference from the briefly stated
opinions of Mr. Ryan and Mr. Masefield is that Defoe used suggestions
received from Knox personally. But that he made use of Knox's printed
work they do not appear to have recognized.[27]

The adventures of Knox on Ceylon were first published in 1681 with
the approval of the Royal Society; the title was as follows: "An Historical
Relation of . . . . Ceylon . . . . together with an account of the detain-
ing in Captivity the Author and divers other Englishmen now living
there, and of the Author's Miraculous Escape." The book is divided into
four parts, the first three of which are descriptive of the island and its
inhabitants. The fourth part, however, is a narrative of Knox's fortunes,
relating the circumstances of his captivity, the chief points of interest
of his life there, and his escape.

That Defoe shortly after 1719 was reading this account by Knox is
clear from the fact that he summarized the story in "Captain Singleton,"
published in June, 1720, subsequently to parts one and two of "Robinson
Crusoe," but previously to part three. There is, then, an inherent probability that Knox's story, being known to Defoe and containing suggestions
of which he stood very much in need, contributed to the composition of
"Robinson Crusoe."

It has been intimated that Knox's experience is the only one of the
kind which approaches Crusoe's in the matter of time covered. To this
should be added that with few exceptions it is the only one related in the
first person with proper attention to the sequence of events and to the
passage of time. At the beginning of his captivity every detail is interesting, but as his daily life falls into a routine it becomes tiresome to
repeat; hence we find Knox making such statements as these:[28] "In this

[27] James Ryan, Editor's Preface to *An Historical Relation of Ceylon* by Robert
Knox (1911), xxii; John Masefield, *A Mainsail Haul* (1913), p. 132.

[28] P. 227. All references to Knox are to Ryan's edition of 1911, published by
Maclehose and Son, Glasgow.

place I lived two years. . . . ";[29] " . . . . I had been now some seven or eight years in this land. . . . ";[30] "In this manner we four lived together some two years very lovingly and contentedly . . . . ";[31] "It was now about the year 1673 . . . ." This way of accounting for the passage of time is exactly in the manner of Crusoe, who remarks:[32] "I had now been thirteen days on shore . . . ";[33] "I was now in the twenty-third year of residence in this island . . . ";[34] "It was now the month of December";[35] "I was now entered on the seven and twentieth year of my captivity. . . ." Notice that Crusoe refers to his condition as one of 'captivity.'

There are similar expressions common to both which have to do with their arrangements to secure food and shelter. Says Knox: "Now having settled all business about my allowance, my next concern was to look after a house more convenient, for my present one was too small to dress my victuals in, and to sleep in too . . . ";[36] ". . . . and so (I) began to settle myself . . . . seeming to be very well contented in this condition";[37] "I soon came to be well furnished. . . ."[38] Likewise Crusoe says: "Having now brought my mind a little to relish my condition . . . . I began to make things as easy to me as I could";[39] "And now I began to apply myself to make such necessary things as I wanted . . . ";[40] and much more of like import. These parallel passages are not cited as proofs in themselves of Defoe's debt to Knox, but merely as evidence that this relation of Knox's with which we know Defoe was familiar has narrative devices and situations identical with those of "Robinson Crusoe." So similar in tone are the two works that many such passages could be transferred bodily from one to the other without noticeable effect upon them.

Besides these similarities of style and tone we find other general likenesses in the substance of the two relations. The island experiences of each, for instance, begin at almost the same time. Young Knox on his father's ship had sailed from the Downs for the East Indies Company in 1658; on the 19th of November, 1659, the vessel was disabled in a

[29] P. 231.
[30] P. 233.
[31] P. 245.
[32] I, p. 61.
[33] I, p. 199.
[34] I, p. 201.
[35] I, p. 255.
[36] P. 211.
[37] P. 226.
[38] P. 266.
[39] I, p. 73.
[40] I, p. 74.

"mighty storm" at Masulipatam, and was ordered to Cottiar, Ceylon, where Knox, his father, and fourteen of the crew were taken captives by the natives. Crusoe's wreck occurred upon the 30th of September, 1659. Shortly after the beginning of their isolation both are afflicted with the ague, a disease of which the elder Knox died a year or so later. Both Knox and Crusoe are supplied with Bibles[41] and other books of a pious character, and both open their Bibles at random to auspicious passages. Both spend much time in prayer and religious meditation.

In each case the wearing out of clothing gives rise to the problem of securing more. Like Crusoe, Knox builds two or three houses, one of which he surrounds with a hedge[42] to keep out spying eyes. He furnishes oil for his lamp from the cocoanuts;[43] Crusoe, it will be recalled, used goat's tallow in a lamp of his own contrivance. The conditions of Knox's captivity were far from rigid; he was allowed to live much as he liked, to engage in trade, and to accumulate property. He purchased a piece of ground at Eladetta where three of his comrades lived with him,[44] enjoying the increase of his land much as Crusoe's growing colony lived upon his bounty.

Now arises for Knox the problem of whether or not marriage with native women is to be permitted. Nearly all of Knox's comrades take wives;[45] finally two of the three living with him marry and, according to agreement, discontinue their residence upon his property. Knox and his remaining companion, Stephen Rutland, with whom he finally escapes, continue bachelors. It will be recalled that about the time of Crusoe's rescue, his island began to be inhabited by a constantly increasing number of people. Besides Friday's father there were the five English pirates left behind at Crusoe's departure, several Spaniards, and a number of savages, both men and women. So that the situation was not unlike that on Ceylon. In both cases deliverance appeared remote; in both the situation was complicated by the presence of none but native women. Knox and his fellows insist that those who take wives shall move elsewhere to eliminate the dissension arising from the presence of these women. There had been disputes "concerning the lawfulness of matching with heathens . . . . and whether the Chingulay marriages were any better than living in whoredom; there being no Christian priests to join them together, and it being allowed by their laws to change their wives

---

[41] *Ceylon*, pp. 203-7; *Robinson Crusoe*, I, pp. 70, 103.

[42] P. 226.

[43] *Ceylon*, p. 211. Many other accounts, however, tell of methods of lampmaking.

[44] *Ibid.*, p. 232 ff.

[45] Pp. 232, 234 ff.

and take others as often as they pleased. But these cases we solved for our own advantage after this manner. That we were but flesh and blood . . . . and that . . . . we were cut off from all marriages any-where else, even for our lifetime, and therefore that we must marry with these or with none at all. . . . These reasons being urged, there was none among us that could object aught against them, especially if those that were minded to marry women here, did take them for their wives during their lives, as some of them say, they do; and most of the women they marry are such as do profess themselves to be Christians."[46]

Likewise the old Spaniard whom Crusoe left in charge of his island saw immediately[47] that "the having of women . . . . would presently be attended with inconvenience and might occasion some strife," and there-fore insisted that each man should take but one woman and "that having taken one, none else shall touch her." So, he continued, " 'though we cannot marry any of you, yet 'tis but reasonable that while you stay here, the woman any of you takes should be maintained by the man that takes her, and should be his wife; I mean,' says he, 'while he continues here.' " When Crusoe returns, a French Catholic priest with him argues vigorously against this lax sort of arrangement, urging that unbound by any sort of contract these Englishmen may at pleasure "abandon these women, disown their children . . . . " and remarry.[48] They are, he insists, "no less than adulterers, and living in adultery."

In "Robinson Crusoe" these discussions lead to formal marriages by the priest of the white men and their savage partners, and to the con-version of both husband and wives, a process which involves much theological catechising and dialogue exactly in the vein of Defoe's "Family Instructor." Crusoe's chief reason for enforcing more regular marriages is that the women may be protected from the caprice of the men and be equal partners in the bargain. To one familiar with Defoe's suggested academy for women in the "Essay on Projects" (1697) this interest in the welfare of wives will be no surprise. Here in "Robinson Crusoe" we find him reverting to one of his favorite themes;[49] all he needs is the situation outlined by Knox, and from his own previously developed materials he spins out the long theological dialogues between Atkins and his wife, and the account of their conversion and baptism.

When Knox escapes, the population on Ceylon has been increased by some eighteen children of these white men and native women. Likewise

[46] P. 234.
[47] Robinson Crusoe, II, p. 75. See also Purchas, III (1905), p. 16.
[48] Robinson Crusoe, II, pp. 125-6.
[49] Moll Flanders and Roxana are in a sense pleas for the education of women. Defoe's moral treatises include the Family Instructor in three parts, and the Religious Courtship.

Crusoe at his second and final departure found that the children of mixed parentage numbered "near twenty in all."[50]

Crusoe's management of his goats may owe as much to Knox as to Selkirk. The latter we know from all the accounts of him had goats which furnished him with both food and clothing. His manner of securing them is singular; his ammunition having given out he was compelled to chase them down afoot. This he was well able to do, his simple mode of life having "clear'd him of all gross humours" and made him exceedingly fleet of foot. To this Steele adds that Selkirk made a practice of crippling the kids so that though still good for food they were unable to run swiftly in after life. These maimed goats lived in herds about his house.

For a number of reasons Crusoe, though he had plenty of ammunition, found it advisable to keep tame goats about him. But his procedure is not that of Steele's Selkirk, but of Knox. Instead of maiming the kids, he built pens for them, and by breeding increased his flock as he wished. Those needed as a beginning for his herd he captured by means of traps or pits dug in the earth and covered with vegetation upon which the goats would feed and thereby be betrayed into venturing upon the fragile covering; this covering presently would give way and drop the beast captive into the pit beneath. Both the plan of breeding goats and the method of capture are very similar to devices mentioned in Knox's "Ceylon." He tells of the methods of the natives for capturing wild hogs,[51] the principal one of which is to make a trap consisting of a pit covered with deceptive earth and vegetation. The scheme of securing a permanent supply of goats Knox himself practiced. Says he, about the year 1672 "we fell to breeding up goats: we began with two, but by the blessing of God they soon came to a good many; and their flesh served us instead of mutton."[52]

One reason for taming goats advanced by Crusoe is that some day he will be old and unable to hunt his food, at which time the tame herd will be his source of supply. These reflections of a possible time of senility grow upon him; later Friday comes to comfort him in that respect. Knox likewise ponders on the day when he shall no longer be able to dress his own food[53] or to supply his other needs; he is urged to marry, but instead adopts one of the children of his English comrades.

Among the devices of the Sinhalese described by Knox which may have proved useful to Crusoe are the making of pottery and cane baskets;[54]

[50] *Ceylon*, p. 277; *Robinson Crusoe*, II, p. 107.
[51] *Ceylon*, p. 43.
[52] P. 238.
[53] *Ceylon*, p. 245.
[54] *Ibid.*, p. 138.

like Crusoe they used the baskets as receptacles in which to store grain; the earthenware they hung from the ceiling of their houses as substitutes for shelves. The Sinhalese also had wooden pestles and mortars[55] for beating their rice, which they ate boiled with salt. Their way of butter-making may be significant. Knox tells how they made it;[56] Crusoe tells what he made his of. Knox tells how the Sinhalese dry their fish and of their use of other dried flesh. One of Crusoe's commonest foods is fish which he dried and eat dry.

Both Knox and Crusoe comment upon the diversity of religions represented in their small neighborhoods. Says the former:[57] "Although here be protestants and papists, yet . . . . they are as good friends, as if there were no such parties. And there is no other distinctions of religion there, but only heathens and Christians: and we usually say, We Christians." Crusoe remarks:[58] "My island was now peopled . . . . we had but three subjects, and they were of three different religions. My man Friday was a protestant, his father was a pagan . . . . and the Spaniard was a papist. However, I allowed liberty of conscience throughout my dominions."

In spite of his position of comfort secured through years of persistence and thrifty management, Knox longs to get away and return to England, as Crusoe similarily situated longs for rescue. The former after nineteen years carries out successfully his plan of escape with his friend, Stephen Rutland, to the Dutch on another part of Ceylon. On their way they carry knives and axes at their sides,[59] a practice which Crusoe and Friday adopt. A passage suggestive of Crusoe's experience with footprints tells how Knox and Rutland are careful to avoid walking on the sand or other soft ground lest their footsteps should be seen; when compelled to walk on sandy ground they go backwards[60] in order to deceive any possible pursuers as to the direction of their flight. Along the way they indulge in a pipe of tobacco;[61] this is his only mention of the weed and it may have no connection with Crusoe's interest in securing pipes and tobacco.

When Knox and Rutland reach the Dutch colony of Arrepa[62] they are barefoot and have "great long beards," so that the people gaze at them and wonder who they are. Like Crusoe, Knox is able to speak Portuguese.

---

[55] *Ibid.*, p. 138.

[56] *Ibid.*, p. 154.

[57] *Ibid.*, p. 304.

[58] *Robinson Crusoe*, I, p. 269.

[59] *Ceylon*, p. 260.

[60] *Ibid.*, p. 261. This very circumstance is mentioned by Defoe in *Captain Singleton*, p. 281.

[61] *Ibid.*, p. 261.

[62] *Ibid.*, p. 274.

by means of which language he manages to communicate with the Dutch. The Governor has a tailor fit him with clothes, and later at Batavia the "General" has two "sutes of apparel"[63] made for them. Crusoe speculated on how his appearance would excite attention back in his native Yorkshire;[64] he had no shoes, and his beard he had "once suffered to grow till it was about a quarter of a yard long." Immediately upon being rescued, he is supplied with apparel, especially "a very good suit of clothes,"[65] by the ship's captain. Both men with one companion each return immediately to London; Knox has been absent twenty-three years and Crusoe thirty-five.

Thus far we have considered the similarities between "Robinson Crusoe" and Knox's only work published in Defoe's lifetime. Many of these similarities are not in themselves very convincing. It is only when we remember that Knox's "Ceylon" was well-known to Defoe and that a few months later (June, 1720) we find him in "Captain Singleton" not only relating the story of Knox's captivity openly but also using further details from it to furnish incidents for Singleton's story, that they become of more than superficial importance. These matters were known to Defoe and could not fail to find some place in Crusoe's endeavors to work out the problem of existence on his island.

b. *Possible Influence of Knox's Manuscript Journal*

There are, however, other points of connection between the adventures of Knox and those of Crusoe which are not so readily to be accepted. When on April 25, 1719, was issued what came to be the most widely read fictitious narrative ever produced in England, Robert Knox was a retired mariner above seventy-eight years of age living in London. Following his deliverance from Ceylon he had been on frequent voyages to the East Indies with only occasional stops in London; but about the end of the century he retired from his seafaring career and thereafter lived constantly in London until his death, June 19, 1720, two weeks after the appearance of "Captain Singleton," and two months before part three of "Robinson Crusoe."

After so much fruitless speculation and assumption that Defoe interviewed Selkirk, it might appear futile to consider a possible meeting between Defoe and Knox. And yet there are reasons why such a meeting is infinitely more probable than the other, expressly for which Defoe is said to have gone to Bristol. It has been asserted by Mr. Masefield, whose acquaintance with seventeenth and eighteenth century seamen is an intimate

---

[63] *Ibid.*, pp. 278, 280.
[64] *Robinson Crusoe*, I, pp. 165-6.
[65] *Ibid.*, I, p. 306.

one,[66] that Defoe knew Knox and got from him many first hand suggestions for "Robinson Crusoe."[67]   But Mr. Masefield here seems to be
relying upon a similar statement in Ryan's preface of Knox's works, which
remarks bluntly, "Defoe knew Knox."   For this important declaration
unfortunately no other proof is offered than that Defoe quotes from the
"Ceylon" in "Captain Singleton," that Quaker William "who contrived
to serve both God and Mammon (in "Singleton") . . . . smacks somewhat strongly of Knox himself," and that the introspective and religious
passages of "Robinson Crusoe" "strongly resemble Knox's account of
his own religious difficulties in captivity."[68]   But this gets us a very little
way toward establishing a direct connection between the men; for the
quotation from the "Ceylon" and the utilization of its religious and introspective passages depend upon no personal contact with its author,—
the "Ceylon" was open to anyone who wished to read it.   And though
Ryan's opinion that Quaker William "smacks" of Knox implies a knowledge by Defoe of some of Knox's questionable undertakings as a slave
trader and a privateer after the publication of the "Ceylon," the resemblances of that shrewd and tactful Quaker, with his keen sense of humor,
to the narrow and blundering Knox are too slight to be of any considerable
weight.   If Ryan had any more certain evidence, he does not mention it;
and the privately printed biography of Knox by Donald Ferguson, though
inaccessible, probably throws no further light upon the question.

There is, however, indication of some sort of acquaintance between the
two men, and if it could be established would be of considerable interest
and importance.   Every biographer of Defoe has confessed the paucity of
our information about his private life.   For long stretches we have little
to guide us except such fugitive traces as were left through his political
activity or through the succession of his published compositions.   Of
his intercourse with other men we know almost nothing; if he had any
friends or acquaintances we know little of who they were.   If, then, this
fellow-dissenter could be shown to have been to any degree conversant
with Defoe, the link would be worth establishing aside from its bearing on
the composition of "Robinson Crusoe."

The presumption that two men of such similar religious tendencies
should, with opportunities of meeting covering forty years, have some
slight acquaintance with each other contains no great improbabilities.
Knox had other acquaintances of literary attainments, such as Sir Chris-
topher Wren and Robert Hooke.   Nor was he uncommunicative about his

[66] See his admirably annotated edition of Dampier's *Voyages* (1906), and his
delightful narratives of seventeenth century seamen in *A Mainsail Haul* (1913).
[67] *A Mainsail Haul*, p. 132.
[68] Preface to the *Ceylon*, p. xxii.

adventures, embittered somewhat by what he considered mistreatment at the hands of Sir Josiah Child and the East India Company. That he pondered upon his nineteen years of solitude on Ceylon we know from the rambling entries in his autobiographical notes which Mr. Ryan has now made accessible in his edition of Knox's writings (1911). These disconnected descriptions may be considered as elaborations of matters too slightly treated in the "Ceylon." That relation, written during the voyage home from his captivity, did not tell many things of interest to his readers. Knox lacked the journalistic instinct, the sense for "news" which Defoe exhibited so masterfully in Crusoe's story. He did not see, for instance, that people would be deeply interested in even the minor details of his struggle; in his methods of dressing his food, of building his houses, and of supplying his other needs. But the questions which were propounded personally to him later showed him his error. Although the copies of the "Ceylon" were all bought up "& many more would have bin if were to be had & [although] it hath bin translated into Dutch and french," Knox had given his bond that neither himself nor his agents should "ever reprint the same." Unable, therefore, to publish a revised edition of his work, he probably gave out such oral information as he had opportunity for, and certainly recorded some such items in his manuscript. For instance, following a lengthy account of his particular friend, John Loveland, who died on Ceylon, Knox appends this note: "I have added this because I have heard some of Mr. Loveland's relation have wished to heare more of him. Robt. Knox."[69] Many other details of how he and his comrades lived were no doubt added by way of answer to similar queries. A man thus anxious to dispense miscellaneous information would hardly shy at any opportunity of telling his misfortunes to curious and appreciative listeners even though they had no personal interest in the relation. We know that he conversed with Dampier who repeatedly mentions that Captain Knox told him this or that.[70]

Having cleared the ground a little by showing that there is nothing inherently improbably in assuming an acquaintance of some sort between Knox and Defoe, we shall next consider those circumstances which would seem to make that assumption probable. The most obvious way to proceed is to look for evidence that Defoe was familiar with facts about Knox which are not recorded in the "Ceylon." In 1719 Knox had in his possession his personal copy of the "Ceylon," in which was folded a manuscript of 137 folio pages entitled "Concerning Several Remarkable Passages of my Life that hath hapned since my delivery out of my

[69] P. 367.
[70] Dampier, I, pp. 507, 511, and elsewhere.

Captivity." These notes which close with the year 1711 have been called by Mr. Ryan, the recent editor of Knox's writings, his "Autobiography." Besides this, six pages of manuscript notes, telling among other things certain facts of his life preceding his captivity, are placed in the front of the volume; they are dated 1696. The earlier parts of the manuscript record tell only of the meeting with his brother and sister and their children upon his unexpected return from Ceylon, and of his succeeding voyages, principally in the services of the East India Company, for the next twenty years. On two occasions his voyages are for slaves. Afterward, to raise his fortunes and to revenge himself on the East India Company for what he considered unfair treatment, he made a privateering expedition to the East. Later parts of the manuscript degenerate into a sort of diary or journal, recording occasional events of importance, such as the great storm of 1703 and the thanksgiving for the victory at Ramillies. Frequently Knox jots down disconnected descriptions of his life on Ceylon, or of meditations thereon; toward the close the journal becomes a mere series of moral reflections, interlarded with quotations and illustrations from the Old Testament, upon the problems and the vanities of life as he saw it about him.

How soon the manuscript autobiography was inserted in the "Ceylon" we do not know. It is certain, however, that "My booke of Ceylon with manuscripts of my owne life" were by the terms of his will (dated 1711) left to his nephew, Knox Ward "who beareth my name," and who bequeathed them to the Bodleian Library where they were discovered in 1910. The next year Messrs. Maclehose republished the "Ceylon" with the manuscript additions and a preface by Mr. James Ryan.

Now it is obviously impossible to ascertain whether or not Defoe used any facts gained orally from Knox. There is the possibility, however, that some evidence that Defoe either conversed with Knox personally, read his manuscript, or talked with some one who did know him, may be gained by checking Defoe's narrative with those recently published notes.

It has been remarked that Selkirk is not Crusoe; it may be added that Knox is not Crusoe, nor is Ceylon Crusoe's island. But there is considerable resemblance between the careers of Robert Knox and Robinson Crusoe (or Kreutznaer)[71] both preceding and following their island ex-

---

[71] The name Robinson may conceivably have been suggested by Knox's christian name. Mr. Aitken (*Notes and Queries,* 7th Ser., I, p. 89) found a Cruso family at Lynn in which the first name Robinson had passed from father to son from time immemorial; but as this was in 1886, it is not impossible that the custom began subsequently to 1719. Crusoe is no doubt from Timothy Cruso, an eminent dissenting minister who had been at the Newington Academy with Defoe. The latter, however, pretends that it is a corruption of the German name Kreutznaer. Wack-

periences. Each goes to sea against the wishes of his father. The elder Knox, who was a seaman and thus knew the hazards of sea life, had determined for his son a career on land as a tradesman, and consented to his son's importunities to be allowed to go to sea only after the intercession of others who argued that "commondly younge men doe best in that calling they have most mind to be in." Crusoe's impatience to go to sea against the desires of his father, who wished him to remain at home and be content with a middle station in life, is well known.

Both Crusoe and Knox begin their career with a successful voyage, and both become captives upon the second voyage. Crusoe first set out to sea in 1651, as nearly as we can judge. This voyage to Guinea, upon which he was the guest of the master, was a successful one. But attempting to repeat it, he found his good fortune at an end; for the ship was surprised "in the grey of the morning" by a Turkish rover who carried all on board into Salee and made them slaves. Knox's first voyage was to Fort George and Bengal, the latter a port at which in later years Crusoe was to spend some time; he was, like Crusoe, a companion of the captain (his father), and the voyage was a brief and profitable one. He likewise attempted another voyage to the Orient which ended as we have seen with his becoming a captive to the Sinhalese upon Ceylon.[72]

After Crusoe escapes from Salee and becomes a planter in Brazil he sets out upon a slaving voyage to Africa; it has already been mentioned that Knox became a slaver subsequently to his deliverance from captivity. The similarities in the island captivities we have considered previously.

Upon deliverance from his island, each returns to London where he finds himself a stranger after twenty-three or thirty-five years absence, during which had occurred both a great fire and a great plague. Each looks up his relatives. Knox finds his brother and his sister, who married to a second husband had several children. Crusoe going into Yorkshire finds "all the family extinct" except two sisters and two of the children of one his brothers. No provision had been made for him in the disposition of his father's estate, so that he (like Knox, whose brother was unable to pay him the part of his portion due him) had to look else-

---

witz asserts that the derivation is impossible. But it may have more point than investigators have observed. Kreutznaer is not far from the German word Kreu(t)zen, to cross or to cruise, and C(k)reu(t)z, a cross. It is interesting that a Cruso family of Leek (Wright, *Defoe*, p. 233) had for its motto, "Sub cruce." Cf. an imitation of *Robinson Crusoe, Der Teutsche Robinson oder Bernhard Creutz* (1722).

[72] It should be stated here that the elder Knox, who had previously been employed about the Barbary coasts, meditated upon his escapes from Turkish pirates. *Ceylon*, pp. 198, 9.

where. His benefactress, the widow who had been intrusted with the surplus earning from his first voyage to Guinea, "was become a widow the second time, and very low in the world." But, says Crusoe, "I made her easy as to what she owed me, assuring her I would give her no trouble."[73] Likewise Knox,[74] finding his brother unable to pay what he owed him, notwithstanding his poverty was able "franckely to remitt it to him."

Soon after his arrival in London Knox visited the East India Company where the "committy of said company" welcomed him and bestowed a gift of 20 pounds upon him. Crusoe met a similar reception[75] upon his return; for the master of the ship upon which he came, "having given a very handsome account to the owners" of his service to them, they invited him to meet them and made him "a very handsome compliment upon the subject," and a present of almost 200 pounds sterling.

For the rest of their careers there is little beyond a general similarity. Crusoe first settles down for several years of quiet before revisiting his island and setting out for the East Indies upon a trading voyage covering several years more. Knox, meanwhile, has returned to his trading in the Indies, and during the last decade of the century must, so to speak, many times have been in the vicinity of the imaginary Crusoe. Finally in 1700 and 1705 Knox and Crusoe, respectively, retire from the sea to spend their last days in London. Both comment[76] upon their ages and their expectation of death. Knox was still alive (as Crusoe is supposed to have been) in 1719 when parts one and two of "Robinson Crusoe" were published, though before part three with its preface signed by Rob. Crusoe saw the light, he had passed away.

The "Ceylon" and the "Autobiography" of Knox themselves resemble "Robinson Crusoe." When we consider the six manuscript pages devoted mainly to telling the events of his life before he was captured, and prefixed to the "Ceylon" which relates his island experiences, and the manuscript autobiography which follows, telling of Knox's adventures subsequent to his escape and trailing off into meditations and reflections strongly saturated with pious ejaculations and quotations from the Bible, there is apparent a close parallel to parts one (early life and island story), two (farther adventures), and three (serious reflections) of Defoe's story.

Proceeding from these general matters to a specific comparison of the contents of Knox's manuscript with Defoe's narrative, we find a number of details common to them which were either not mentioned at all in the

[73] *Robinson Crusoe,* I, p. 311.
[74] Knox, p. xxxii.
[75] *Robinson Crusoe,* I, p. 311; Knox, pp. xxxvi, 309.
[76] Knox, p. 382; *Robinson Crusoe,* II, p. 319.

"Ceylon" or were treated but slightly.[77]   Knox's second voyage following his return from Ceylon is to Madagascar for slaves where the natives after a period of friendliness treacherously seize the ship's boat capturing Knox and eleven of his men. The ship is three miles away at sea, but the captives manage to escape to it.[78]   When Crusoe leaves his island after the second visit, his ship touches at Madagascar and similarly to Knox's has trouble with the natives. The latter are at first friendly, but later make a surprise attack upon Crusoe and eleven of his men who are ashore in the ship's boat; as in the case of Knox the ship itself is a league away, but comes in near enough to aid in the escape of those on shore.[79]

Sailing from Madagascar Knox goes to St. Helena where the ship's crew run away with the vessel leaving him on shore. From Madagascar Crusoe goes to Bengal where he is left at the demand of the seamen. Other points of similarity between the careers of the two men have been dwelt upon earlier.

Having finished his narrative of his later voyages, Knox, as has been said, repeats with further elaborations many of the details of his life on Ceylon. He mentions, for instance, that he had no pens, ink, or paper, and hence could not record his experiences until after his escape; Crusoe had these writing materials at first and so was able to record events as they occurred, though later his ink gave out. Knox dwells at length upon his schemes to make his clothing last.[80]   His hat held out longer than anything else; his breeches were less permanent, and since his hair grew to his waistband and rendered shirts unnecessary he converted them into breeches. Shoes and stockings he dispensed with.   Later when his Dutch benefactors gave him European clothing he wore them awkwardly (as did both Crusoe and Selkirk) until accustomed to them again. Crusoe's devices do not greatly resemble those of Knox at every point. Knox was never reduced to the necessity of using animal skins; in fact, he later adopted the Sinhalese garb. But these matters are of importance as showing the similarity of the situations of the men; that they worked out their problems in a somewhat different manner is no very great evidence that the account of one did not influence the other.

[77] The summary of Knox's island experience in *Captain Singleton* apparently was made directly from *Ceylon*; at least no points not contained therein are introduced. Defoe keeps closely to Knox's diction except when condensing that account greatly; he reduces to twelve pages what Knox had used a hundred or so pages for. It may be noted here, however, that *Singleton* has other traces of Knox's influence which will be considered in a subsequent chapter.

[78] Knox, p. 313; *Robinson Crusoe*, II, p. 190.

[79] Other voyagers testify to the treachery of the natives of Madagascar.

[80] Knox, p. 393.

Knox tells[81] of his food (like Crusoe's it was principally rice and goat's flesh) ; of carrying his wood and water; and of beating his rice from the husk. He continues, "I washed all my pots and pans, in which I grew very expert." He roasted, boiled, and baked in an earthen pan ("made for my purpose") with fire on top and bottom. He made his own flour with a mortar. Crusoe mentions doing all these things, telling specifically how he made his earthenware substantial enough to put next the fire, and how he baked his bread with fire above and below his improvised pan. Knox's house which he built at Elladata was equipped with earthen pots, stools, and a table,—all of which Crusoe made for his dwelling. His house had two rooms; one which he called his "ketchen"[82] his boy slept in. Crusoe mentions calling one of his rooms his kitchen.

One of the most striking similarities between Knox's manuscript and "Robinson Crusoe" is the account of making planks. Speaking of the scarcity of boards owing to there being no saws, Knox says that the Sinhalese "make but two be the tree never so big, for they cut the tree through with axes into two sides or peeces and then with an ax and adds they chop it thine into a board; which was too much worke for me to doe." He adds, however, that since he had nothing else to do, the time required was no drawback. Crusoe's procedure was identical with this. Commenting upon his lack of tools, he says that "if I wanted a board, I had no other way but to cut down a tree, set it on an edge before me, and hew it flat on either side with my axe, till I had brought it to be thin as a plank, and then dub it smooth with my adze. It is true, that by this method I could make but one board out of a whole tree. . . . But my time or labour was little worth, and so it was as well employed one way as another." It is only fair to add that Dampier reports a procedure quite like both these which is practiced at Mindanao in the Philippines; this we shall consider presently.[83]

No one, I think, has ever suggested that Defoe needed any sources for the "Serious Reflections of Robinson Crusoe," since it has little narrative. It is, however, surprisingly similar in both tone and content to Knox's reflective passages. Just as part two of "Robinson Crusoe" gives way to the "Serious Reflections," so Knox's account of his later adventures dwindles into serious reflections upon the significance of his experiences and like matters. Knox, also, has his "Strange Surprising Adventures" (the "Ceylon"), his "Farther Adventures" (the autobio-

[81] Knox, pp. 395-6.
[82] *Ibid.*, p. 397.
[83] Knox, p. 402; *Robinson Crusoe*, I, p. 74; Dampier, I, p. 332.

graphical portions of his manuscript), and his "Serious Reflections" (following the autobiography).[84]

Those who have had the patience to read part three of "Robinson Crusoe" know that it is divided into a series of chapters each of which deals with a single topic, such as solitude and honesty, and a separate section called "A Vision of the Angelic World." Though several of these chapters, as the essay on honesty, have no counterpart in Knox, others are but more elaborate treatments of topics which he had touched upon significantly. Take for example the first chapter of the "Serious Reflections" of Crusoe, "Of Solitude (:) How incapable to make us happy, and how unqualified to a Christian life." This subject, upon which he spends fifteen pages, Knox had covered in a paragraph or two. He remarks that since his captivity he had heard "many discourse as if it were scarce possible to retaine any sence of religion where there is not a publicke worship. . . but I thanke God I have not found it so . . . . for God is a spiritt & they that worship may be as sincere in a wilderness as in a crowded congregation." Not the sanctity of the place nor the numbers present, he continues, can make him an acceptable worshipper; nor can his devotions "be the less excepted to the omnipresent God" because he is in a remote part of the earth. After demonstrating that the private devotions of many men have been honored by God, he goes on to say that in "these solitary states of life we are free from many temptations as drinking; sports . . . . & play houses and commonly publicke conversations few come better out then they were when they entred in."[85]

Thus in a page Knox dismisses the matter. Not so with Defoe whose hero goes into the matter of solitude more extensively and discourses of the true solitude of the mind and soul which is different altogether from that of the body. Man may, he thinks, "be properly said to be alone in the midst of the crowds and hurry of men and business." Of the freedom from temptations, especially those of playhouses, Crusoe had remarked when narrating his island life. Conversation occupies him in chapter three of the "Serious Reflections": "Of the Immorality of Conversation . . . " where he discusses at length the evils of conversation and the remedy therefor.

[84] For these contemplations and meditations Knox offers a whimsical apology. "These notions and contemplations," says he, "I have scribbled . . . . for my own use, & to please myselfe, & wheather hereafter they are ever or never read by any one it is equially the same to me, as to a dead beast what use his skine is put to, wheather to make a muffe or a ruffe for ladyes necks or made into shooes, or a pare of bellows, or a cover for a Bible . . . "

[85] Knox, p. 411.

After the remarks on solitude Knox feels led to protest against atheism.[86] Crusoe discusses atheistical conversation and atheism. Knox next meditates upon the "heats and differences amoungst men of the same religion in essentialls, about cerimonious circumstances used tharein." The meditation extends over a half dozen pages.[87] Crusoe devotes an essay of seventy pages to the "Present state of Religion in the World," in which he remarks these dissensions among professed Christians.[88] "How many self-contradictory principles do they hold?" he asks. " . . . How does one side burn for what another side abhors? And how do Christians . . . doom one another to the devil for a few disagreeing clauses of the same religion, while all profess to worship the same Deity, and to expect the same salvation?" Then he shows how those differences (which Knox thought would be avoided if men would eschew "traditions of churches" and "opinions of men," and follow "Gods holy word") arose among men who were all trying to follow the Bible.

Finally Knox's entry of December 31, 1706, in which he described briefly but significantly the thanksgiving for the victory of Ramillies, and his later comments upon the hollowness of military glory, are suggestive of Crusoe's satiric description of that very thanksgiving. "'Tis now the fashion," declares Knox,[89] "to call our victories & campanes, & generals for their conduct . . . glorious . . . In the pulpets when they proclame our glorious victories, ascribe it to second causes as conduct of generals," a glory which he thinks belongs to God alone. Crusoe, having surveyed the fallen state of religion throughout the Christian nations, turns to England in hopes of finding at home what he had searched for in vain in many other parts of the world,—hopes inspired by the proclamation appointing "a general thanksgiving for a great victory obtained by the English forces . . . over the French at (   )."[90] Thereupon follows an elaborate description of the day's events, description which dwells chiefly upon points mentioned by Knox in his journal. The latter's entry is as follows. "December the 31th Anno 1706 Tewsday, this day the Queene in great state rode in a ryall coach attended by boath houses of parliament, the house of Lords boath Spirituall & Temperall being in theire parliament Robes, to the Cathedrall of St. Paules, it being a general thanksgiving day through England, where Dr. Burnett, Bishop of Salsbury preached; all ceremonies were performed as firing guns; ringing bells: &

[86] Knox, p. 423; *Robinson Crusoe*, III, pp. 84ff., 302ff.

[87] Knox, p. 425ff.

[88] *Robinson Crusoe*, III, p. 128ff.

[89] P. 438.

[90] A reference to Ramillies so obvious that editors have inserted the name there in some editions.

bonfires for the great late victory obtained by the Duke of Marlborough &c., at Ramelies in flanders."[91]

Crusoe's discussion of the day extends to the following facts: "the queen would be there herself, and all the nobility"; there was an "infinite crowd of people"; the service was sung within "the church"; cannon were fired and the crowd gave "huzzas"; the day closed with drunkenness, bonfires, and "the squibs and crackers of the street."[92]

That Defoe had first hand acquaintance with this day of thanksgiving is more than probable, since he was an ardent admirer of Marlborough and an earnest advocate of the war. But what suggested the occasion to him in 1720? Certainly not the fact that his discussion stood in need of that particular sort of illustration. It is possible, of course, that this is an exception to Defoe's usual disregard of chronology in the story, and that an event of 1706 is used because Crusoe who returned from abroad in 1705 would be likely to have witnessed it; the "Serious Reflections," however, makes no attempt at observance of chronology at other points and probably does not here. Does it not at least seem possible that the event was suggested to Defoe either by conversation with Knox or by a perusal of his manuscript, especially since, as we have already seen, so many topics are common to these two compilations? Both men, moreover, repeatedly make comparisons with like occurrences in the Old Testament. Defoe alludes to Solomon's dedication of the temple, to Josiah's great feast of the reformation, to the escape of the Israelites from Pharaoh at the Red Sea, and to the rejoicing of Moses thereat,—all of which he vainly expected to see duplicated. Knox bluntly declares that he can "find nothing like this in the old Testament but all victoryes and glory is ascribed to God alone." Whereupon he cites divers instances.

It is evident from the foregoing discussion that Defoe, being as we know familiar with Knox's "Ceylon," utilized it in "Robinson Crusoe." There is, further, sufficient resemblance between the unpublished manuscript notes of Knox and Defoe's story to justify tentatively assuming that Defoe probably got other material either directly or indirectly from him.

III. *The Influence of Dampier's "Voyages"*

a. *Upon the "Farther Adventures"*

If we think of Selkirk as having suggested to Defoe the idea of writing a story of desert island life, and of Knox as having provided him with a concrete embodiment of that idea, we shall not go far astray. Defoe's next need would be a large storehouse of details of life under unusual

---

[91] Knox, p. 387.
[92] *Robinson Crusoe*, III, p. 142.

circumstances from which he could clothe the skeleton furnished by
Selkirk and Knox. Exactly such a storehouse of details is Dampier's
"Voyages."[93]

That Defoe was acquainted with the works of Dampier is no new
statement; he mentions them in the "Complete English Gentleman." Various writers have spoken in a general way of Defoe's debt to these voyages,[94] but no one, I think, has determined exactly what Defoe got from
Dampier, or indeed whether he certainly got anything from him. It is not
very difficult, however, to discover points both in the island story and in the
farther adventures of Crusoe which were taken directly from Dampier.
Obviously the more difficult task is to demonstrate this true for the island
story; I shall, therefore, first show that Defoe was indebted to Dampier for
parts of the later experiences of Crusoe, after which what I have to say
concerning the borrowings from him in the island story ought to be
received with less hesitation.

The reader will recall that when Crusoe bids final farewell to his island
and, after a brief stop at his old port in Brazil, sets out for the East Indies
by the usual route around the Cape of Good Hope and past Madagascar,
he is finally put ashore at the instance of the disgruntled crew at Bengal.[95]
Dampier, at the beginning of volume two of his voyages, is at Achin[96] on
the island of Sumatra. He had related, in the previous volume, his
adventures in crossing the Pacific from the west coast of North America
to the East Indies and to Sumatra. From Achin he makes a voyage east
to Tonquin Bay and China, and returns; but fearing that the reader will
weary of an account of that voyage, he leaves it for a later writing and
closes with his voyage from Achin home to England.[97]

Achin is no great distance from Bengal, and Crusoe and Dampier are
not far apart at this point. Each is a long way from home; how shall he
get back to England? Crusoe considers two ways:[98] " . . . . I might
travel here by land over the great Mogul's country to Surat, might go
thence from Bassora by sea, up the Gulf of Persia, and from thence
might take the way of the caravans over the desert of Arabia to Aleppo
and Scanderoon, from thence by sea again to Italy, and so overland into
France. . . . " Or he could "wait for some English ships[99] . . . . from

[93] William Dampier, *A New Voyage Round the World*, 2 vols. (1697, 1699);
A Voyage to New Holland, in two parts (1703, 1709).

[94] See Wackwitz, pp. 6, 13ff.

[95] *Robinson Crusoe*, II, p. 209.

[96] Dampier, II, p. 2.

[97] *Ibid.*, I, pp. 505, 521.

[98] *Robinson Crusoe*, II, p. 209.

[99] *Robinson Crusoe*, II, p. 210.

Acheen (Dampier's "Achin"), on the island of Sumatra, and get passage on board them for England."

Precisely these same routes home had been considered by Dampier in much the same language. Captain Bowrey importuned him "to go his boatswain to Persia.[100] . . . From thence he intended to pass with the caravan to Aleppo, and so home for England." There was also the possibility of taking ship directly for Engand,[101] as Crusoe saw.

Now Dampier chose the latter way and sailed from Bencouli on the *Defense*, January 25, 1691. But Crusoe rejected both routes, and, instead of returning home at all, set out upon identically the same course to Tonquin and China which Dampier had made from Achin, but which, out of consideration for the reader, he refrained from describing in his first volume published in 1697. Two years later, however, Dampier published his second volume, at the beginning of which he reminds the reader of the omission of that account, and proceeds to give a detailed relation of the voyage. This relation Defoe follows closely from the time Crusoe set out from Bengal until he passes northward from Macao to Nanking, and so out of Dampier's course. It is more than probable that he also made use of Dampier's map of the East Indies;[102] for some of the matters gathered by Defoe from Dampier appear more clearly on the map than in the text.

Prior to this voyage Crusoe and his partner, whom he picked up at Bengal, purchase a Dutch ship from some men who pretend to be her owners but who later transpire to be only members of the crew, the captain having been murdered with three of his men by Malayans.[103] These rogues had run away with the ship to Bengal leaving other members of her crew ashore,[104]—a circumstance which later brought the unsuspecting Crusoe and his men into danger of being summarily hanged as pirates. This episode clearly has its foundation in the misfortunes of a Captain Johnson related at length by Dampier.[105] Captain Johnson, having bought a Dutch ship on the East coast of Sumatra, was ashore with his carpenter to cut some timbers to refit her when a band of armed Malayans set upon them and murdered them both. The remainder of the crew, after beating off an attack upon the ship, was considerably puzzled about what to do with the vessel whose owner and commander was dead. They did not,

[100] Dampier, I, p. 503.

[101] *Ibid.*, I, p. 519ff.

[102] *Ibid.*, I, p. 282. Though unsigned, this map is probably by the well-known Dutch map-maker, Herman Moll, who about this time moved to England; at least the large map of the world in the front of the volume is by him.

[103] *Robinson Crusoe*, II, p. 215ff.

[104] *Ibid.*, p. 216.

[105] Dampier, II, pp. 110-118.

however, either steal her or set up as pirates, and I should not feel so certain of Defoe's use of the incident did it not occur as part of a series of borrowings which are indisputable.

In the voyage to Tonquin both Dampier and Crusoe meet with storms in passing through the straits of Malacca, and both touch at the mouth of the Cambodia River.[106]   It is at this latter place that Crusoe is attacked upon suspicion of being a pirate.   He barely escapes in season to avoid painful consequences; Dampier a little later describes the Cambodia River and speaks of pirates thereabouts.[107]

Fleeing from this encounter Crusoe's party "stood out to sea[108] eastward," later changing their course to north northeast[109] toward the bay of Tonquin and Macao. Just before reaching the bay, they[110] judge it to be the better part of valor to lie awhile in "a small river" to avoid any ships which might still be looking for them. About them they find a barbarous and thievish population. Dampier's map,[111] besides agreeing otherwise with Crusoe's distances, shows the little river just southwest of the entrance to Tonquin Bay, and his text speaks[112] of such a river and of the treachery of the natives thereabouts. But to this I shall return later.

At this point Defoe, as in the case of the choice of routes home from Bengal to England, betrays in his diction his dependence upon Dampier. From the small river, he says,[113] *"we coasted northeast to the point of land which opens the great bay of Tonquin. . . . "* Likewise Dampier had said, in words which it is absolutely certain that Defoe was following, that leaving the river of Cambodia "on our larboard side,[114] *we coasted along to the eastward . . . . to the point of land that bounds the S. W. part of the bay of Tonquin. . . . "* Because of slight differences in the two sentences we must not become confused and imagine that they say different things; the sentences not only resemble each other in phraseology, but their meaning is precisely the same. Both men are travelling northeast (or eastward), both arrive at the point of land,—the same point of land (which appears also on Dampier's map),—which lies at the southwest boundary of Tonquin Bay. The subtle difference lies in the fact that Defoe mentions only the direction in which he is going, whereas Dampier

[106] *Robinson Crusoe,* II, p. 217; Dampier, II, p. 4ff.
[107] Dampier, II, pp. 105, 6.
[108] *Robinson Crusoe,* II, p. 223.
[109] *Ibid.,* p. 225.
[110] *Ibid.,* pp. 226-7.
[111] Dampier, I, p. 282.
[112] *Ibid.,* II, pp. 7-8.
[113] *Robinson Crusoe,* II, p. 227.
[114] Dampier, II, p. 6.

in addition thereto mentions the situation of the bay which they are reaching.

Having arrived at this point of land under Dampier's guidance Crusoe finds himself "surrounded with enemies." The natives,[115] he asserts, "were among the most barbarous of all the inhabitants of the coast, having no correspondence with any other nation, and dealing only in fish and oil . . . . and it may be particularly seen that they are . . . . the most barbarous of any of the inhabitants, viz., that among other customs they have this as one, viz., that if any vessel have the misfortune to be shipwrecked upon the coast, they presently make the men all prisoners or slaves. . . . " This he takes freely from Dampier who remarks:[116] " . . . . I have been informed, that if a ship is cast away on this kingdom, the seamen that escape drowning and get ashore become slaves to the king." He then recounts briefly of a Captain John Tiler who "was thus served." "The seizing of ship-wrackt-men," he continues,[117] "has been also a custom at Pegu (just north of this region). . . . "

Crusoe, we have seen, found these people isolated from intercourse with the outside world, dealing only in oil and fish, "and such gross commodities." Dampier expresses the belief[118] that when they enter into commerce with other nations they will give up their practice of impressing wrecked seamen into slavery ; among their products he mentions oil (which they fish for), and pitch and tar. With these hints as to the character of the inhabitants Defoe invents an exciting account[119] of how they attempted to serve him and his companions, setting upon them as they were mending a leak in their vessel. Just when the natives think the crew is their prey, one of the seamen, who is equipped with pitch for paying the ship's seams, hurls that boiling liquid upon the attackers with a large ladle and drives them away.[120]

b. *Upon the Island Story*

Beyond doubt, then, Defoe was utilizing Dampier's "Voyage" in Crusoe's "Farther Adventures" written prior to August 20, 1719. It is not unreasonable to suppose that he made use of the same source in Crusoe's "Strange Surprising Adventures" published but four months earlier; that he did so in "Captain Singleton" prior to June, 1720, I shall

[115] *Robinson Crusoe*, II, p. 227.
[116] Dampier, II, p. 7.
[117] *Ibid.*, II, p. 8.
[118] *Ibid.*, II, pp. 7-8.
[119] *Robinson Crusoe*, II, pp. 228-231.
[120] Possibly this account owes something to Knox's treatment on Ceylon; for his ship was being repaired when the natives enticed him and his fellows ashore and made them captives.

show in a later chapter. It has been thought significant that the second edition of Rogers's "Voyage" containing the story of Selkirk appeared in 1718, approximately a year before the publication of part one of "Robinson Crusoe"; but that the sixth edition of Dampier's "Voyage" came out in 1717[121] has not been remarked in connection with Defoe's story. Such a number of editions is sufficient testimony of the wide-spread popularity of Dampier's books which, with their fresh treatment of many far-away places, informed with keen insight and characterized by careful observation, were increased in value by the maps of Herman Moll. Dampier, moreover, was hardly less connected with the adventures of Selkirk than was Rogers, having been concerned both with the expedition upon which Selkirk set out and the one which brought him back.

Mr. Aitken has commented[122] upon the resemblances of the map of the world delineating the voyages of Crusoe to that in Shelvocke's "Voyage" (1726). But as Crusoe's map appeared[123] seven years previously to Shelvocke's it is difficult to see any point to the comparison. Something of more significance is the resemblance of Crusoe's map to the one by Moll in Dampier's "Voyage." In title, proportions, general features, and courses marked out as sailed by Crusoe and Dampier, respectively, they are much alike.

In the light of these considerations, if we find indications of Defoe's borrowing details from Dampier for the island portion of Crusoe's story, we shall be less skeptical of acknowledging Dampier as the rightful source in the absence of any more probable origin for those details. Wackwitz and Wright have indeed pointed out that the story of the Mosquito Indian's experiences as a solitary inhabitant of Juan Fernandez was recorded by Dampier.[124] But neither has gone farther. That Dampier's adventures on the east coast of South America and in the West Indies and in other parts of the world are a veritable mine of information and suggestion for one writing a novel of desert island life in those regions has been ignored. Traces of Defoe's use of his history of those adventures appear throughout part one and portions of part two of "Robinson Crusoe" in addition to those already considered pertaining to the voyage from Bengal to Tonquin Bay.

The early episodes of Crusoe's career culminate in his becoming a slave at Salee. Upon escaping from thence he made his way southward in a boat; near Cape Verde a Portuguese vessel rescued him and his companion Xury, and carried them to Bahia de Todos los Santos, the principal

---

[121] This was used by Mr. Masefield as the basis for his text.
[122] Introduction to *A New Voyage Round the World*, p. ix.
[123] In August, 1719, in the *Farther Adventures*.
[124] Wackwitz, p. 6; Wright, *Defoe*, p. 231.

port in Brazil.[125]   Here Crusoe became a sugar planter, but was lured by the enormous profits of the slave trade into a voyage to Guinea, which voyage as every one knows ended in shipwreck and twenty-eight years of island solitude.   After his rescue he found that part of his income from his Brazil sugar plantation had been distributed to the Monastery of St. Augustine; [126] and upon revisiting Bahia, he helped deliver a man from the clutches of the inquisition by sending him and his family to the island colony.[127]

Defoe could, of course, have got his information about Brazil from many sources, but none other is so probable as Dampier's "Voyage to New Holland," published in two parts, one called volume three of his previously published "New Voyage" appearing in 1703, and the other, designated simply as a continuation, appearing in 1709.[128]   On this voyage to what is now known as Australia, he not only saw Portuguese ships passing from near Cape Verde to Brazil but actually sailed that route himself, going directly to Crusoe's port,[129] Bahia de Todos los Santos, where he stopped awhile.   He also described the region in his usual manner.   His description of Brazil and its port, Bahia, gives in a succinct form all that Defoe needed for his account of Crusoe's life there.   He tells of the sugar industry;[130] of the profitable trade of selling negro slaves;[131] of the establishments of Catholic orders;[132] and of the inquisition, the clutches of which he narrowly avoided.[133]   These are precisely the points made use of by Defoe.   Both Dampier and Defoe, moreover, allude to the restrictions upon trade with vessels other than Portuguese.[134]

For the island story Dampier furnishes multitudes of ideas many of which Defoe certainly used.   He tells of a number of islands along the northeast coast of South America resembling Crusoe's island.   Of islands stocked with goats and tortoises (Crusoe's chief articles of food in the

[125] Crusoe later calls it by another name, Sao Salvador, which was occasionally given it by the Portuguese.

[126] Robinson Crusoe, I, p. 313.

[127] Ibid., II, p. 182.

[128] For convenience I shall refer to them as volumes three and four of Dampier's "Voyage."

[129] III, pp. 47-91.

[130] III, p. 55.

[131] III, p. 61.

[132] III, pp. 51, 89-90.

[133] He tells (III, p. 53), moreover, of an English merchant there among the Portuguese,—a suggestion which makes Crusoe's friendly reception plausible. Crusoe's neighbor, Mr. Wells, may have got his name from a Mr. Wells also mentioned by Dampier in another part of his narrative (II, p. 110ff.).

[134] Dampier, III, p. 54; Robinson Crusoe, II, p. 181.

earlier days of his island life) he mentions several. Especially noteworthy is the isle of Aves off the north coast of Venezuela. This small and un-inhabited island Dampier describes[135] as being "not above 4 miles in length" and as having a "riff or bank of rocks" which extends from the east end about three miles into the sea. Upon these rocks a French fleet was lost; from the wreck "masts, yards, timbers, and many things" else were driven on shore. Crusoe's island, it will be remembered, had a ledge of rocks extending into the sea from the east end, upon which a Spanish vessel was wrecked; contents of that vessel also were driven ashore.[136]

The isle of Aves is not, to be sure, at the mouth of the Orinoco River; instead it is some leagues northwest. But Defoe seems to have had no particular island in mind. Tobago, an English island near Trinidad, is sometimes said to have been the one Defoe meant; but this is erroneous, since Tobago is northeast of Trinidad and in 11 degrees and some minutes north latitude, whereas Crusoe says plainly[137] that his island was in the region of nine degrees and twenty-two minutes north latitude, and that he could see Trinidad west and northwest of him. Our maps no longer show a group of small islands south and southeast of Trinidad, plainly represented hovering about the mouth of the Orinoco upon seventeenth century maps; at least they so appear on Dampier's map.[138] It is probable that Defoe had vaguely in mind one of these unnamed and undescribed islands,[139] and that he invented or borrowed from other islands such physical features as he needed. His reason for locating Crusoe in the vicinity of the Orinoco River cannot be known definitely; but it is rea-sonable to suppose that this region possessed unusual interest to him from its having been explored by one of his favorite historical characters, Sir Walter Raleigh, an account of whose voyages he issued within a year after the publication of "Robinson Crusoe."

[135] Dampier, I, p. 49ff.
[136] Robinson Crusoe, I, p. 206ff.
[137] Ibid., I, pp. 69, 239.
[138] Dampier, I, p. 24.
[139] Since writing this paragraph I have discovered that precisely this same idea has been advanced by a writer in La Mercure de France, 15 November, 1922 (reprinted in The Living Age, 30 December, 1922, p. 776ff.). One reason given by that writer for rejecting Tobago as the island which Defoe had in mind is of no importance, namely, that Tobago was inhabited in 1655. The important question is not whether it was inhabited, but whether Defoe thought it was; and that he did not think so is made evident in Captain Singleton, where (p. 165) he asserts that it was without inhabitants. The article by Mr. Freeman (in Travel, February, 1920) is of no importance, offering no solution of the problem, and propagating much error.

Some of the features of Crusoe's island were undoubtedly borrowed from Juan Fernandez, the scene of Selkirk's adventures; others were not improbably taken from some of these islands described by Dampier. The latter relates, as has been mentioned, rescuing the Mosquito Indian who had been three years alone on Juan Fernandez and who devised a number of ways of getting food. Upon meeting another Mosquito Indian in Dampier's party, the lonely man greeted him with all the tokens of unaffected joy exhibited by Friday at the meeting with his father.[140] One of the happiest touches of Defoe in the story is the naming of Friday. It may be true as one writer has pointed out[141] that the name "Friday" occurs in the register of St. Dunstan's parish (near Canterbury) in the eighteenth century, where the names "Cruzo" and "Defoe" also appear in the late seventeenth century. But not improbably Defoe in naming his savage was (as he implies) imitating the voyagers, who made a practice of naming islands and capes for the day upon which they were discovered. Dampier followed this practice in giving the name St. Matthias to an island discovered by him.[142] Crusoe's man came to him upon a Friday, and from thence received his name. That a little while previously Crusoe confessed having lost all trace of particular days so that he could not have known when the event actually happened does not affect the matter at all.

I have suggested similarities between the isle of Aves as described by Dampier and Crusoe's island. Another island nearby Aves is "Bonairy" which Dampier mentions being stocked with goats.[143] Of islands similarly stocked with goats he speaks again and again;[144] once he mentions an island which has no goats.[145] References to tortoises are perhaps more numerous than to any other one thing in Dampier. He tells where they are to be found[146] and describes them in detail,[147] mentioning their manner of breeding,[148] their length of life,[149] and their mode of travelling and of laying eggs.[150] He tells also how they are to be caught and what kinds are best for eating.

The whole region along the northeast coast of South America is described by Dampier. The Caribbee Indians who travel about from place to

---

[140] Dampier, I, p. 86; *Robinson Crusoe*, I, p. 265.
[141] *Notes and Queries*, 7th Series, I (February 20, 1886), p. 158.
[142] Dampier, IV, p. 113.
[143] *Ibid.*, I, p. 48.
[144] *Ibid.*, I, pp. 56, 72, 74-5, 77-8, 86-88.
[145] *Ibid.*, I, p. 58.
[146] *Ibid.*, I, pp. 2, 9, 38, 39, 56, 57, 58, 75.
[147] *Ibid.*, I, pp. 103-110, 133, 146, 159, etc.
[148] *Ibid.*, I, p. 160.
[149] *Ibid.*, I, p. 108.
[150] Dampier, I, 75, 194-8, 215.

place among the nearby islands, St. Martha and other points on the coast, and Trinidad island (which he touches), all find a place in his relation.[151] This area is said by Crusoe to be inhabited by Caribbees as far as St. Martha.[152,153]

Of fowls upon his island Crusoe mentions especially parrots, penguins, and pigeons. One of the best known incidents of the story is the training of a parrot to speak. Dampier tells of parrots repeatedly, remarking upon one occasion that they "prate prettily" and that his men got one each.[154] Pigeons, penguins, and other fowls are given attention in his pages. Crusoe's dogs,[155] one of which came to him out of his own wreck and the other out of the wreck of a Spanish vessel, are partially matched by an English dog mentioned by Dampier;[156] this animal was, against the wishes of the fond crew, given upon request to the governor of Guam as a present.

A number of Crusoe's devices for his safety and comfort were suggested by Dampier. The former built a "periagua or canoe" after directions given by the latter, who no less than a dozen times speaks of "pereagoes or canoes," excluding references to canoes only.[157] Dampier three times tells how they are made,[158] remarking that those of cedar are best. "They are nothing," he says,[159] "but a tree itself made hollow boatwise with a flat bottom. . . ." At another place he describes the method of

[151] *Ibid.*, I, p. 58.

[152] *Robinson Crusoe*, I, p. 240. Professor Trent finds Crusoe's remark obscure, though admitting that he must have meant St. Martha, now a river or city of Columbia. (See his edition of *Robinson Crusoe*, 1916, p. 355). But there can be little doubt that he refers to that city, which appears clearly on Dampier's map (I, p. 24) and which is mentioned by Dampier in his narrative. As Professor Trent seems to infer, Defoe speaks of the place in *Captain Singleton* also.

[153] Purchas (XVI, p. 301ff.) has an account of Trinidad by Francis Sparrey "left there by Sir Walter Raleigh" in 1595. Sparrey speaks of an island near the mouth of the Orinoco, called Athul, of which he says: "If I had had company to my liking, I could have found in my heart to have stayed there and spent my life . . . There is no want neither of fish, tortoyses, . . . foules . . . It hath wood great store, fruites all the yeere in abundance . . . The island is small, and for feare of the Caribes, there is nobody." Another uninhabited island "to the south southwest of Orenoco," he reports being used as "a bayting place for the Caribes, when they had stollen people, which they meant to eate." He goes on to tell that he and some others went there "somewhat strong" to kill any of these cannibals, but they found none. See Günther, p. 49.

[154] Dampier, II, ii, pp. 128-9. See also I, p. 39, and IV, pp. 73, 101, 164.

[155] *Robinson Crusoe*, I, pp. 70, 212.

[156] Dampier, I, p. 302.

[157] Dampier, I, pp. ii, iii, 26, 29, 40, 85, 136, 185; II, part ii, pp. 4, 18, 51.

[158] *Ibid.*, I, pp. 29, 85, 214-5.

[159] *Ibid.*, I, p. 29.

fashioning them from large trees,[160] and of getting them to the water afterward. Crusoe, upon deciding to contrive "a canoe, or periagua," proceeds to cut down a huge cedar tree[161] which he shapes and makes hollow, and so has "a very handsome periagua." His failure in getting the canoe to the sea after it is built is too well known to need recounting.

The methods employed by Defoe's hero in plankmaking may be from the unpublished manuscript of Robert Knox, as has been said; if not, they are undoubtedly from Dampier's report of the Philippines. The native carpenters at Mindanao, he says,[162] have no saws; "but when they make a plank they split the tree in two, and make a plank of each part, planing it with the ax and ads. This requires much pains, and takes up a great deal of time; but they work cheap" and the planks are very good.[163]

The use of ladders to enter dwellings Dampier mentions twice;[164] on the second occasion he tells in some detail of the method of house-building practiced by the natives of the Bashi Islands, whose dwellings are like Crusoe's in being upon a hill-side with inaccessible precipices at the flanks and having entrances equipped with ladders. The houses of these people, he says, are low. "The sides, which are made of small posts, watled with boughs, are not above 4 foot and a half high." Their. dwellings being bound by precipices, they need only to draw up the ladder "if they be assaulted, and then there is no coming at them from below, but by climbing up as against a perpendicular wall; and that they may not be assaulted from above, they take care to build on the side of such a hill, whose backside hangs over the sea, or is some high steep, perpendicular precipice, altogether inaccessible . . . . and the natives, whether for fear of Pyrates, or foreign enemies . . . . care not for building but in these fastnesses."

Crusoe, it will be recalled, found "a little plain on the side of a rising hill, whose front . . . . was steep as a house side, so that nothing could come down" upon him from above.[165] In the space before this hill (which he calls a rock) he pitched his tent, enclosing it with a half circle of posts which, with the rock in the rear, made it inaccessible either to man or beast. "The entrance to this place," he says, "I made to be not by a door, but by a short ladder to go over the top, which ladder I

---

[160] *Ibid.*, I, p. 214-5.

[161] *Robinson Crusoe*, I, p. 139.

[162] Dampier, I, p. 332.

[163] It is possible that Knox, who a number of times conversed with Dampier, was influenced in his account of board making among the Sinhalese either by talking directly with Dampier or by reading the passage quoted above in his published narrative.

[164] Dampier, I, pp. 151, 428. For other accounts of this custom see Hakluyt, V, p. 485, and Purchas, X, pp. 156, 185.

[165] *Robinson Crusoe*, I, p. 63ff.

lifted over after me, and so I was completely fenced in, and fortified . . . . from all the world. . . . " Some time later, having converted his pale into a wall by placing turf against the posts, he "raised rafters from it (the wall) leaning to the rock, and thatched or covered it with boughs of trees." As will appear in the following chapter, Defoe borrowed a number of ideas from Dampier's account of the Bashians to use in "Captain Single- ton."

Other devices used by Crusoe and mentioned or described by Dampier are the making of rafts, earthenware, umbrellas, baskets, and truncheons. Dampier describes several kinds of rafts[166] and the manner of construct- ing them, to be used either with sails or oars. Crusoe built rafts upon which to carry ashore the goods plundered from the wreck, using both sails and oars. Dampier, though he mentions earthenware,[167] does not give any specific suggestions which Defoe may have used; those, as we shall see, probably came from another source. Umbrellas[168] and baskets[169] are mentioned but not described by Dampier. Truncheons are spoken of twice;[170] Crusoe took one with him into a tree for protection during his first night's lodging.

Such articles of food as melons and grapes found by Crusoe on the island are mentioned repeatedly by Dampier,[171] who once speaks of rusk and bisket.[172]

One of the most graphic incidents in "Robinson Crusoe" is the finding of foot prints in the sand. Strange as it may seem, the literature of travel is not rich in such experiences. I have called attention to Knox's device in escaping from the Sinhalese of walking backwards on the sand that his tracks might delude any possible pursuers as to the direction of his flight. Another source suggested as the origin of Crusoe's experience is Smeeks's "Krinke Kesmes"; the Dutch boy castaway in that work speaks twice of tracks in the sand. But his remarks lose much of their significance for the student of Crusoe's story when their nature is understood. The boy was a member of a ship's crew sent to an island to search for some seamen cast away there awhile before. The rescuers found no one, says the boy,[173] although they saw some tracks of bare feet in the sand.[174]   Later the

[166] Dampier, I, pp. 142-3.
[167] Dampier, I, p. 250; II, p. 63.
[168] Ibid., I, pp. 407-8.
[169] Ibid., I, p. 150.
[170] Ibid., IV, pp. 77, 118.
[171] Ibid., I, pp. 134, 392; II, part ii, p. 49. See also Hakluyt, VIII, pp. 298, 392, and IX, p. 11.
[172] Dampier, I, p. 303.
[173] The Narrative of the El-Ho (1921), p. 2.
[174] The original (see p. 111) is, " . . . dog zaagen eenige drukkingen van bloote voeten in 't zand."

boy becomes separated from his comrades, and in searching for them thought he saw "footprints" (literally "footsteps").[175] In both of these cases the footprints are presumably those of friends, and are suggestive not of fear but of hope. There is, furthermore, nothing of the prominence or interest attached to them by Smeeks which Defoe gives to Crusoe's finding of footprints.

It is possible, however, that either Knox or Smeeks may have suggested to Defoe the idea of having Crusoe find footprints of savages in the sand; but neither mentions them as discovered under the circumstances attending Crusoe's discovery, namely, that of fear that they may be evidence of danger from the presence of an enemy. It is this very fact which gives unusual importance to a passage in Dampier's narrative dealing with the discovery of foot prints; for precisely this element of fear, missing in both Knox and Smeeks but present in "Robinson Crusoe," enters into it. The incident is this. Dampier and some others, being ashore to kill cattle on the isle of Pines (near Cuba), landed on a sandy bay where they saw "much footing of men and boys; the impressions seemed to be about 8 or 10 days old."[176] "This troubled us a little," said Dampier, who strongly suspected them of being the tracks of Spaniards; "but it being now their Christmas, we concluded that they were gone over to Cuba to keep it there, so we went after our game. . . . " The element of fear is, of course, mild in comparison to that in "Robinson Crusoe," but it is there. Like Crusoe, the party find footprints which trouble them and about which they hold some sort of consultation, deciding them to be traces of an enemy.[177]

As a contribution to Crusoe's island adventures we may consider finally Dampier's severe illness with the fever, brought on like Crusoe's ague by exposure to wet weather. Defoe, as we have seen, was probably indebted to Knox for the idea of Crusoe's ague, but for its treatment he appears to be more indebted to Dampier whose cure wrought by a Malayan doctor was by quite as violent means as those employed by Crusoe.[178]

Many of these suggestions from Dampier Defoe could have got elsewhere. But since he certainly used Dampier's "Voyages" in the "Farther Adventures" (published four months after the island story) and since

---

[175] P. 119, " . . . my dagt ook dat ik voestappen zag, doch deeze verdweenen weeder."

[176] Dampier, II, part ii, p. 34.

[177] It is probable that Crusoe's chart of the seasons on his island (I, p. 117) was worked out by Defoe from suggestions given by Dampier, II, part iii, p. 77ff. There he remarks that the rainy seasons come and go with the sun in its northward and southward movements.

[178] I, p. 503.

some of these details, notably the method of canoe making, are from Dampier, it is unquestionable that this storehouse of suggestions open to his hand was utilized to a very great extent by Defoe. Here and from Knox and the published accounts of Selkirk's affairs Defoe got his chief incidents for the island story.

This discussion of Defoe's obligations to Dampier began with demonstrating that the voyage from Bengal to Tonquin Bay related in the "Farther Adventures" was modelled closely after an account of Dampier's voyage over that route. There remain a few other points from Dampier used by Defoe in the "Farther Adventures." On the way from his island to Bengal Crusoe stopped at Madagascar where his men were attacked by the natives.[179] The reason for this attack was the abuse of a native woman by one of the seamen; the latter is slain by the enraged savages. To avenge his death his comrades burn a native village. A very common matter with Dampier is his recording of irregular conduct between his men and the native women; and not infrequently are reported violent means taken by the natives in revenge.[180]. On two occasions he speaks also of the burning of native villages.[181]

Other matters which suggest incidents in Defoe's story are: Captain Swan's being left behind in the Philippines by his rebellious crew (as Crusoe was at Bengal) ;[182] Dampier's friendly relations with French Jesuit missionaries to China;[183] his descriptions of hideous Chinese idols;[184] his mention of chinaware, lacquer ware, and silk,[185] and of the manners of the mandarins;[186] his descriptions of the Spice Islands;[187] and his repeated mention of the Spanish vessels trading between Manila and Acupulco.[188] Both the Spice Islands and the Manila-Acupulco ships figure prominently in "Captain Singleton" and are mentioned in "Robinson Crusoe."

Finally Dampier personally may have contributed a few features to the character of Crusoe. He tells us how his desire to "ramble" and to see the world led him to go to sea ;[189] and once when near drowning in a storm

---

[179] II, p. 189ff.
[180] Dampier, I, pp. 364-7, 374, 548; II, 161.
[181] Ibid., I, pp. 145, 223.
[182] Ibid., I, pp. 372-4.
[183] Dampier, II, pp. 93-7.
[184] Ibid., I, pp. 396-7; II, p. 56.
[185] Ibid., I, pp. 250, 409; II, pp. 61-3.
[186] Ibid., II, p. 84.
[187] Ibid., I, pp. 311, 316, 318, 364, 447.
[188] Ibid., I, pp. 260, 291, 303, 384.
[189] Ibid., II, part ii, p. 2.

at sea, he repents of his roving life, looking with sad reflection upon his misspent days.[190]

IV. *Le Comte and Crusoe's Adventures in China*

Having carried Crusoe to the Chinese coast, Defoe could make no further use of Dampier's works, and so turned elsewhere for ideas. Crusoe's stay in China, though several months in length, leads to little either of description or narrative. He and his partner sail to Nanking, but, with a ship suspected of being manned by pirates, they decide on the more prudent course of retiring southward along the coast to a lesser known port, called in the story Quinchang, a name which Crusoe admits to differ from that given it by others. Here they dispose of their cargo, make a short journey to Nanking overland, and set out for Peking in company with some Jesuits. From Peking they depart by caravan toward Archangel. This portion of the story occupies approximately twenty pages. The action is not very important, and the comments upon the country are of a general character.

For his purpose Defoe might have turned to a number of suitable accounts of China. Though many descriptions of that empire were old and defective, others were recent and in the main accurate. The Jesuits were zealous in sending out missionaries to China, and the late seventeenth century was especially prolific of their reports. There was, also, the interesting account of China by a native of the country, Dionysius Kao; this was translated into English and published with Ides's "Travels" (1706), a book known to Defoe. Another work suggested by Mr. Aitken as a possible source of this portion of "Robinson Crusoe" I have been unable to find any record of: Le Duc's "Voyage à la Chine" (1700).[191]

Just which account may have been most useful to Defoe would be a difficult matter to determine had he not, in the "Serious Reflections of Robinson Crusoe," especially referred to the Jesuit Father, Le Comte.

---

[190] It is interesting to note some stylistic resemblances between Defoe and Dampier, such as the frequent use of "viz." The use of the word "fright" as a verb has been thought distinctive of Defoe, and has been relied upon by some investigators as evidence of his authorship of certain works. But it is used by Dampier even more than by Defoe. (Dampier, I, p. 439; II, part ii, p. 23; III, pp. 146; IV, pp. 134-5, 140; he says "frighted," "affrighted," and "to fright." Knox likewise occasionally says "frighted.") Twice Dampier remarks, "I shall not trouble the reader with an account of every day's run," Crusoe's phraseology (though found also in Le Comte's *China*). And both Crusoe and Dampier speak of the errors of our hydrographers and mapmakers (Dampier, I, pp. 100, 193), and discuss the northeast passage to America (Dampier, I, p. 274; *Crusoe*, II, p. 211).

[191] *Robinson Crusoe*, I, p. lv. It is possible that this is an error for Le Comte.

Speaking of the state of religion in China he says,[192] "Father Le Comte gives us the pictures of some of their house idols." Louis Le Comte was one of the French Jesuit missionaries to China in the latter part of the seventeenth century; his "Memoirs and Observations made in a late journey through the Empire of China" was translated into English in 1697. This work, with some suggestions from Dampier, supplied Defoe with all the information he needed for Crusoe's brief remarks on China.[193]

Le Comte travelled from Siam to China by much the same route as did Crusoe and Dampier; but instead of stopping at Macao, as the missionaries were accustomed to do, he went on to Ningpo, whence he travelled to Peking. Crusoe, as we have seen, sailed up to Nanking from Macao, but later retraced his course to the place which he inaccurately called Quinchang. Whether or not Defoe had a real harbor in mind we do not know; it is not improbable, however, that he was referring to Le Comte's "Nimpo," or Ningpo, since he says the Jesuit fathers were in the habit of stopping there on the way from Macao to Peking, and he himself relates that Crusoe a little later went up to Peking with Father Simon, a French Jesuit comparable to Le Comte. Both Le Comte and Crusoe comment upon the convenience of this port for voyages to Japan. Both mention the danger of thieves; and Crusoe's guard at Quinchang resembles that granted to Le Comte.[194]

In his remarks upon China in general Crusoe emphasizes the density of the population, relating that Father Simon regards Peking as bigger than London and Paris combined. Le Comte, likewise, speaks at length of the amazing number of inhabitants;[195] Peking he estimates to contain 2,000,000 persons, or twice as many as Paris. Both Crusoe and Le Comte are inclined to scoff at the reputed wonders of China, explaining that were these features brought into comparison with those of Europe they would appear but mean.[196] Crusoe enters into a lengthy discussion of the state of Chinese civilization, commenting especially upon her military forces and her commerce.[197] One line of German or of French cavalry, he thinks, could overthrow all the horse of China; and he wonders why the Czar of Muscovy did not choose to attack China, of which he might soon have been emperor, instead of Sweden whose king defeated him at

[192] *Ibid.*, III, p. 125.

[193] A brief assertion of Defoe's indebtedness to Le Comte for Crusoe's observations on China has been made in a recent German dissertation which I had not seen until this study was written: Albert Lüthi's *Daniel Defoe und seine Fortsetzungen zu Robinson Crusoe* (1920), p. 66.

[194] Le Comte (1697), pp. 29, 87; *Robinson Crusoe*, II, p. 245.

[195] *Robinson Crusoe*, II, p. 247; Le Comte, pp. 55-58.

[196] *Robinson Crusoe*, II, p. 253; Le Comte, p. 64.

[197] *Robinson Crusoe*, II, p. 253ff.

Narva. Le Comte likewise has a mean opinion of Chinese civilization. Chinese troops look well on parade, he says, but are easily disorganized in battle. At another place he remarks having often reflected how easily Louis XIV could have subdued China.[198]

I do not mean to imply here that Defoe knew no more of China than Le Comte told him; but certainly he gave in "Robinson Crusoe" only offhand elaborations of Le Comte's suggestions. The latter explains the circumstances which led China to esteem so highly her own progress in the arts and sciences, and which extended her reputation in other lands. With this inspiration Crusoe launches into a heated attack upon the civilization of China, the force of which carries over into the "Serious Reflections."[199]

Their learning Crusoe finds as contemptible as their military establishment. ". . . . they have globes and spheres," he says, "and a smatch of the knowledge of the mathematics; but when you come to inquire into their knowledge, how shortsighted are the wisest of their students! They know nothing of the motions of the heavenly bodies; and so grossly, absurdly ignorant, that when the sun is eclipsed they think 'tis a great dragon has assaulted and run away with it, and they fall a-clattering with all the drums and kettles in the country to fright the monster away, just as we do to hive a swarm of bees."[200]

Le Comte is plainly the source for all this. He describes the Chinese astronomical observatories at length, illustrating his discussion with a plate of diagrams.[201] It is well, he thinks, that the Chinese make their boasts of astronomical excellence 6,000 leagues from Europe where it is impossible to demonstrate to them their errors. The Chinese, he continues, have long studied astronomy, but should be ashamed of the little improvement they have arrived at. So ignorant are their astronomers that they are still unable to form an exact calendar, preferring their antiquated instruments and methods to the modern ones introduced by Europeans. But then, he goes on to say, "provided their salaries be paid as usual . . . . they are in no great trouble about the changes which happen in the sky." To explain eclipses "they have fancied that in the heavens there is a prodigious great Dragon, who is a possessed enemy to the sun and moon, and ready at all times to eat them up." Whereupon they resort to the beating of drums to drive the dragon away. Again near the end of his book,[202] Le Comte mentions the custom of attempting by

---

[198] Le Comte, pp. 75, 309.
[199] Le Comte, p. 123ff; *Robinson Crusoe*, II, p. 253ff; III, p. 119ff.
[200] *Robinson Crusoe*, II, p. 255.
[201] Le Comte, p. 64ff.
[202] *Ibid.*, p. 489.

noise to frighten away the dragon which at eclipses they imagine holds the sun or moon between his teeth intending to devour it and therewith satisfy his hunger.

Crusoe and his partner delay their departure from Quinchang to Peking until Father Simon is joined by another missionary from Macao; then the party travels in the retinue of a mandarin, "a kind of viceroy." The state in which the mandarins journey and the homage which they expect from the inhabitants of the places through which they pass is noted by Crusoe much as by Le Comte.[203] The former says that the people are expected to furnish supplies for the mandarins and all their retinues when they travel; Le Comte says that the people offer supplies, but apparently out of respect for the mandarins, and at another place he speaks as though the expenses of those viceroys are borne by the emperor,[204] though this may not apply to the sustenance they require upon journeys. It may be that this slight disagreement with Le Comte arose from Defoe's recollection (unconscious, perhaps) of a statement in Knox's account of the Sinhalese, to the effect that when the king's chief officers travel the people must bear his expenses.[205]

Crusoe's attack upon the insufferable pride of the Chinese has warrant in Le Comte's account, but when the former proceeds to picture a country gentleman who joins their party for a few miles, riding in a state of "perfect Don Quixotism, being a mixture of pomp and poverty," he seems to be getting beyond the Jesuit. Le Comte indeed does say[206] that the mandarins of meaner quality never go on the street unless mounted and attended by several footmen. He also describes the long and cumbersome habit of the Chinese, telling of the *surtout* "the sleeves whereof are extream wide" and trail upon the ground; of the bonnet or cap with "a great flake" of red silk falling down to its edge; of the elaborate vest girdled by a broad silk sash the ends of which hang to the knees. And these features agree with Defoe's description of this fellow's garb as having "all the tawdry trappings of a fool's coat, such as hanging sleeves, tassels, and cuts and slashes on almost every side."[207] But Defoe goes much further in his satire, giving an excellent portrait of this "greasy

---

[203] *Robinson Crusoe*, II, p. 256; Le Comte, p. 163ff. Several pages following 160 in Le Comte are wrongly numbered. The references here are to the pages as numbered by the printer.

[204] Le Comte, p. 270.

[205] Knox, *Ceylon*, p. 84.

[206] *Robinson Crusoe*, II, p. 258; Le Comte, pp. 163-4.

[207] Le Comte's repeated mention (pp. 163, 4) of the mandarin's use of umbrellas is suggestive of Crusoe's umbrella. The latter is said to have seen them in Brazil. Other possible sources of the idea will be mentioned later in this chapter.

Don" whose dirty calico and taffeta vest "as greasy as a butcher," testified "that his honor must needs be a most exquisite sloven." The description of the man's horse, attendants, country seat, and meal, extending over a couple of pages, is either largely Defoe's own invention or else a borrowing from some other source than Le Comte.[208]

Shortly after the party arrives at Peking, Crusoe and his comrade conceive the idea of going back to England by land through Tartary, Siberia, and Russia, for which journey Defoe is compelled to look elsewhere for guidance. Some other obligations to Le Comte, however, need to be pointed out. Crusoe's description of the Chinese wall is one of these. Most of the accounts of that wall dwell upon its dimensions and strength. Both Le Comte and Crusoe do that; but they also do something else which is not so customary; they comment upon the uselessness of extending the wall over mountains and precipices which are more difficult for an enemy to scale than the wall itself after it has been reached. Says Crusoe: " . . . . a very great work it is, going over hills and mountains in a needless track, where the rocks are impassable, and the precipices such as no enemy could possibly enter, or indeed climb up, or where, if they did, no wall could hinder them." Le Comte's remarks are similar: ". . . . how ridiculous was it of them to carry this wall to the top of some precipices which the birds can scarce reach . . . . and on which it is impossible the Tartarian horse should ascend . . . ." He continues by saying that even if the enemy could scale those heights such a low and thin wall would be no obstacle to them.[209]

Crusoe's description of a house made of porcelain resembles in part Le Comte's account of the porcelain tower near Nanking. The former structure is a dwelling, not a public building, and is near Peking. Defoe explains the wonder as merely a "timber house" plastered (within and without, apparently) with "China ware, that is to say, it was plastered with the earth that makes China ware." Le Comte's tower is made of 'thick timbers" incrusted with chinaware. In other details the two accounts agree and disagree.[210]

Crusoe defends the Jesuit missionaries as unselfish and devoted sincerely to the conversion of the Chinese, though he regards the native

[208] Attention should be called to the fact here that the Muscovite ambassador to China, Ides, entered Peking attended by a mandarin and his train. The influence of Ides's account of his journey upon *Robinson Crusoe* will be discussed presently.

[209] *Robinson Crusoe*, II, p. 267; Le Comte, p. 76. Crusoe contemptuously compares this wall to the one in Northumberland built by the Romans; the latter he was shortly after to describe in the *Tour*.

[210] *Robinson Crusoe*, II, pp. 265-6; Le Comte, p. 80. Other writers had described this porcelain tower, notably Dionysius Kao, whose account Defoe almost certainly had read.

Christians as attached principally to those features of the Catholic worship which were most like their former idolatry. Le Comte dwells upon the untiring and unselfish devotion of these missionaries, and admits that there is some ground for fearing that the converts were more attached to the symbols and forms of worship than to the Christian doctrines.[211]

When Crusoe gets to the Amur river he remarks of a story that the mouth of this river is choked with monstrous bulrushes three feet around and twenty or thirty feet high. It is possible that he is here confusing two statements in Le Comte, one of which says that the harbor at Nanking is rumored to be "choaked" with sand, and the other that a nearby river is full of islands overgrown with large bulrushes which the natives use for fire wood.[212]

It is interesting to note that Le Comte's book, which Defoe uses here in the "Farther Adventures," may have contributed to Crusoe's island devices. The possibility of its having suggested the idea of umbrellas has been mentioned upon a previous page. Crusoe makes pottery (earthenware) in a way very similar to the Chinese; his account and Le Comte's both mention the use of the wheel and the method of firing and cooling the product.[213]

Finally Le Comte furnishes a cue which may have inspired Defoe in contriving a lamp for his hero. He tells how the Chinese use the tallow-like substance from a certain tree for the oil; the wicks they make by wrapping a stick with the porous inner part of a rush. Owing to this awkward construction of the wick, the light is dimmer, more smoky, and more odorous than where cotton wicks are used.[214] Crusoe made use of goat's tallow and a wick made of oakum.

V. *Ides and the Journey from Peking to Archangel*

Crusoe's adventures had now grown sufficiently to fill the volume and it was time for Defoe to think of getting his septuagenary hero home, preferably by some new route. There remained still untravelled by him the vast domains of the Czar of Muscovy, and hither then Crusoe turns his face, intending to traverse those incalculable distances back to European ports from whence he might take ship for England.

To guide him in this trackless expanse, through deserts, through regions infested with wild beasts and still wilder men, whom shall he

[211] Le Comte, pp. 392, 398. Such ideas as these, however, may be in part from Dampier.

[212] *Robinson Crusoe*, II, p. 279; Le Comte, pp. 89, 110.

[213] *Robinson Crusoe*, I, p. 159; Le Comte, p. 159. Defoe, it should be remembered, probably knew something of the manufacture of such clay products from his business adventure at Tilbury.

[214] Le Comte, p. 101ff. Cf. Knox's *Ceylon*, p. 418.

employ? Let it be understood that after he reaches Archangel, he passes without incident to Hamburg, and from thence overland to the Hague, where he embarks for London. For such a journey summed up in half a page we need look for no source. So that our search here should concern itself only with the journey from Peking to Archangel. For this purpose the "Three Years Travels from Moscow overland to China" by E. Ysbrant Ides,[215] ambassador from the Czar of Muscovy to the Emperor of China, is admirably suited, and as a matter of fact was relied upon almost exclusively for the materials of this journey.

Other works might have been of service to Defoe, such as the accounts of travels into Russia contained in Hakluyt and Purchas, Olearius, and Mandelslo. All of these books, were, as we know, in Defoe's library, and known to him. Details from Olearius and Mandelslo Defoe used in "Singleton" and in other portions possibly of "Robinson Crusoe" itself. But the only suggestion which this work may have contributed to Crusoe's adventures in Russia has to do with an Armenian merchant who accompanied the caravan to Moscow intending from thence to float down the Volga to Astrakhan.[216] One of the prominent episodes in Olearius is the account of his voyage down the Volga to Astrakhan;[217] there accompanies the relation an extremely large map of the Volga showing its course from its source to the Caspian Sea. Le Comte relates that some French Jesuit missionaries had gone to China by way of Poland, Russia, Siberia, and the greater Tartary, to the East Ocean; and the preface to the English translation of his book remarks that caravans are said to pass yearly between Peking and Moscow.[218] Either of these suggestions may have led Defoe to send Crusoe over that course.

Defoe, however, owes little to any other work than Ides's for this unusual journey, Ides and his retinue travel from Moscow to Peking, taking advantage of the rivers and other waterway channels wherever possible, and going in general directly east until well into Siberia, when they turn southeast toward China. Crusoe's caravan of horses and camels traverses the same route (though going in the opposite direction), passes through the same towns, and makes the same sort of comments upon the country and its inhabitants. Just how closely Defoe adjusts Crusoe's progress to Ides's chronology I have not fully determined. It is evident,

[215] Originally in Dutch, but translated into English and published at London in 1706.

[216] *Robinson Crusoe*, II, p. 261.

[217] Adam Olearius, *Voyages & Travels of the Ambassadors* (1662), p. 150ff.

[218] Le Comte, Introduction (unpaged), p. 3. See also Purchas, V, pp. 257-262; and XIV, p. 272ff. Hakluyt had recorded Jenkinson's voyage down the Volga to Astrakhan.

however, that upon the whole he has watched Ides's account of distances and of the time required to pass from point to point. For example, in traversing the "barbarous uninhabited road" over dismal rocks from Udinsk to "Jarauna," Ides states that he left the former on April 6 and arrived at the latter on the 29th. Crusoe and his party upon leaving "Jerawena" passed "a frightful desert" from which, after a march of twenty-three days, they emerged into a land of towns and castles, the only place mentioned being Udinsk.

Practically the only points in this portion of the story which Defoe could not have obtained from Ides come either before Crusoe gets out of China (where he is still under the sway of Le Comte) or after he is forced to leave Ides's route at Tobolsk; Crusoe's path is northwest to Archangel and Ides's is southwest to Moscow. Between this point of departure and Archangel Defoe's geography apparently runs wild; for some of the towns and rivers which he finds in that region are discoverable upon no maps which I have seen, either ancient or modern. Whether Defoe, weary with his subject resorted to a halfhearted attempt to invent names of non-existent towns and streams, or whether his spelling (studiedly careless all through the later portion of part two) degenerates so that we cannot penetrate the disguise with which he has clothed these places, is unknown.

This journey from Peking to Archangel covers the last half hundred pages of Crusoe's "Farther Adventures." Ides's account stretches to more than twice that length. Though he returns to Moscow over the route by which he went to Peking, his report of the homeward trip is brief, and it is to the account of the original journey that Defoe is chiefly indebted. Naturally the latter omits much that might have been purloined from Ides; for, as Crusoe repeatedly tells us when tempted to dwell in more detail upon the customs and manners of the Russians and the Tartars, he is relating his own adventures, not writing a description of the peoples among whom he travels. The story, moreover, was attaining sufficient length to make a book of good dimensions, and there was no need of further padding. Attention should also be called to the large map of Tartary, Siberia, and Russia which Ides's work contained. With its dotted line showing the course of the journey, it was as useful to Defoe as the narrative of the journey itself.

As soon as his caravan, consisting of over three hundred horse and "upwards of a hundred and twenty men," passes the Chinese wall, Crusoe finds dangerous marauders on hand.[219] Ides keeps a guard as a defense against 3,000 men who threaten him at the Chinese frontier.[220] Soon

[219] It should be mentioned that Crusoe and Ides on his return journey both depart from Peking in the month of February.

[220] *Robinson Crusoe*, II, p. 268ff; Ides, p. 82.

Crusoe's party enters a great desert noted by Ides; both accounts mention the necessity of night vigils here. Both speak likewise of the opportunity of buying surplus camels at this point, give warnings against straying from the caravan, and remark in passing through Naun (sic) that it is on the frontier of China.[221] Crusoe's guard sent out by the Chinese government is paralleled by Ides who goes north (on his return) from the Sadun River to Nerchinsk under the protection of a hundred Chinese soldiers.[222] Crusoe's desert between Naun and Argunsk is Ides's Tartarian wilderness.[223] Each mentions Argunsk as being on the border of the Muscovite domains; Ides makes the statement definitely, but Crusoe feigns a faulty memory:[224] "I think the first city, or town, or fortress, whatever it might be called, that belonged to the Czar of Muscovy, was Argunsk, being on the west side of the river Argun." Ides does not so exactly locate Argunsk, but his valuable map showed it to be, even as Crusoe says, on the west bank of the Argun.

Crusoe remarks that upon entering Muscovy he observed that the eastbound rivers ran "into the great river Amour, or Gamour." As the only river which he mentions thereabouts is the Argun, he cannot be straying far from the statement of Ides that the Argun falls into the Amur.[225] Both Crusoe and Ides speak of rivers which flow north,[226] a circumstance which the former uses as evidence of a northeast water passage of whose existence Defoe was convinced fifteen years earlier.[227] Crusoe's remark that the Tartars are said to be the Gog and Magog of the Old Testament might have come originally from Hakluyt,[228] but in any case Ides repeats the legend and so probably brought it anew to Defoe's attention.[229]

The way from Argunsk to Nerchinsk, "a continued desert or forest" (vague terms), cost Crusoe twenty days travel; Ides found it rough and spent fifteen days in covering it.[230] From Nerchinsk Crusoe hastens on to "Jerawena," passing through "Plotbus" (Ides's "Plotbischa") and by "a great lake called Schaks-Oser." Ides travelling in the opposite direction passes, of course, from "Jarauna," by "Lake Schackze-Oze," through

---

[221] *Robinson Crusoe,* II, p. 271; Ides, pp. 82-3.
[222] *Robinson Crusoe,* II, p. 275; Ides, p. 83.
[223] *Robinson Crusoe,* II, p. 277; Ides, p. 46.
[224] *Robinson Crusoe,* II, p. 277; Ides, p. 46.
[225] *Robinson Crusoe,* II, p. 279; Ides, p. 46.
[226] *Robinson Crusoe,* II, pp. 279-80; Ides, p. 42.
[227] *The Storm,* p. 62.
[228] Hakluyt, III, pp. 371, 413.
[229] *Robinson Crusoe,* II, p. 280; Ides, p. 101.
[230] *Robinson Crusoe,* II, p. 281; Ides, p. 47.

"Plotbischa" to Nerchinsk. Shilka, apparently considered a town by Defoe, is unmentioned by Ides, but shows as a river only on his map.[231]

In the desert between "Jerawena" and Udinsk, Crusoe spends twenty-three days, passing abundance of sable-hunters by the way. It has already been remarked that Ides likewise is twenty-three days traversing this wild region whose inhabitants, he says, are sable-hunters.[232] Crusoe mentions the governor of Udinsk, and says that the towns and castles thereabouts have Muscovite garrisons. Ides does not allude to such governor or garrisons, but opposite his account of Udinsk is a full page view of Nerchinsk, showing the governor's castle, and his map indicates the garrisons.[233]

It was Crusoe's hope that as he came nearer to Europe he would observe in the people evidences of civilization and Christianity. On the contrary, he confesses, "I found myself mistaken . . . . for we had yet the nation of the Tonguses to pass through, where we saw the same tokens of paganism and barbarity, or worse, than before . . . . for rudeness of manners, idolatry, and multitheism, no people in the world ever went beyond them. They are clothed all in skins of beasts. . . . You know not a man from a woman, neither by the ruggedness of their countenances or their clothes. . . ." These people he encountered between Udinsk and Yeniseisk, exactly where Ides found them. The latter speaks of their doeskin and dogskin clothes, and of the similarity of dress worn by men and women. Of their religious superstition he comments at length, telling of a visit to one of their sorcerers or "diabolical artists." Ides, as Crusoe, is a zealous Christian and is often disgusted with the degrading idol worship of the natives.[234] Especially is this true of his account of the region between the Obi River and the Yenisei. Similarly Crusoe says:[235] "All the country between the river Obi and the river Yenisei is as entirely pagan . . . . as the remotest Tartars."

Passing through Yeniseisk, Crusoe observes that it is on the Yenisei River; Ides touches and describes both town and river.[236] But from the Obi to Tobolsk, the capital of Siberia, the courses of the two parties differ so much that Ides's account becomes of comparatively little use to Defoe. For the ambassador, utilizing water courses wherever available, sails on the Irtus a great way north to the junction of the Irtus with the Obi upon which he travels southward again. Quite naturally

[231] Robinson Crusoe, II, p. 291; Ides, pp. 40-42.
[232] Robinson Crusoe, II, p. 294; Ides, p. 41.
[233] Robinson Crusoe, II, p. 294; Ides, p. 40.
[234] Robinson Crusoe, II, p. 295; Ides, pp. 28-33.
[235] Robinson Crusoe, II, p. 296.
[236] Robinson Crusoe, II, p. 296; Ides, p. 27.

Crusoe's caravan of camels and horses has no reason for travelling hundreds of miles out of its course merely to follow this waterway; hence he remarks simply, after leaving the Obi, "I have nothing material to say of my affairs till I came to Tobolsk."[237]

In such a well known city as Tobolsk Defoe is again on familiar ground, and is in no need of Ides's description of the place. Crusoe remains all winter in this northern city, keeping his horses and camels in underground stables and taking them nearly to Archangel with him in the following summer. The long Siberian winter goes pleasantly for him in the company of exiled Russian nobles. One of these, a prince, he offers to convey in disguise among his company to freedom; the prince, however, declines in favor of his son whom Crusoe takes with him to Hamburg.

Leaving Tobolsk Crusoe is compelled to avoid cities where troublesome sentries may discover his noble guest; hence he again departs from Ide's route. But the latter could serve him little farther anyway, since their destinations are different. Many suggestions, however, Ides still furnishes and his map is as useful as ever. There is, for instance, his reference to the plundering Kalmuck-Tartars, from which Defoe spins many circumstantial details.[238] Ides also mentions the practice of travelling by dog-sleds in winter when snow and ice allow passage over streams and ditches, a means rejected by Crusoe in words very like Ides's.[239] The principal cities mentioned by Ides in this region are Tiumen and Solikamsk, both of which are carefully avoided by the philanthropic Englishman with his fugitive prince. Both Crusoe and Ides remark that Solikamsk is on the Kama River, and that this river separates Europe from Asia.[240]

It is, perhaps, owing to Ides's statement that annually travellers go in small ships down (northwest) the Dwina River to Archangel that Crusoe chooses that course.[241] Before he reaches the Dwina, however, his geographical details become of doubtful accuracy. He must cross an immense territory barren of features on the maps of that day. His Kermazinskoy probably is Korchemskoi, and his Lawrenskoy is Jarensk. Veuslima, given by him as a town, resembles somewhat Veslena shown as a river on some modern maps; there is also a city now called Veslenskoi. But Ozomoys, what and where is it? It is unlike the names of other Russian towns in that area, nearly all of which end in "sk." Likewise the Kirtza River is unidentifiable. When Crusoe's caravan reaches the Vichegda River where it begins the water course to the Dwina and to

[237] Robinson Crusoe, II, p. 297.
[238] Robinson Crusoe, II, p. 313ff; Ides, p. 10.
[239] Robinson Crusoe, II, p. 297; Ides, pp. 2, 14-15.
[240] Robinson Crusoe, II, p. 311; Ides, pp. 4-5.
[241] Robinson Crusoe, II, p. 318; Ides, p. 2.

Archangel (and where presumably the camels are at last disposed of), the path is direct and furnishes no further difficulty for us.

Just where Defoe got his information for this closing portion of Crusoe's Russian journey I do not know. It is clear from the foregoing, however, that he relied upon Ides's record both for Crusoe's route from Peking to Archangel and for his remarks upon the physiography of the region and the character of its inhabitants.

VI. *The Picaresque Influence upon "Robinson Crusoe"*

To what extent was Defoe indebted to Head and Kirkman in the composition of "Robinson Crusoe?" Not all of those who refer to the story as picaresque mean that Crusoe is a lineal descendant of Lazarillo de Tormes or of Meriton Latroon; many intend only to convey the idea that he shows traces of rascality, while others apparently assume the picaresque and the adventure story to be the same thing. There have been writers of respectable reputation who assert plainly that "Robinson Crusoe" is to some extent at least indebted to the "English Rogue." The opinion of Professor Cross, noticed in the preceding chapter, is that by sending their hero "on a voyage to the East," Head and Kirkman "began the transformation of the rogue story into the story of adventure as it was soon to appear in Defoe." For this general statement he gives no definite evidence; Latroon went to foreign lands for adventure, and Crusoe went likewise to foreign lands for adventure; therefore (Professor Cross appears to reason) the former gave the cue to the latter. But it is not at all certain that Defoe was indebted to the "English Rogue"; at best the picaresque story was but one of the factors contributing to Defoe's art, and surely not the one most prolific of foreign adventure. The narratives of travel had been sending their heroes to foreign lands for hundreds of years before the "English Rogue" was written. We know beyond cavil that Defoe was most intimately acquainted with many reports of travellers. The very fabric of "Robinson Crusoe" is, as we have seen, from such works. To assume, then, that he was indebted to a single work which he may possibly have never read, when there lay before him a great body of literature dealing exclusively with foreign adventure, —literature which time and time again leaves its mark on his pages,—is to reject what is positive for what is mere conjecture. It may be argued that this literature of travel is a record of facts, whereas "Robinson Crusoe" is fiction, and that in its composition Defoe would naturally turn for his models to other works of fiction. But two facts make this assumption highly improbable.

The first of these is that not all the books of travel were authentic; indeed so much of untruth was there in them that each author felt the necessity of insisting upon the uniqueness of his own relation in that it was true. The true character of Mandeville's "lying travels" was known in Defoe's day;[242] and Mandeville's disciples were legion. A century and a half before the publication of "Robinson Crusoe" the writer of the preface to the account of Hans Stade's adventures affirms[243] as his opinion that the book was not a compilation from "the statements of other men," but a reliable relation of Stade's own experiences. He admits, however, that "travellers have, with their unlimited lies and spreading of false and invented stories, brought matters to such a pass, that but little belief is accorded, even to those honest and truthful men who come from foreign lands." It has, therefore, become a popular saying that "whosoever would lie, let him lie about things far off and out of the country, for nobody will go thither to verify his statements. . . ."[244]

The introduction to the first English translation of Le Comte's book on China complains of false travels which too frequently pass for truth, though they are either "romances, novels, or hypotheses."[245] Further testimony to the untrustworthy character of many books of travel is given by Henry Nieuhoff, who in publishing his brother's "Travels in Brazil" assured the reader[246] that John Nieuhoff had not been infected "with that disease, so incident to travellers, to relate fables instead of histories, it having been his constant practice, to adhere most religiously . . . . to the naked truth. . . ."

Nor is it safe to assume that because a writer complains of other narratives of pretended travellers his own is authentic. A good illustration of this fact is afforded by the "Voyage of François Leguat" by Maximilien Misson, which after two centuries of credence has recently been demonstrated to be a fabrication,[247]—a disconcerting situation for the Hakluyt Society which not long ago reissued the work, and for zoologists and botanists who have incorporated into the body of their sciences Misson's invented descriptions of animals and plants. And yet this "Voyage" is as vehement in its protest against false accounts as is any of the others cited. Says the pretended editor:[248] "Indeed, said I to myself, there's such a one (I can scarce forbear naming fifteen or twenty)

[242] W. Chetwood, *The Voyage of Richard Falconer* (1734), preface.

[243] *The Captivity of Hans Stade,* in Hakluyt Society publications, 1st series, volume 51, pp. 5-7.

[244] *Hans Stade,* p. 7.

[245] Louis Le Comte, *Journey through China* (1697). The Introduction is unpaged.

[246] John Nieuhoff, *Brazil and East Indies* (1703?), preface.

[247] Geoffroy Atkinson in *Publications of the Modern Language Association,* XXXVI (1921), p. 509ff.

[248] *The Voyage of François Leguat* (ed. 1891), p. lxxvii.

. . . . have had the impudence to impose on the public, and their ridiculous falsities have been very well receiv'd. Why therefore is it not lawful for an honest man to tell things which are true. . . . Wretched romances, and ill-contriv'd fables, find a vent; why may not my true romance have as favorable a fate?"

The second reason why Defoe would have turned to more or less authentic models is that he was writing not an acknowledged work of fiction, but a professedly authentic story of adventure. No better proof of this is needed than the fact that the well-known contemporary attacks upon the story attempted to show that it could not be true. Defoe was doing precisely what the authors of "Leguat's Voyage" and of "Krinke Kesmes"[249] were doing, namely, investing a fabrication with all the machinery for securing credence given to authentic narratives of travel. He would, therefore, imitate not an acknowledged fiction, but works generally accepted as true.

It is evident, then, that without direct and forceful evidence of a specific nature to the contrary, we must accept as probable the assumption that Defoe was indebted for the theme of foreign travel not to the "English Rogue," but to the tradition of Hakluyt and Purchas.

There have not been lacking, however, attempts to point out particular details which "Robinson Crusoe" owes to the "English Rogue." The most noteworthy of these is that of Dr. Wackwitz whose study of Defoe's masterpiece has previously been considered. This writer, besides citing some general resemblances of Crusoe's travels to those of Latroon, such as their setting out upon a voyage, and their experiencing shipwreck and capture by Turkish pirates, centers his attention upon the likeness of the shipwreck scenes.

This leads us to a study of the first episode in the story: the shipwreck off Yarmouth shortly after Crusoe's departure from Yorkshire. It will be recalled that young Crusoe had, at the solicitation of a comrade, taken passage from Hull to London upon a coastwise trading vessel. After considerable delay caused by contrary winds, the ship reached Yarmouth road where a most terrifying storm forced those aboard to take refuge in a boat sent to them from a neighboring vessel. Their own vessel foundered and they with difficulty escaped to shore.

Between Defoe's account of this storm and Head's account of the one experienced by Latroon, Wackwitz finds many parallels. To begin with both crews are forced to the pumps owing to the ships springing

[249] See the unpublished preface to *Krinke Kesmes* in which Smeeks attempts to show that his story is not a fabrication. Parts of this preface are given by Mr. Hubbard in his Introduction to the *Narrative of the El-Ho* (1921), pp. xxv, xxxi.

leaks, and in both cases the pumps are ineffective.[250] Wackwitz continues:
"E. R.: Some were sent down into the hold who quickly returned to us
with the symptoms of death on their countenances; R. C.: One of the men
that had been down on purpose to see cried out we had sprung a leak;
another said there was four foot water in the hold.—E. R.: One was
at his prayers that never till then knew what a prayer was; R. C.: I saw
what is not often seen, the master, the boatswain, and some others more
sensible than the rest, at their prayers.—E. R.: By this time I understood
what had passed; that is, our ship had sprung a leak, and was ready to
sink; R. C.: Then I understood for the first time what was meant by a
ship foundering in the sea.—E. R.: Our master ordered some eight guns
to be fired; R. C.: The master ordered to fire a gun as a signal of distress."

Further parallels are cited, and in them Wackwitz does not limit his
discussion to the Yarmouth storm, but includes also the one which later
cast Crusoe upon his island. It should be observed in this connection
that Wackwitz for his resemblance relies quite as much upon likeness of
diction as upon similarity of ideas and incidents. For in several of his
citations the phraseology is the only thing in common. His selections
wrested from their setting, moreover, hardly give a fair conception of
their relation to the whole.

Another account which has been suggested as Defoe's source for the
description of this Yarmouth storm is apparently unknown to Wackwitz.
This account, which is even more strikingly similar to Crusoe's than is that
in the "English Rogue," but which Defoe could not have read, is contained in the autobiography of Thomas Shepard, a divine eminent for
his services to the Massachusetts colony and for his share in founding
Harvard College. Nearly a century before "Robinson Crusoe" was
written (to be exact, in 1634), Shepard experienced a Yarmouth storm
under practically the same circumstances as did Crusoe; the similarity
of this storm to Crusoe's has been pointed out by E. E. Hale.[251] As
Shepard came to Boston shortly afterward, there is not the slightest probability of Defoe's having read his autobiography which remained unpublished until 1832. Nor did Mr. Hale believe that Defoe was indebted
to the manuscript of Shepard; he did, however, think that Defoe had an
oral account from someone else who experienced this "Windy Saturday"
off Yarmouth, and utilized it in "Robinson Crusoe." This Mr. Aitken
has admitted as a possibility.[252]

[250] *Entstehungsgeschichte von D. Defoe's "Robinson Crusoe,"* pp. 30-31.
[251] E. E. Hale, *Daniel Defoe and Thomas Shepard* in the *Atlantic Monthly*, liv (1885), p. 85ff.
[252] Introduction to *Robinson Crusoe*, I, p. lvi.

Without directly replying to the contentions of either Dr. Wackwitz or Mr. Hale, we may see the situation in a better light if we approach it from another angle. Before considering Defoe's indebtedness to another writer for details of any event occurring in England or upon the English coasts, one ought to investigate Defoe's firsthand information of the region; that knowledge gained through his extensive reading and travelling and abundantly set forth in two places: his account of the great November storm of 1703, and his "Tour thro Great Britain." The latter work devotes five pages to a discussion of the dangers of the coast at Yarmouth and to a description of the physical features which make it dangerous.[253]

It has been stated that Crusoe's ship met contrary winds[254] immediately after its departure from the Humber; so that six days elapsed before it reached Yarmouth where it was obliged to remain at anchor in the road seven or eight days owing to contrary winds from the southwest.[255] During this time many ships (colliers) came into the road from Newcastle. On the eighth day, the wind increased until "it blew a terrible storm indeed." Ships were everywhere in distress. After a long struggle against storm and increasing water in the hold, Crusoe's comrades fired guns as a signal of distress. Another ship just ahead ventured out a boat to help them, but though they got into the boat they were unable to make way to the other vessel. They were able, however, "partly rowing and partly driving" to get the boat northward, "sloping towards the shore almost as far as Winterton Ness." Their progress to the shore was slow and they did not reach it "till being past the lighthouse at Winterton, the shore falls off to the westward towards Cromer, and so the land broke off a little the violence of the wind." From thence they walked to Yarmouth where quarters were found for them by magistrates of the city, who likewise granted them sufficient money to go either to London or back to Hull.[256]

More than one writer has commented upon the circumstantiality of this account, pointing out that Defoe is not content with getting his hero on land merely, but that he goes on to relate in detail just how and where he got on land. Well might he speak with precision about a place which he knew so thoroughly. The coast to the north of Yarmouth, he says in the "Tour,"[257] "is particularly famous for being one of the most dangerous . . . . in all England . . . . and more so, because of the great number of ships which are continually going and coming this way, in their

[253] Tour, I (1724), i, pp. 104-8.
[254] I, p. 6.
[255] I, p. 9.
[256] Robinson Crusoe, I, p. 13.
[257] Tour, I, i, p. 104ff.

passage between London and all the northern coasts of Great Britain. . . .
The reasons for these dangers . . . . are found in the situation of the
country . . . ." which he proceeds to describe at length, speaking among
many other points of the shore falling away to the west at Winterton
Ness, of Cromer's being west of Winterton, and of the four lighthouses
north of Yarmouth; these are to warn sailors against "running into Cromer
Bay, which the seamen call the Devil's Throat."   Proceeding from Yarmouth northward toward Cromer, Defoe observed "in all the way from
Winterton, that the farmers . . . . had scarce a barn, or a shed, or a
stable; nay . . . . not a hogstye . . . . but what was built . . . . of
the wreck of ships." The description closes with an account of a terrible
storm which Defoe says occurred there in 1692; it is not, however, greatly
like Crusoe's storm.

If it be objected that the "Tour" was written five years after "Robinson
Crusoe" from data accumulated (as Defoe asserts) during 1722 when
he set out upon a journey especially for the purpose, there are two sufficient replies. The first is that no one in the world knows whether Defoe
took such a tour in 1722, or whether he merely pretends to have done so
to lend continuity and interest to a mass of otherwise heterogeneous
material. The assumption of a journey allows him to fall into the narrative method so congenial to his powers. The second reply is that in many
parts of the "Tour" he simply elaborated points which he has introduced
casually into his earlier writings, just as in this case of Yarmouth; in
"Robinson Crusoe" the description of the physiography of the coast is
incidental to the narrative—in the "Tour" it is an end in itself. Moreover,
Defoe exhibited twenty years before the "Tour," and fifteen before
"Robinson Crusoe," this same detailed familiarity with the Yarmouth
coast.

The "Storm," (1704) mentions repeatedly Yarmouth, Hull, Newcastle,
and other ports on the east coast of England, and the whole is a rich collection of storms, shipwrecks, and calamities of every sort. And here it
is that we shall find Defoe's real "source" for the storms in "Robinson
Crusoe." Instance after instance is cited to show the devastation caused
by this storm of 1703. We read[258] that "the Russia fleet . . . . was absolutely dispers'd and scatter'd, some got into Newcastle, some into
Hull, and some into Yarmouth roads; two founder'd in the sea; one or
two more run ashore, and were lost; and . . . . their convoy, foundered
in Yarmouth roads, all her men being lost, and no boat from the shore
durst go off to relieve her . . . . but all her men perished."

[258] Defoe, *The Storm* (1704), p. 64.

Of a great fleet of colliers from Newcastle, he relates[259] that some ran into the Humber ; some got shelter under the high lands of Cromer (which "broke off a little the violence of the winds" for Crusoe) ; and others got into Yarmouth roads, where were four hundred colliers (from Newcastle, of course), "and coasters from Lynn and Hull." Crusoe was aboard a Hull coaster, and he mentions the arrival of a large number of ships from Newcastle.

Commenting upon the openness of the road at Yarmouth, Defoe remarks[260] how extraordinary it was that anything should be safe there considering how crowded it was with ships and "how almost everything quitted the road, and neither anchor nor cable would hold." Consequently, he continues in the "Storm,"[261] "We expected terrible news, and every one was impatient till they saw the accounts from thence . . . . as there was a very great fleet there, both of laden colliers . . . . and others."

There follow in the "Storm" several accounts of shipwreck which collectively furnish all the details which appear in Crusoe's storm. One in particular, relating to Yarmouth, appears at the end of the volume.[262] This relation is a letter purporting to be "From on board the *John and Mary,* riding in Yarmouth Roads during the great storm." That vessel, says the supposed narrator (who for all we know may have been the actual narrator), was delayed a week on its way from Newcastle to Yarmouth by contrary winds and storms which (as in the case of Crusoe who was delayed similarly on the way thither from Hull) later subsided. He reports that he and his men found Yarmouth roads occupied by a great fleet of colliers, the "Russia Fleet," "and about a hundred sail of coasters, Hull-men, and such small craft." Shortly after, they were "got to an anchor, moor'd, and set all to rights" when the wind freshened, and the mate feared they would have "a blowing night of it." They did what they could to prepare for it, striking their topmast (like Crusoe's shipmates) and making "all tite and fast upon deck."[263] At eleven that evening, he continues, the breeze "freshen'd again, and blew very hard ; we rid it out very well till twelve, when we veer'd out more cable, and in about half an hour after, the wind increasing, let go our sheet anchor; by one a clock it blew a dreadful storm, and though our anchors held very well, the sea came over us in such a vast quantity, that we was every hour in danger of foundering. . . . Our mate would then have cut our mast by the board,

---

[259] *Ibid.,* p. 64.
[260] P. 67.
[261] P. 210.
[262] P. 266ff.
[263] P. 267.

but I was not willing and told him, I thought we had better slip our cables, and go out to sea, he argued she was a deep ship, and would not live in the sea, and was very eager for cutting away the mast. . . . Abundance of ships . . . . came by us; some with all masts gone . . . . my men said they saw two founder'd together . . . . a Russian ship came foul of a collier, and both drove away together out of our sight." Some ships just ahead "fir'd their guns for help, but twas in vain to expect it; the sea went too high for any boat to live." Towards morning he began to think they would "ride it out there, or founder," when a ship's long boat drove against them (his men "said there was some people in the boat"), causing both their anchors to give way. They immediately began to drive; but the "tide of ebb had begun to flow" and shortly after at daybreak the wind abated. The writer closes his account by saying that "we stood in for the shore, and coming under the lee of the cliff near Scarbro, we got so much shelter, as that our small bower anchors would ride us."[264]

Here we have directly from Defoe's pen (or at least under his editorship) an account sufficiently like Crusoe's to form its basis. Though there are differences, they are only such as an author might make to disguise the resemblances. One storm occurs at night, the other during the day; the first account is of a Newcastle collier which finds Hull-men in the road, the other is of a Hull-man which finds Newcastle colliers in the road. In one account the ship's anchors finally are forced loose, thus allowing the ship to drive; in the other the anchors hold, but the ship springs a leak. The first ship rides out the storm; the second founders and the crew is rescued by the boat of another ship. It will be noticed that several of these differences are in fact resemblances, being nothing more than different choices of the same two possible courses of action.

The positive resemblances of this account of the wreck in the "Storm" to that in "Robinson Crusoe" are many and striking. Both ships are from the north; each has been delayed about a week on the way to Yarmouth; each finds a crowded harbor; each mentions Hull-men and Newcastle colliers among the ships present; each strikes its topmast and makes all "tite" ("snug," Crusoe) on deck in preparation for the storm; in each case the wind is from the southwest; both accounts mention veering out more cable ("to the bitter end," Crusoe); both ships put out the sheet anchor; both are partially submerged by the waves ("shipped several seas," Crusoe); both are in danger of foundering (Crusoe's does founder); in each case the mate wishes to cut the mast away, but is opposed by the captain; and both accounts speak of slipping cables (not his own in

[264] P. 269.

Crusoe's case), and the advantage of light ships over those deep-laden. In each case the narrator turns from his own situation to view the desolation about him, and cites similar detail in the same order; (1) ships without masts; (2) foundering ships; and (3) ships driving away to sea. Each mentions the firing of guns as a distress signal. And finally, in each case, the gaining of security is effected under the shelter of a high shore, recounted in words very much alike. One party "stood in for the shore, and coming under the cliff near Scarbro, ... got so much shelter, as that" their anchors would hold; Crusoe relates that he and his comrades were unable to reach the shore, "till being past . . . . Winterton, the shore falls off to the west ward towards Cromer, and so the land broke off a little the violence of the wind." The only substantial differences in the two reports are that the first one lacks the complication of a leaky vessel and the consequent loss of the vessel and rescue of the crew, and the subjective features such as the muttered fears of the master, the prayers, and the emotional struggles of Crusoe himself. But other accounts of wrecks in the "Storm" supply those features in good measure.

Two of these other accounts tell of leaky ships, one of which drove forty-eight hours after springing a leak, and later drove on shore; all those on board were saved.[265] And the closing page of the book relates the fortunes of a ship without masts and in danger of foundering whose commander in despair took his life.[266] Several of the relations deal with the emotional reactions of the seamen. One writer, ostensibly Miles Norcliffe, tells of the consternation of the crew. Says he:[267] "Here we all pray'd to God to forgive us our sins, and to save us, or else to receive us into his heavenly kingdom." He also emphasizes the awfulness of the situation of the drowning men. Though this report is not literally true in all details, Defoe remarks that it is inserted "because it seems to describe the horror and consternation the poor sailors were in at that time."

Some minor details of Crusoe's relation are to be found in several of the other letters in the "Storm." His chronology allows fourteen days between his departure from Hull and the shipwreck at Yarmouth (six days enroute from Hull and eight days waiting in Yarmouth road), the wind blowing heavily all of the time. This agrees very closely with the situation preceding the great storm of 1703, of which Defoe remarks[268] that the wind had blown with great fury "for near fourteen days" before the storm proper. The letter from Milford Haven speaks[269] of guns being

[265] P. 253.
[266] P. 272.
[267] P. 194.
[268] P. 62.
[269] P. 167ff.

fired for help throughout the night, commenting upon the fact that "when day appear'd, it was a dismal sight to behold the ships driving up and down . . . . without masts, some sunk."

Another seaman writes of the experiences endured by his ship and its crew.[270] This was in the Downs. When the storm threatened so that the men-of-war about them "struck their top-masts, and rode with two cables an-end," they "made all as snug as we could and prepared for the worst." There follows a paragraph concerning the dreadful danger of themselves and others. Ships drive by without masts, and guns are fired as distress signals from several parts of the road. In spite of the noise can be heard the "cries of poor souls in extremities." More ships are driven from their anchors. A large man-o'-war drives past, all masts gone, bent for destruction on the Goodwin Sands; "she had neither anchor, nor cable, nor boat to help her; the sea breaking over her, in a terrible manner. . . . The cries of the men, and the firing of their guns . . . . every half minute for help, terrified us in such a manner, that I think we were half dead with the horror of it." They rode all this while with "two anchors a-head, and in great distress." To fire guns for help, the writer continues, "I saw was to no purpose, for if any help was to be had, there were so many other objects for it, that we could not expect it." In this case the master urges cutting away the masts, and is opposed by the mate; the former carries out his desires and the ship rides easier, "having two new cables out, and our best bower and sheet anchor down." They were finally compelled to slip their cables and run out to sea where without masts or sails they wallowed miserably. They saw several other ships in like condition, but giving aid was out of the question. One ship foundered before their eyes. He continues: "Another dismal object we met with, which was an open boat full of men, who, as we may suppose had lost their ship. . . . [271] What became of them any one may guess; if they had been within cables length of us we could not have help'd them."

Finally the cue for the charitable action of the Yarmouth magistrates in providing for the present needs of the unfortunate seamen and in furnishing them with funds to continue their journey is given in the "Storm," which relates that the mayor of Deal[272] not only fitted out boats with which were rescued above two hundred men "whose lives a few minutes after, must infallibly ha' been lost," but that afterward he devoted himself to the care of the destitute men. He furnished them with food,

[270] P. 26off.

[271] Precisely the situation of Crusoe and his fellows who had deserted their sinking ship in an open boat; they likewise found it impossible to be aided by other ships, and so had to take their chances alone.

[272] Pp. 201-3.

lodging, and clothing, and "gave them all money in their pockets, and passes to Gravesend." Crusoe remarks simply that he and his comrades "were used with great humanity . . . . by the magistrates of the town, who assigned us good quarters . . . . and had money given us sufficient to carry us either to London, or back to Hull, as we thought fit."[273]

Any one who doubts that here are the materials out of which Defoe constructed the Yarmouth storm experienced by Crusoe must be skeptical indeed.[274] With such a storehouse of material of his own at hand, material which there is no manner of doubt that he utilized in "Robinson Crusoe," it was needless for him to turn to any other source for details, especially to an acknowledged romance not particularly rich in storms. The accounts of storms in the literature of travel were available by the score, but even they were unnecessary to a writer whose narratives of sea calamity are second to none in vividness and richness of detail.

It is well known that Defoe used again and again the same anecdotes, ideas, and incidents. He wrote so rapidly that it would have been strange had he not done so. The "Tour" repeats a number of incidents which had appeared earlier in the "Storm," notably the account of a man and two boys of Helford Haven who in the storm of 1703 guided a ship laden with tin safely into the mouth of a creek in the isle of Wight (much as Crusoe, by the way, guided his raft into the mouth of the creek on his island).[275] Many of the details of the "Complete English Tradesman" are repeated in the "Complete English Gentleman." The anecdote of the matching of genealogies by Aubrey, Earl of Oxford, and "old Lord Craven," from the former work, is quoted almost verbatim in the latter.[276] The "Complete English Tradesman" has also a particularly interesting anecdote of "a terrible revenge" taken by "a certain lady,"[277] who was affronted by a tradesman in London, in a matter of love." The special importance of this lies in the fact that it was taken from the supposedly fictitious "Moll Flanders,"[278] though to suit a different purpose it undergoes a slight change in the later version. Whether Defoe introduced a true incident into his novel, or whether in his nonfictitious "Tradesman" he relates one invented by him as though it were true, we do not know.

[273] P. 13.

[274] The bearing of these relations published by Defoe in 1704 upon Crusoe's later storm which cast him away upon his island has not been considered here. But this later one has many resemblances to the one off Yarmouth, especially as to its length, and to the attempted escape of the crew in boats.

[275] Storm, pp. 196-9; Tour, I, iii, p. 115.

[276] Tradesman, p. 245; Gentleman, pp. 14-15. See also the True-Born Englishman, closing line of part I.

[277] Pp. 154-9.

[278] Moll Flanders, I (ed. 1903), pp. 88-94.

The comments in part three of "Robinson Crusoe"[279] upon the forced joviality of the man of crime, into the midst of whose songs and laughter sighs inevitably creep, are repeated with many of the same details in "Moll Flanders."[280]   Both "Robinson Crusoe" and the "Gentleman" record the incident of Captain Vratz[281] (a German, though miscalled a "Polander" by Defoe in each case) who, waiting to be executed for the murder of Thomas Thynne and being "spoken with by the minister to prepare himself for death," replied that "he did not doubt but God would have some respect to him as a gentleman."   So likely is it that a prolific author should reshape and adapt portions of his own previous writings that the reappearance in the "Memoirs of Captain Carleton" of an incident in "Robinson Crusoe" has been thought strong evidence of Defoe's authorship of these memoirs.[282]

The question of whether or not Defoe composed the letters in the "Storm" or whether he merely edited them cannot be answered until we find whether the work as a whole is an authentic relation or not.   In either case Defoe would hardly hesitate to make any later use he saw fit of the narratives which it contained.   The most superficial examination of the book reveals that it is deeply rooted in fact; and fifteen years later the distinction between those parts which are authentic and those which may have been invented would have been wholly obliterated.

Defoe, then, would not be in need of any details from the accounts of storms in the "English Rogue."   What he did stand in need of, however, was a larger scheme of activity, a skeleton outline of adventure to guide him, and ideas for the development of his hero's character.   These, in spite of the opinions of Cross and Wackwitz to the contrary, the "English Rogue" does not furnish to "Robinson Crusoe."   It is true that Latroon goes to the East Indies, that Crusoe goes to Guinea, and that both are captured by Turkish rovers.   But the circumstances otherwise differ so materially that only when these common traits are wrested from their setting does their resemblance appear.   Latroon is a convict being exported to the West Indies when storm and shipwreck drive him to the coast of Spain.   During the storm (which as I have shown bears no relation to Crusoe's), instead of being in despair as the conscience smitten Crusoe is, the impudent rogue takes charge of the disordered crew and sets them all at the pumps.   Crusoe's going to Guinea and being captured by Barbary pirates can be paralleled by dozens of seventeenth century ac-

[279] P. 68.
[280] I, pp. 84-5.
[281] *Robinson Crusoe*, III, p. 174; *Gentleman*, p. 30.
[282] C. E. Doble, *Academy*, XLIII (20 May, 1893), p. 439; W. P. Trent, *Defoe*, p. 210, note 10.

counts of travellers and merchants, which resemble in many details the fortunes of Defoe's hero.

Hakluyt relates the story of Thomas Sanders who was captured by the Moors of Tripoli in 1583, dwelling at length upon his experiences and those of other Christians, especially of eighteen men who escaped in a boat and drifted along the shore in search of sustenance for twenty-one days before recapture.[283]   Several relations of Turkish slavery appear in Purchas. One tells how Sir Henry Middleton,[284] captured by the Turks and carried to Moha, managed to escape in a tub; another recounts how a certain Master Pemberton escaped in a canoe, to be picked up later by an English ship.[285]   In the volume dealing with northern Africa Purchas gives a considerable treatment of the Barbary pirates.[286]   Other works dealing with that matter abounded on every hand.

Attention has been called earlier to the expeditions of the English government against Salee pirates during the seventeenth century, and to the tracts published with lists of those held captive there and with other matters relating to their treatment. Similar to Crusoe's account of his two years as a Salee captive are the experiences suggested by these works: "True Account of Thomas Phelps . . . . in Barbary, and of his strange Escape . . . . London, 1685;" "Travels in the Kingdoms of Fez and Morocco during eleven years' Captivity;"[287] D'Armand's "History of Algiers," treating at length of the fortunes of Christian slaves; and Simon Ockley's "Barbary," which promises the account of the author's miraculous escape from slavery there, but fails to give it. Robert Knox, whose career, as we have seen, somewhat closely resembles Crusoe's, was not himself in danger of Barbary pirates; but his father had often been in such danger, and meditated thereon during his captivity in Ceylon.[288]

Crusoe's account of this part of his adventures is general. His treatment, he says, was not so dreadful as he apprehended; for, instead of being carried to the emperor's court with his comrades, he was kept as the slave of the pirate captain, whom he calls his patron. His hope was that he would be taken to sea with his master where he might be recaptured by Europeans. But as he was kept at home, he was forced to use his own ingenuity in escaping. This was made possible by the indulgence of his master who trusted Crusoe, a Moor, and another youth, "the Maresco," to sail out of the port in his own boat on fishing expeditions; on one such oc-

---

[283] Hakluyt, V, p. 292ff.
[284] Purchas, III, pp. 157-8.
[285] *Ibid.*, III, pp. 29-30.
[286] *Ibid.*, VI.
[287] In Captain John Stevens, *New Collection of Voyages*, 1708.
[288] *Ceylon*, pp. 198-9.

casion, having passed the castle at the mouth of the port without exciting suspicion, Crusoe threw the Moor overboard and turned his course southward toward Cape Verde.[289]

It is evident from the abundance of such material that Defoe needed no especial suggestion for having Crusoe taken by Barbary pirates. But when he came to the particular details of that episode he apparently turned to Ogilby's "Africa" (1670). This massive folio volume which Mr. Aitken thought Defoe might have used in the composition of "Captain Singleton" has, besides a large map of Africa and a smaller one of Fez and Morocco showing Salee, a double page view of Salee itself, with the harbor and the castle (the only specific feature mentioned by Crusoe) prominently displayed.[290] The castle is mentioned also in the text. Ogilby, moreover, has a concise account of the Salee pirates, and of the condition of Christian slaves taken by them.[291] Crusoe, as has just been said, had two hopes: he might be retaken at sea by Christians, or, failing in that, he might escape. This is precisely the situation of the slaves as given by Ogilby, who goes on to say [292] that these slaves "generally lead a miserable life . . . . only some one by good fortune, that lights upon a mild patron, is more gently handled." This good fortune had fallen to Defoe's hero who had a mild master, called by him his patron. Ogilby's mention of a "Morisco" may possibly have suggested Crusoe's "Maresco."[293]

Before quitting the subject of Salee pirates Ogilby inserted an illustrated report of an encounter between English seamen and Barbary pirates. The former sail into the mouth of the Salee port and spend some hours there trying to get into communication with their countrymen and to find an opportunity of doing damage to the enemy.[294]

But whether or not Defoe made use of Ogilby's book in this portion of "Robinson Crusoe," it is interesting to note a curious lack of attention to historical accuracy. For, as Ogilby tells us,[295] Salee was embroiled in a civil war from 1650 to the end of 1655. Crusoe pretends to have been there from September 1, 1653 (?)[296] to September 19, 1655; yet he says

[289] Robinson Crusoe, I, p. 23ff.

[290] Ogilby, p. 178; Robinson Crusoe, I. p. 24.

[291] Ogilby, pp. 153; 218-9.

[292] Ogilby, p. 153.

[293] Ibid., p. 223. See Professor Trent's comment on this word in his edition of Robinson Crusoe (1916), p. 338.

[294] Ogilby, pp. 218-9.

[295] Ogilby, pp. 182ff.

[296] For a study of the chronology of Robinson Crusoe and its contradiction and errors see Professor W. T. Hastings's article in Modern Language Notes (1912),

nothing of this trouble, though during much of his sojourn there, the city was actually under bombardment. When making his escape, he is allowed to pass out of the harbor as freely and securely as though he had been in London. "The castle," he says, "which is at the entrance of the port (and is so shown on Ogilby's illustration of Salee), knew who we were, and took no notice of us."[297]

The fact that Crusoe is unware of this war reported by Ogilby is no indication that Defoe was not using the latter's book. He is even more careless of chronology and of historical events in other parts of the story. For example, young Crusoe does not mention the English Civil wars, though he lived at York and was nearly old enough to have participated in some of the later campaigns. Worse still, he has his father previously to 1651 speak of his (Crusoe's) brother having been killed in a battle which was not to occur until 1658. While making such blunders as these with regard to English affairs Defoe would have troubled himself little about minor inconsistencies in an incident of far off Morocco.

This discussion of Defoe's probable debt to Ogilby and other truthful records of Barbary slavery has led us somewhat astray from Wackwitz's contention, to which we shall now return. The experiences in captivity of the two men, Latroon and Crusoe, differ in the extreme. Crusoe had a lonely but peaceful two years at Salee before he made his escape to the Brazils. Latroon, on the other hand, underwent the more usual tortures and experiences of the slave market which Christians ordinarily met at the hands of those Mediterranean peoples.

The fact is that the resemblances between the "English Rogue" and "Robinson Crusoe" arise, not from any indebtedness of one to the other, but from the circumstance of both authors having turned to the accounts of travellers for their materials. Wackwitz has acknowledged this in the case of each individually. From the books of travel Head has borrowed details to furnish out Latroon's East India adventures. And if Head should turn to books of travel, why should not Defoe who had in his earliest writings manifested the keenest interest in the affairs of foreign lands? Nor need we assume that Head's action suggested this course to him. Professor Chandler's admission [298] that Latroon's journal of the voyage from Surat to St. Helena is in Defoe's manner, means nothing. It is also in the manner of Dampier, Rogers, and literally hundreds of

---

p. 161. The special importance and purpose of Professor Hastings's work there is to show that the story cannot be in any thoroughgoing sense an allegory of Defoe's own life.

[297] *Robinson Crusoe*, I, p. 23.

[298] *The Literature of Roguery*, p. 217 (note).

other voyagers who could not have been under any sort of obligation to Head and Kirkman.

Until further and positive proof to the contrary is submitted, we are, therefore, justified in assuming that Defoe composed "Robinson Crusoe" independently of any materials in the "English Rogue," and that it owes nothing whatsoever, either of theme, characterization, or detail, to the picaresque story.

VII. *Minor and Possible Influences*

a. *Minor Influences*

It may be said with a fair degree of certainty, I think, that the more immediate influences upon the composition of "Robinson Crusoe" come from works first published in Defoe's own day. This is natural. The older works of travel, such as the collections of Hakluyt and Purchas, Defoe at some time or other had read; they formed the background of his geographical knowledge. But their details had become dim in his memory; they had been, furthermore, largely superseded by more recent works. So that for the concrete facts of his narrative he would naturally turn to current accounts. One suspects, however, that an occasional detail stuck fast in his memory and crept into his stories.

1. *Hakluyt and Purchas*

Such an incident may be that recorded by Hakluyt[299] of some ship-wrecked men, who like Crusoe spent their first night ashore sitting in trees where they were safe from men and beasts. Their whole adventure is suggestive of a number of Crusoe's experiences. It was in 1593 that their ship, the *Tobie,* driven by bad weather ran aground upon the coast of Barbary, just outside of Gilbraltar. " . . . . one of the men coming speedily up, sayd, Sirs, the ship is full of water." They cut away the main mast in vain, for the ship split in sunder. With nothing but death ahead the men committed themselves "unto the Lord and beganne with doleful tune and heavy hearts to sing the 12 Psalme, Helpe Lord for good and godly men &c." Their singing ended suddenly, for the "waives of the sea had stopped the breathes of most of our men." All were drowned except twelve who "by God's providence partly by swimming and other meanes . . . . gote on shoare," about a fourth of a mile away. They found the place uninhabited, but nevertheless took the precaution of sleeping in trees, as has been said. Later they discovered Moors to whom they delivered themselves and by whom they were carried through Salee (the scene of

[299] VII, p. 124ff.

Crusoe's bondage, who remarks that he was not carried up to the emperor's court as his comrades were) to Morocco.[300]

2. Henry Pitman's "Relation"

The suggestion was made years ago[301] that Defoe may have got his ideas for Will Atkins from an account of the adventures of John Whicker, published in 1689 as part of "A Relation of the great suffering and strange Adventures of Henry Pitman." Mr. Aitken with his usual caution accepted this tentatively.[302] It is not clear just how much Professor Arber intended to imply, but apparently he meant that Whicker's account of three "unprincipled and loose kind of fellows" who, attempting to seize control of the ship upon which they were and to put their comrades in bonds, were taken in ambush, may have been the inspiration for Crusoe's deliverance "by Pyrates." If this is his meaning his position is conservative and safe; for no other account of the rescue of a castaway through the agency of pirates is known previously to "Robinson Crusoe." But that the whole narrative of Pitman and Whicker's experiences in the West Indes has much in common with Crusoe's story no one has remarked.

Pitman inadvertently allowed himself to become entangled in the clutches of Jeffreys and Kirke for participation in the Monmouth uprising of 1685, and with many others suffered the fate of being transported to Barbados, an English island in the West Indies. There with eight comrades he contrived to escape in a boat (much as Crusoe escaped from Salee). Having concerted their plans and provided food, sailing directions, and other necessities, they set out and for a number of days sailed southwest in a leaky vessel. Driven by thirst they attempted to land on the island of Margarita (northwest of Trinidad), but, seeing cannibal Indians awaiting them with fires ready kindled, they went on to Tortuga. On this "desolate and uninhabitable island" they were forced to live as castaways for three months. Tortoises were their chief article of food; these they roasted on spits, drying and storing away for winter what they did not eat.

---

[300] Other shipwrecks reported by Hakluyt and Purchas which are not dissimilar to those experienced by Crusoe are these: that of the *Revenge,* from which but one man gains the shore alive, reported by Linschoten (Hakluyt, VII, p. 84); that of a French vessel wrecked upon the Bermudas, reported by Henry May (Hakluyt, X, p. 200); that of Captain John Drake (Hakluyt, XI, p. 94); that of Master Piero Quirino (Purchas, XIII, p. 417); that of Peter Carder (Purchas, XVI, p. 136ff); that of Alvaro Nunez on the coast of Florida (Purchas, XVII, p. 45ff); and that of Sir Thomas Gates (Purchas, XIX, p. 5ff.).

[301] Edward Arber, *An English Garner,* VII (1895), p. 374.

[302] Introduction to *Robinson Crusoe,* I, p. lv.

Upon the approach of the wet season they built houses or huts. For crockery two or three earthen jars found thereabouts served them. They attempted to make earthenware sufficiently durable to boil turtle in. Crusoe wanted an earthen vessel which would bear liquid and stand exposure to fire, and after a long series of experiments succeeded in supplying that want.[303] These people, unlike Defoe's hero, found no clay, and were forced to use fine sand tempered with turtles' eggs; but none would endure the drying process. Other food than tortoise meat was furnished by fowls the eggs of which laid in the sand and the flesh were edible. Crusoe found tobacco on his island; Pitman found another weed, a sort of "wild sage," which "for want of a pipe" he smoked in a crab's claw.

At the end of the three months Pitman was rescued by a vessel which stopped at Tortuga, but Whicker and the others were left to continue their solitude a while longer. Then came the incident which Professor Arber suggests as a source for Defoe's story.

Some privateers, unaware of its occupants, landed on the island. Through treachery three members of this party seized the firearms, placed the other members under their power, and planned to secure all the money at hand. One of the others, however, managed to gain his liberty by cutting the bands which held him, and roaming about the island for sustenance stumbled upon Whicker's party. It will be recalled that as the time of Crusoe's stay upon his island drew to a close there came to the island a ship the mutinous crew of which had deposed the captain and turned pirates; they brought the captain and a few of his loyal followers ashore to dispose of them. Then it was that Crusoe made his presence known to the mistreated captain and his men, and offered to help them regain control of the ship and the crew. In like manner Whicker and his comrades went to the aid of these mistreated men. As in "Robinson Crusoe," they lay in ambush and seized the pirates as they came ashore. All were secured except one who remained on board; and when his situation was made clear to him he also surrendered,—a procedure precisely parallel to the action in "Robinson Crusoe." Shortly after (in both stories) the trouble makers are left ashore, and the castaways set sail for England in the delivered ship.

In this account we have material which may have contributed to Crusoe's escape from Salee, to his island life, and to his final deliverance. That Defoe used it in the last case is almost certain; and this fact makes it the more probable that he used Pitman's relation for the other two portions of the story. It may be of significance that one of Pitman's comrades

---

[303] *Robinson Crusoe*, I, p. 132ff.

was named Atkins. His first name, however, was not William, but Jeremiah; and instead of being one of the trouble makers (as Will Atkins is in "Robinson Crusoe"), he is one of those who aid in the frustration of the base attempt of the three privateers.

Pitman's pamphlet was published in 1689, after the accession of William and Mary made it more expedient to acknowledge participation in Monmouth's affairs. Defoe would no doubt have had an interest in such a relation; for he too, we have good reason to believe, was among the supporters of Monmouth and so stood in danger of a fate similar to that of Pitman and Whicker. One of his companions of the Newington Academy was hanged on this score; and how Defoe escaped we do not know.

3. Misson's "Voyage of Leguat"

The "Voyage of Leguat" (1707),[304] a desert island fiction (though not known nor, apparently, suspected of being such in Defoe's day) which Defoe was to employ in the composition of "Captain Singleton," furnished a few incidents which appear somewhat transformed in "Robinson Crusoe." The imaginary hero, François Leguat, with seven companions, is reported to have maintained his existence for a number of years on the island of Rodriguez. One incident in the struggle of these unfortunate men to support life has to do with their attempts to grow grain. After touring the island in search of a better location, they return to their first abode and clear the ground for sowing.[305] Unfortunately the seed which they had brought with them from Holland had *not* been sealed in earthen pots, and hence was spoiled by the sea air.[306] More had been procured, however, at the Cape of Good Hope. Only five seeds of "ordinary" and five of watermelon, three of succory, three of wheat, some artichokes, and some turnips came up. Melons "prodigiously large and excellently well tasted" were produced. The three grains of wheat produced two hundred ears from one plant, the other two perishing; but these proved tare,—a fact which troubled them because they found themselves "depriv'd of the pleasure of eating bread."

Crusoe, it will be recalled, found some stalks of barely and of rice growing near his habitation. At first this discovery seemed unexplainable,[307] but later he remembered shaking the husks from a sack after rats

---

[304] Maximilien Misson, *A New Voyage to the East-Indies by François Leguat and his companions. Containing their adventures in two Desart Islands*, 1707. Dated 1708.

[305] *Leguat*, p. 55ff. References are to the edition prepared by Captain Pasfield Oliver for the Hakluyt Society, 1891.

[306] Crusoe stored his grain in earthen vessels. (I, p. 133.)

[307] I, p. 84ff.

had apparently devoured all the grain. He was, therefore, astonished sometime later to see "about ten or twelve ears come out, which were perfect green barley." "I carefully saved the ears of this corn," he continues," . . . . and laying up every corn, I resolved to sow them all again, hoping in time to have some quantity sufficient to supply me with bread." Besides the barley, he found twenty or thirty stalks of rice.

Some other resemblances of the Leguat story to "Robinson Crusoe" are interesting and may be significant. For instance the preface to the former anticipates a common criticism of the latter, in stating that the relation will contain no observations upon the manners and customs of peoples since a desert island does not allow such digressions.[308]

Settling upon Rodriguez Leguat and his comrades have left them the following provisions,[309] not unlike those which Crusoe gets for himself from the wreck: "biskets," fuzees, powder, bullets, saws, hatchets, nails, hammers, and some other such articles. The supposed narrator remarks[310] that had there been women the population would have increased rapidly. Crusoe's statement that he "was like to have few heirs" may be a glance at this remark or at the polygamous George Pines; or it may be an independent reflection with no such connection.

Leguat's party made umbrellas of tree tops; [311] found great turtles[312] (not water turtles, however) ; had Scripture reading and other religious devotions daily;[313] frequently taught parrots to speak;[314] used turtle fat to burn in lamps;[315] and built a bark in which to attempt an escape. Though they had no tools, pitch, tar, cordage, compass, or anchor, necessity enabled them to surmount every obstacle.

b. Possible Influences

1. "The Bucaniers of America"

A hitherto unnoticed resemblance to "Robinson Crusoe" is to be found in a book certainly known to Defoe: "The Bucaniers of America."[310] This work, a copy of which was in his library, had an unmistakable

[308] Pp. lxxxii-iii.

[309] P. 51.

[310] P. 54.

[311] Pp. 59, 60.

[312] P. 71.

[313] Pp. 99, 100.

[314] P. 115.

[315] P. 105.

[316] This work consisted originally of one part, Exquemelin's (sometimes written Esquemling) account in Dutch; this was translated into English in 1684. The following year Basil Ringrose contributed another story of these free-booters, which became known as volume two. Shortly afterward two other narratives of pirate life were appended; and all four appeared together in the eighteenth century editions of the work.

influence upon Defoe's account of Captain Avery and of the fictitious Singleton. Part three of the "Bucaniers," written by the Sieur Ravenau de Lussan, begins with an autobiographic account explaining why the narrator went to sea.[317] He discourses as follows.

". . . who is he that can penetrate into the secrets of nature, and give a reason for some sort of inclinations she works in the minds of mortals; as for myself, I confess I am not able to give an account of the depth of my desires; and all that I can say, is that I have always had a most passionate disposition for travel. Scarce was I seven years old, when, through some innate motions whereof I had not the mastery, I began to steal out of my father's house . . . and I have often given my parents the trouble to look after me in the suburbs . . .This rambling sort of humor was accompanied with another, which . . . wrought in me an ardent desire to see some siege or battle. . ."

After some experience he took part in the bloody siege of St. Guislane. He continues:

". . . though my parents, who could not well brook this my gadding humor, were in hopes the fatigues of war would cure me of it, they were mistaken in the matter; for I was no sooner got upon the stones of Paris, but I grew weary of being there. I had nothing but voyages in my head, and those that were longest . . . appeared to me to be best.

"There was nothing omitted on the part of my parents . . . to divert me from my resolutions; but as to many young men . . . it may be said . . . that what they will, God wills; and to say the truth, I was overruled by my inclination herein. . ."

Similar to this is Crusoe's explanation for his reckless adventures; he dwells upon his unfortunate humor for travel which though it brought him so much misery could not be controlled. His efforts to secure the permission of his parents to go to sea are too well known to need further discussion.

We should not forget, however, that many men have gone to sea against the wishes of their parents, and particularly that Dampier was possessed of a rambling disposition, and that Knox records the fact of his going to sea against his father's desires. No account other than this of the Sieur Ravenau de Lussan, however, parallels closely Crusoe's report of his departure from home; and Knox's account was not published in Defoe's day.[318]

[317] II (1771), p. 106ff. For a partial list of the books in Defoe's library see the *Athenæum*, 1 June, 1895, pp. 706-7.

[318] Mr. O. F. W. Fernsemer, in the *Journal of English and Germanic Philology* (XIX, p. 94ff.) argues that Crusoe's rambling disposition was probably the German "wanderlust" inherited from his father. This suggestion, characteristic of an article which attempts to discover the origin of *Robinson Crusoe* in the Palatine emigrations of 1709, needs no comment.

2. *"Strange News from Plymouth"*

The incident,[319] reported by Crusoe as having occurred shortly after his departure for the second visit to his island, of the rescue of a storm-driven ship with a starving crew has considerable resemblance to "Strange News from Plymouth,"[320] an account published in 1684. The latter tells of a ship from the Indies which was becalmed in mid-ocean; the crew and passengers, driven by hunger, were compelled to cast lots to determine the order in which they were to be eaten by their fellows. Among the passengers was a family consisting of a man, his wife, their two children, and a servant, who suffered with the rest. In order to avoid killing his wife the man committed suicide. Later the ship reached port, but most of those aboard were then dead from starvation. The woman, however, survived. This relation, signed "J. G.," is vouched for by two seamen, one of whom is, strangely enough, Will Atkins. The incident in "Robinson Crusoe" is of a vessel driven far out of its course; those aboard had suffered the extremities of hunger. The little food to be had was hoarded by the crew, so that the passengers fared badly. Among the latter was a woman, her son, and their servant; to preserve the life of her son the woman sacrificed her own life, refusing her share of their slender nourishment. The son and the maid survived, and joined the colony on Crusoe's island.

3. *Grimmelshausen's "Simplicissimus"*

In a continuation of his "Simplicissimus" (1669), Hans Jacob Christoph von Grimmelshausen relates an episode of desert island life similar to Crusoe's. This episode, which apparently is in part indebted to Neville's "Isle of Pines,"[321] begins with a shipwreck from which Simplicissimus and a companion escaped to an island where they managed to provide food and shelter. The companion later died of intemperance and left Simplicissimus alone on the island. Among the details of the narrative which are most suggestive of "Robinson Crusoe" are the following.

Simplicissimus kept a record of the passage of time by cutting a notch on a post every day and on Sunday a cross. Out of wood which resembled iron he made shovels and other tools, and without lathe or wheel he contrived earthenware vessels. As the island was without beasts, he was compelled to use bird-skins for clothing. Other devices

[319] *Robinson Crusoe*, II, p. 24ff.

[320] *Harleian Miscellany*, IX (1810), p. 80; *Strange News from Plymouth: or a . . . Relation of a Voyage from the Indies. . .*"

[321] Compare the discussion of marriage in the German story (English translations of 1912, p. 414) with the chief feature of the *Isle of Pines*, which was translated into German in 1668,—the year before *Simplicissimus* was published.

have a general·similarity to the shifts to which Crusoe was driven. Having only a mild counterpart in Defoe's story, however, is the element of the supernatural which appears early in the Simplicissimus narrative and which finally dominates it.[322]

Whether or not Defoe knew the story of Simplicissimus we cannot say; no evidence other than its internal resemblances to "Robinson Crusoe" has been advanced to show that he did. Though Grimmelshausen's book went through numerous German editions, translation into foreign languages was slow; no English version of Defoe's day is known. But in spite of our having no evidence that he knew the German language, Defoe conceivably may have read this episode in the story of Simplicissimus.[323] Such an assumption, however, is not necessary to an understanding of the materials of "Robinson Crusoe."

4. Smeeks's "Krinke Kesmes"

No treatment of the composition of "Robinson Crusoe" would be complete which did not take into account the episode of the El-ho or Freeman in Hendrik Smeek's "Krinke Kesmes," published at Amsterdam in 1708. Krinke Kesmes (Kesmes is an anagram for Smeeks) is an imaginary island in the south seas, the inhabitants of which, like those of Bacon's "New Atlantis," have many interesting educational, political, and social features. Embedded in the description of the island is a sixty-eight page narrative of the adventures of the El-ho, a dutch boy who, having been by accident left on a nearby island and having maintained his existence by various means, some of them resembling Crusoe's, was after an indefinite period captured by a savage tribe from whom he was rescued by the inhabitants of Krinke Kesmes. It is this island story which alone concerns us here.

Smeeks's book apparently attracted little attention until after the publication of "Robinson Crusoe," the unprecedented popularity of which led to successive Dutch editions of "Krinke Kesmes"[324] and to various German translations. But so great was the vogue of Defoe's story that no claims of priority or charges of plagiarism were advanced; the magic name of Robinson Crusoe was seized upon by any one with an adventure story to issue or reissue—all were swept into the current of the English work. Here is a story, they said, which is *like* "Robinson Crusoe,"—

[322] Hans Jacob Christoph von Grimmelshausen, *The Adventurous Simplicissimus* (1912), p. 407ff; Wright, *Defoe*, p. 233.

[323] See the discussion of the "Krinke Kesmes" of Smeeks for Defoe's acquaintance with foreign languages.

[324] 1721, 1732, 1776.

whether it originally appeared earlier or later than "Robinson Crusoe" was of no moment. Hence Seek's book was dubbed the "Holländische Robinson," just as "Leguat's Voyage" of the previous year (1707) reappeared in 1723 as "Der Französischer Robinson." So that when, in the last century, students of Defoe turned to tracing the antecedents and imitations of his masterpiece, they listed Smeeks's story as an imitation, supposing the edition of 1721 to have been the first one. Not until 1907 was the importance of the book as a possible source of "Robinson Crusoe" pointed out by W. H. Staverman.[325] Other studies, notably by Hoogewerff[326] and Léon Polak,[327] attempted to show that Defoe had actually made use of the El-ho's story. Polak, I believe, was the first to call the attention of English readers to the matter by a paragraph in "Notes and Queries," in 1914.[328] Two years later Professor Trent tentatively admitted the possibility of Defoe's indebtedness to Smeeks.[329] More recently still Mr. L. L. Hubbard has brought the question prominently before American and English students by translating into English the El-ho's story and comparing it with passages from "Robinson Crusoe."[330]

By translating the El-ho's story Mr. Hubbard has done a service to every student of Defoe's literary methods. It is unfortunate, however, that he has seriously weakened his case for Smeeks by overstating it. Many of his parallel passages from "Robinson Crusoe" serve only to confuse the reader. An example of Mr. Hubbard at his worst may be found at page 39; there the El-ho, in relating his encounter with seven black bulls, remarks, "This was the first game that I had seen." In the column opposite is given Crusoe's statement, "The first shot I made among these creatures, I kill'd a *she-goat*." To the El-ho's "I was there for refreshments" (p.3) Mr. Hubbard cites Crusoe's "going on shore for refreshments,"—not from the island story at all, but from "The Farther Adventures."

[325] *Robinson Crusoe in Nederland*, 1907.

[326] *Onze Eeuw*, IX (September 9, 1909), p. 399 ff.

[327] *Germanisch Romanische Monatscrift*, VI (May, 1914), p. 304ff.

[328] 11th series, IX (June 20, 1914), p. 486.

[329] See the introduction to his edition of *Robinson Crusoe* (1916), p. xxv.

[330] *The Narrative of the El-Ho Sjouke Gabbes*, 1921. Hubbard's reason for giving the name "Sjouke Gabbes" to Smeeks's unnamed hero, is that (p. xxxiii) he feels the need of some name for the boy and prefers one with a historical background to the anachronistic "Henrich Texel" used in the German edition of 1721. Sjouke Gabbes is the name of a Dutch boy who *may* have gone astray on the coast of Australia in 1697, and who *may* have been the actual character upon whose experiences Smeeks based his story. But as Smeeks's hero experienced his island solitude neither in 1697 nor in Australia, the whole is too flimsy a conjecture upon which to name him Sjouke Gabbes. I have, therefore, retained the only title Smeeks has given him, namely, that of El-ho, meaning Freeman. Mr. Hubbard's book has recently been reviewed by Professor Julius Goebel in the *Journal of English and Germanic Philology* (XXII, p. 302).

In other words Mr. Hubbard sees in "Robinson Crusoe" all sorts of obligations to Smeeks; to him the Dutch book is more than a mere "source" of Defoe's story,—it is *the* source shamelessly plundered by Defoe of motif, episode, and diction, the origin of which he has "gone far to conceal" by "assimilation and distortion." For these reasons he hales Defoe into court on a charge of plagiarism and literary theft against which no statute of limitation may be pleaded.

When Crusoe tells of catching fish which he "dry'd in the sun" and eat dry, Mr. Hubbard (p. 44) believes him to be echoing and negating the El-ho's statement that his chief food was fish, which he boiled and roasted. Any such reading of meanings into the story is so unsafe that it scarcely needs refutation. And yet I have already cited an account in English of a castaway who put his meats "a drying in the wind, and so eat them raw."[331] I have spoken also of Knox's report that the Sinhalese dried goatflesh and ate it uncooked.

As evidence of Defoe's reliance upon the Smeeks story Mr. Hubbard thinks the account of the killing of a large fowl is highly significant. Says the Dutch boy:[332] " . . . . I saw . . . . an exceedingly large bird . . . I shot him. . . . His bill was curved like an eagle's beak, but was blood-red. His head and breast were of a golden yellow, and on his head he had a very beautiful red tuft. His neck . . . . was green and blue . . . . His legs were very large and black, and on them were very thick and red curved claws. His wings were exceedingly large. . . ." The boy found him excellent eating, and for several days fed himself and his dog from the carcass.

This story Mr. Hubbard strips judiciously and compares with a similarly stripped account in "Robinson Crusoe." I have given somewhat more of the text purposely to show how little the two episodes have in common. Says Crusoe,[333] "I found also that the island was barren, and . . . . uninhabited (except for beasts and fowls, but whether or not good for food he did not know) . . . . I shot at a great bird which I saw sitting upon a tree on the side of a great wood, I believe it was the first gun that had been fir'd there, since the creation of the world; I had no sooner fir'd, but from all the parts of the wood there arose an innumerable number of fowls . . . . but not one of them of any kind that I knew: as for the creature I kill'd, I took it to be a kind of hawk, its colour and beak resembling it, but had no talons or claws more than common, its flesh was carrion, and fit for nothing."

[331] Mandelslo, p. 281.
[332] Hubbard, pp. xlvii, iii.
[333] I, p. 57.

The similarity between the two Mr. Hubbard finds "as convincing as anything." He continues:[334] "Defoe here again is true to his adopted method. He states the facts set forth in the Dutch text, quite in agreement with the general setting down to the last two (facts), which he quite as significantly denies, much in effect as if he had added—'unlike the bird described in Krinke Kesmes.'" And in this unsafe conclusion Polak, if not Hoogewerff, agrees with him.

To anyone familiar with the descriptions of beasts and fowls in the accounts of travellers and geographers of the seventeenth century this sort of argument can have little weight. Nothing is more common than such descriptions of birds and the obvious comment upon whether or not they are edible. Wafer[335] has page after page devoted to the fowls upon the isthmus of Darien; and, in the case of every one mentioned, the account closes with a statement concerning the value of its flesh as food.[336] To a man in Crusoe's position, the all-important question would be, is it good for food? and Defoe is in a sorry strait if his hero cannot make such a comment without exposing him to charges of plagiarism.

Another kind of argument advanced by Mr. Hubbard must be cleared away as of no value. He lays great stress upon the errors in "Robinson Crusoe,"—the contradictions of fact and the inconsistencies of chronology; for in them he finds strong indications of Defoe's desire to disguise the supposed borrowings from Smeeks. Otherwise, asks this writer, why were these errors not corrected in subsequent editions?[337] The answer is clear; the author of a story which is going rapidly through edition after edition and which is being speedily translated into all the languages of Europe does not worry about minor inconsistencies which (as Mr. Hubbard confesses) in no way mar the interest of the story. Especially would this be true of a careless and rapid writer like Defoe. Similar errors appear throughout his other works. Contradictions of chronology in "Cap-

---

[334] Hubbard, p. xlviii.

[335] Lionel Wafer, *A New Voyage and Description of the Isthmus of America* (1704), p. 89 ff.

[336] See also similar descriptions of fowls in Dampier, (I, p. 49), especially those of the "booby" and "man-of-war." The former "hath a strong bill, longer and bigger than a crows . . . her feet are flat like a ducks feet . . . Their flesh is black and eats fishy, but are often eaten by the privateers . . ." The latter "is about the bigness of a kite, and in shape like it, but black; the neck is red . . . His wings are very long; his feet are like other land fowls . . ." These birds Dampier found in great plenty on the isle of Aves, which I have suggested as a prototype of Crusoe's island.

[337] For a discussion of these errors the reader has already been cited to Professor W. T. Hasting's article in *Modern Language Notes*, XXVII (June, 1912), p. 161.

tain Singleton" and "Roxana" are even more glaring than in "Robinson Crusoe," and other slips are in proportion. In the former work, it is related that the hero set out to sea in 1695 (p. 3); at a later time Defoe speaks of the date as 1706 (p. 192); and still later as 1699 (p. 207). Similarly he records the occurrence of a quarrel between Captain Singleton and Captain Wilmot (p. 210-11) which leads to their permanent separation; afterward he forgets about this and mentions the presence of the latter with Singleton (p. 244) as though he had not previously passed out of the story. The contradictions in "Roxana" have been alluded to by Professor Saintsbury as a "chronological muddle."[338]

Mr. Hubbard makes much of the fact that in each story the hero is supplied with food and other necessities three times,—twice from his own property and that of his fellows, and once from a strange wreck. That is, the El-ho on two occasions finds supplies buried by his comrades in the sand, and Crusoe gets supplies from his ship twice: "before and after the shifting of the wreck."[339] But certainly no unprejudiced observer would advance such superficial resemblances as these as indications of Defoe's obligations to Smeeks, for to do so is to argue that the former went out of his way to make his story resemble the latter's. Had Defoe been following the Dutch author here, his narrative would have agreed in substance, not meticulously in details of form which it would have been his first object to conceal.

Much of Mr. Hubbard's argument partakes of this insubstantial character. On page 8 he translates from Smeeks the word "beschuit" as "rusk," and remarks that Crusoe uses "rusk," "bisket," and "bisket-cake." What else Defoe could have used I do not well see, since the slightest acquaintance with the accounts of seamen of the seventeenth and eighteenth centuries shows the general use of both "rusk" and "bisket."[340] Without significance likewise is Crusoe's use of the word "skipper" in a situation slightly similar to the Dutch boy's use of its equivalent, "schipper."[341] The ordinary English terms were master and captain; skipper was, nevertheless, used upon occasion, as both Knox and Dampier reveal.[342] Defoe himself uses the term twice in "Colonel Jacque."[343]

Of more significance is the incident of finding footprints, common to the two stories. It is not sufficient to dismiss the matter, as one reviewer

[338] *The English Novel*, p. 68. Similar contradictions in the *Memoirs of Captain Carleton* will be recorded in a later chapter.

[339] Hubbard xlv.

[340] Dampier (I, p. 103) uses both words. See also *Leguat*, p. 55.

[341] Hubbard, p. 18.

[342] Knox, p. 274; Dampier, IV, p. 188.

[343] *Colonel Jacque*, II, p. 147.

of Hubbard's book has done, by saying that that thrill is as old as Æschylus. Both Dampier and Knox, however, speak of footprints in the sand; and, as we have seen, the former with more probability of being Defoe's "source" than does Smeeks. Crusoe's statements of self-congratulation, such as "I had all that I was now capable of enjoying . . . . " are not very close to the Dutch boy's "I was thankful to God for his goodness. Many times every day I looked with joy upon my stock of victuals."[344] They are instead quite in keeping with the previously discussed remarks of Knox. It may be thought significant that both the El-ho and Crusoe pass through somewhat similar religious experiences. We must not forget, however, that Knox and Selkirk likewise passed through these states. The element of piety, moreover, is prominent in the "Simplicissimus" and the "Voyage of Leguat." Even the bestial George Pines in his later years became a strict moralist. The age was one in which moralizing was conventional. Defoe especially was given to discussions of right and wrong in matters of conduct,—a fact obvious to any casual reader of his serious works.

One of the great weaknesses of Hubbard's evidence is that he attempts to make it prove too much. For example, of the phrases and sentences of a single paragraph (p. 41) of Smeeks's text he finds traces in four widely separated places in "Robinson Crusoe," namely, on pages 95, 151, 160, and 212 of the first edition. It is only when we clear away this rubbish of similarity of diction and errors of chronology and get down to the points of the stories that are unusual and yet alike, and consider the stories in the large that we shall make any progress toward a disentanglement of this puzzling knot. Looking at the larger features of the two narratives, we see a number of similarities. In both the hero maintains himself alone on an island for several years,[345] during which they have some experiences in common. In spite of many differences of detail there is much similarity in the hedges with which they surround their dwellings;[346] their methods of basket-making are much alike.[347] Each, moreover, is served by a storm which drives ashore supplies from a wreck;[348] each plunders a wreck for means of subsistence; each enjoys the companion-

[344] Hubbard, p. 41.

[345] The El-ho loses all track of days and years, and gives us no very precise idea of how long he lived alone.

[346] Hubbard, pp. 29-30; *Robinson Crusoe,* I, p. 63ff.

[347] Hubbard, p. 31; *Robinson Crusoe,* I, p. 118ff.

[348] Hubbard, p. 48; *Robinson Crusoe,* I, p. 91ff. See Lionel Wafer's *Darien* (1704), p. 170, for an account of an earthquake which caused a commotion of the waters similar to that reported by Crusoe following his earthquake; he relates that the return of the water carried vessels far inland from their position in the harbor (at Lima), just as Crusoe's vessel was "strangely removed."

ship of a dog,—Crusoe has two; and each is finally terrified by savages who attack his strongholds. These constitute the more striking likenesses which cannot readily be shown to have been taken from other sources.

The moralizing of the El-ho upon the uselessness of gold is not very close to Crusoe's outburst at the sight of money; the verbal similarity is slight, and the occasion for the remarks are not the same. The Dutch boy munching an apple prefers his possessions to gold; Crusoe finding money discourses upon how little it is really worth.[349] Such reflections are commonplaces in traveller's accounts of out-of-the-way places. Crusoe's wooden spade is less suggestive of the El-ho's wooden shovel and wooden hatchet (9) than of the wooden implements of Simplicissimus; the use of lamps by the El-ho (45) is no more like the device employed by Crusoe than are those reported by Knox of the Sinhalese, by Le Comte of the Chinese, and by Misson of his colonists on Rodriguez. Both Crusoe and the El-ho tell of making baskets of twigs and of storing grain in them; the former, however, plastered his with clay (apparently on the outside), whereas the latter, like the natives of Brazil reported by Purchas, places his earthenware vessels inside the baskets. These natives of Brazil also stored their grain in baskets made of bulrushes.[350]

No castaways of whom I have read enjoyed the companionship of dogs, except the Dutch lad and Crusoe, each of whom finds one aboard a wreck.[351] Dampier, however, speaks of a large English dog aboard his vessel;[352] this dog was beloved by the crew who objected to his being given as a present to the governor of Guam. Knox, also, in his biographical notes (unpublished in Defoe's day, but possibly accessible to Defoe in manuscript), mentions a large dog which he carried with him on a voyage to Madagascar. It is not at all impossible, furthermore, that Defoe chanced upon the idea of a dog for Crusoe independently of any "source." Both Selkirk and Crusoe are reported to have had cats on their islands; and dogs and cats are often associated in our minds; in fact, Crusoe's first mention of his dog is in connection with cats. A similar instance may be found in "Captain Singleton," where Defoe has his hero tell of setting a ship on shore "with neither cat or dog in her."[353] Defoe, moreover, seems to have had a personal fondness for dogs, as is evidenced

---

[349] Hubbard, p. 12; *Robinson Crusoe,* I, p. 62.

[350] Purchas, XVI, p. 518ff. See also Knox, p. 138.

[351] Hubbard, p. 56; *Robinson Crusoe,* I, pp. 70, 212. Crusoe's first dog was aboard his own wrecked vessel; his second was on a Spanish vessel which suffered disaster near his island.

[352] Dampier, I, p. 302.

[353] *Captain Singleton,* p. 215.

by his taking a spaniel with him upon one of the journeys recorded in the "Tour."[354]

Undoubtedly the most significant likeness of the two narratives is the episode of exploiting a wrecked vessel. Each hero goes to the wreck day after day, carrying away food and equipment of various sorts to be stored in his habitation. And finally the coming of the savages is quite similar in the two stories. Even here, however, the accounts differ widely in detail. Crusoe's savages are the conventional man-eating Caribbees of the seventeenth century voyages; they come to his island to feast upon their captives.[355] The Dutch boy's savages, on the other hand, live on the island, apparently; they are not cannibals, and they have no reason for attacking him.

Granting for the moment that Defoe did know and use Smeeks's narrative, the debt is a slight one. It in no way diminishes his obligations to the published accounts of Selkirk, to Knox, to Dampier, and to the others; it simply adds one more to the already numerous works which he used. Mr. Hubbard's enthusiasm has led him to assert too much. He attacks Defoe's title to "originality for the best conception extant of a story of solitary life in the wilderness." Now Defoe is not by anyone whomsoever asserted to be the originator of the idea of desert island life or the author of the first account, true or fictitious, of such life. But that "Robinson Crusoe" is the greatest story of adventure in existence few will deny.

"Robinson Crusoe" is no mere plagiarism or imitation of the El-ho's story; it is indebted to that narrative, if at all, for a few details, just as it is to several other such accounts. To see how slight a basis Smeeks furnishes for Defoe's story one has but to read the two books one after the other. The Dutch cabin boy, hunting around in the forest for his comrades from whom he has become separated, and tracing his way about from apple tree to apple tree, comes to the seashore where he discovers the buried provisions left him by his fellows; thereupon he sets about constructing his habitation, and providing for his other needs; and finally by a series of foolish and unpardonable blunders he is captured by the savages and carried away to live with them. He is not cast ashore in a terrible storm; he does not sleep all night in a tree; nor does he keep a record of time, build caves, construct canoes, or do many other things accomplished by Crusoe. In his story there figure no parrot, no man Friday, no earthenware, no

---

[354] At least such is his assertion. See Profesor Trent's comment in his edition of *Robinson Crusoe* (1916), p. 350.

[355] Purchas, XVI, p. 301ff; Nieuhoff, *Brazil* (1704), p. 1; Pitman (in Arber's *English Garner*, VII, p. 353); and D'Acugna, *Voyages in South America* (1698), p. 34.

pirates; he does not grow grain, make mortars for grinding the grain into flour, bake bread, or tame goats.

It is clear that most of the details of "Robinson Crusoe" which Hubbard and his predecessors have declared to be from "Krinke Kesmes" are from Knox, Dampier, and other English accounts which have already been considered. I have, in fact, purposely deferred introducing this problem until the reader was aware of the nature and extent of the literature of travel, and also of Defoe's indebtedness to it, without acquaintance with which no one is qualified to pronounce upon the subject.

The improbability of Defoe's having known the El-ho's story is accentuated by the fact that it is buried in an obscure book which before 1719 attracted little attention even in Holland. Being a sort of Utopia, the "Krinke Kesmes," furthermore, would be unlikely to attract the attention of Defoe, whose preference for narratives and memoirs of actual occurrences is obvious. Even the obstacle of language, though not insurmountable to a resourceful man like Defoe, is not wholly negligible. For in spite of Defoe's attachment to the cause of William III and his knowledge of Holland exhibited in "Roxana" and elsewhere, we have no positive grounds for assuming that he could read Dutch, the only language in which "Krinke Kesmes" was accessible to him before 1721. That he knew French, Latin, Greek, and Italian he never tired of boasting; but the ability to speak or read Dutch he nowhere mentions.[356]

There is the fact, moreover, that the resemblances of "Robinson Crusoe" to "Krinke Kesmes" are not confined to the printed text of Smeeks's book, but are discernible in the manuscript notes which Smeeks appended to his own copy and which Defoe could not have read. As Mr. Hubbard shows us, the publisher, Ten Hoorn, rejected the introduction submitted by Smeeks, substituting therefor one of his own to which he attached the author's name.[357] In his own copy of the book, now in the Royal Library at the Hague, Smeeks wrote in ink the substance of his rejected preface. It is in this unprinted preface that Smeeks sets about very much in Defoe's manner the task of securing credence for the story.[358] The impersonal attitude which, as the pretended editor, he

[356] A satisfactory discussion of Defoe's statements on the subject may be found in the *Literary Review* (New York), September 9, 1922, p. 12. The article, by Joseph Wood Krutch, is a review of Hubbard's book. The fifth language which Defoe speaks of and which Mr. Krutch is unable precisely to identify is no doubt English itself. I have just discovered that a Dutch grammar is listed by Mr. Aitken as one of the books in Defoe's library (*Athenæum*, 1 June, 1895, p. 706ff.).

[357] Hubbard, p. xxv.

[358] Whether or not Smeeks was wholly romancing we do not know. Apparently, however, the story has no more foundation than *Robinson Crusoe*.

assumes, allows him without immodesty to speak of the book in terms of high praise. After citing a passage from the account of the voyages of Walter Schouten of Haarlem which appears to give a slight foundation for the El-ho's adventures, he remarks, "This demonstrable truth contributes not a little to our belief in the rest, and is a strong witness to the credibility of the El-ho's singular story."[359] He goes on to say that parts of his book have been submitted to the "High and Mighty Dr. N. Witsen."[360] Here we have Smeeks following the custom, very common in the narratives of Defoe, of citing concrete facts and names of actual persons to give the appearance of fact to what is largely fiction. The truth of the matter appears to be that both men were attempting to imitate the authentic records of voyages, and both were resorting to the same means of making their compositions resemble those records; and it is not at all improbable that Defoe owed nothing whatsoever to Smeeks. I have already demonstrated that the resemblances of "Robinson Crusoe" to the "English Rogue" arise not from any interdependence of those works, but from a common reliance upon books of travel. Many narrators of prose fiction have found these accounts of travellers a prolific source of inspiration. The suitability of such works to inspire imaginative minds to produce literature of a higher type has been noted previously.

If, however, any one thinks the resemblances of "Robinson Crusoe" to the El-ho's story are too great to be set down as mere coincidences, let him ponder a still greater coincidence, namely, that within the year in which Smeeks published "Krinke Kesmes" there appeared another fictitious story of desert island life, "Leguat's Voyage" (published in English and French versions simultaneously) ; and at that very time Selkirk was alone on Juan Fernandez waiting for Rogers and Dampier to come to his rescue. That is to say, two fictitious accounts and one actual experience of desert island life existed side by side, each unconcerned with and uninformed of the others. The interest in the accounts of travellers left in solitude was culminating in novels of desert island life. A fictitious episode dealing with such a situation appeared in English in 1668 (Neville's "Isle of Pines") ; one in German in 1669 (Grimmelshausen's "Simplicissimus") ; one in French (and English) in 1707 ("Leguat's Voyage" by

[359] Hubbard p. xxxi.

[360] Witsen, who had been ambassador to England from Holland and who had written *Nord en Ost Tartarye,* was the original printer of Ides's *Travels in Muscovy,* the English version of which, as we have seen, Defoe used for Crusoe's journey from Peking to Archangel.

Misson) ; one in Dutch in 1708 (Smeeks's narrative) ; and finally "Robinson Crusoe" in English in 1719. That Defoe had read the Leguat story before June, 1720, is certain, as will be shown in connection with my study of "Captain Singleton"; but whether or not he ever heard of Simplicissimus or the El-ho is highly conjectural.

The fairest conclusion possible from this incomplete consideration of the case is that the episode of the El-ho related by Smeeks has some general and a few specific resemblances to "Robinson Crusoe"; that it is not at all certain that Defoe either knew or used the Dutch story; and that, if he did so, it was of far less service to him than Mr. Hubbard and others have asserted, since most of the material contained therein was available to Defoe in English works which we are certain that he knew and used.

5. Miscellaneous

Mention should be made of the fact that no traces are apparent of Defoe's use in "Robinson Crusoe" of Villault's "Relation,"[361] which Mr. Aitken suggested as a possible source of the story. Nor need we suppose with Henry Kingsley that Ramusio contributed to Crusoe's "Farther Adventures."[362]

A discussion of Simon Tyssot de Patot's "Voyages de Jacques Massé," which Professor Trent cites as a precursor of "Robinson Crusoe," may be found in Geoffroy Atkinson's study of the "Extraordinary Voyage in French Literature."[363] The hero's experience with the inquisition at Goa and his capture by Algerine pirates mildly suggest events in the lives of both Crusoe and Singleton.

[361] Sieur de Bellefond Villault, *A Relation of the Coasts of Africk called Guinee*, 1670.

[362] Biographical Introduction to *Robinson Crusoe* (Globe Edition), p. xxiii.

[363] II (1922), p. 70ff. Two German dissertations dealing with *Robinson Crusoe* may be grouped together here. Arno Schneider's *Die Entwickelung des Seeromans in Enland in 17. und 18. Jahr hundert* (1901) and Paull Geissler's *Defoes Theorie über Robinson Crusoe* (1896), contribute nothing to our knowledge of Defoe's materials.

A series of articles in recent issues of *Englische Studien* deal with phases of the story which are outside the scope of this study. They are as follows. G. Hübener, *Der Kaufman Robinson Crusoe*, V. 54 (1920), p. 367ff.; Hermann Ullrich, *Zum Robinsonproblem*, V. 55 (1921), p. 231ff.; and S. B. Liljegren, *Defoe's Robinson*, V. 56 (1922), p. 281ff.

A Summary of the Sources of "Robinson Crusoe"

Separate columns indicate those which may be regarded as certain, those which are probable, and those which are possible sources. An * marks works the influence of which upon "Robinson Crusoe" has not hitherto been traced.

PORTION OF THE STORY	CERTAIN	SOURCES PROBABLE	POSSIBLE
Part I			
Crusoe's roving disposition		*"Bucaniers of America"	
Yarmouth storm	*Defoe's "Storm" (1704)		
Salee slavery		*Ogilby's "Africa"	
Island story	Published accounts of Selkirk *Knox's "Ceylon" *Dampier's "Voyages" *"Leguat's Voyage" Pitman's "Relation"	*Knox's manuscript notes	Peter Serrano story "Simplicissimus" "Krinke Kesmes"
Part II			
Voyage from Bengal to China	*Dampier's "Voyages"		
Adventures in China	*Le Comte's "China"		
Journey from Peking to Archangel	*Ides's "Travels"		

VIII. *Preliminary Conclusions*

It is interesting to know how careful Defoe is as a novelist dealing with an historical situation. We have noticed some particulars wherein he is indifferent to such matters. At this point some others may not unprofitably be considered. It is strange that Crusoe says nothing of the civil war, though he was a lad of ten when it began and though he lived at York about which so much of the excitement of the period centered. At approximately the time when Charles I was beheaded Crusoe was reminded by his father of the death of his (Crusoe's) older brother[364] at the battle near Dunkirk which was not to occur for nearly a decade.[365] Had Defoe been at all scrupulous in such matters he might easily have had the brother killed at Edgehill, Marston Moor, or any of the other battles of the war which was barely over.

But similar carelessness characterizes the whole story. Crusoe is, as we have seen, a slave at Salee during a period when that city was being besieged; entirely oblivious of such matters Defoe has him sail peacefully out of the mouth of the harbor, mentioning that the castle paid no attention to him. And this was at a time when the castle was under bombardment night and day. Apparently, then, it is but accidental that Crusoe finds Brazil in possession of the Portuguese in 1654 or 1655; it had but recently passed out of Dutch hands.

Crusoe's stay on his island began a few weeks prior to the Restoration and ended a year before the revolution of 1688; in fact that revolution must have been in progress at the time of his return from Spain. Yet he makes no comment upon those political changes. Nor does he mention those earlier changes wrought by the great plague and the fire of 1665 and 1666, respectively. Later in his second visit to the new world he rescues a French vessel and carries its passengers to Newfoundland, making no mention of the fact that a state of war then existed (1694) between France and England.

This careless disregard of historical accuracy is somewhat strange from a man so well informed of, and so keenly interested in history as was Defoe. But the situation differs with regard to matters of geography. In that field he is, with some exceptions, such as we have noted in the region between Tobolsk and Archangel, Russia, as accurate as could be expected from one living in that day. The reason for this difference is probably that he uses whatever suggestions his sources offer him for particular places, but pays no attention to the political changes which

[364] I, p. 4.
[365] June, 1658.

occurred between the time of Crusoe's supposed adventures and the writing of the accounts from which Defoe made up those adventures.

This leads us to a consideration of Defoe's debt to the literature of travel in the composition of "Robinson Crusoe." There can be no manner of doubt, as the facts submitted in the preceding sections of this chapter prove, that he was widely read in that rich field of narrative, and that "Robinson Crusoe" is firmly based upon such relations. We have seen something of the nature of the specific borrowings from Knox, Dampier, Le Comte, and Ides, and of his groundwork in the Hakluyt tradition in general. It is evident, moreover, that here and in Defoe's own earlier account of the storm of 1703 we have all the elements and materials of "Robinson Crusoe;"[366] so that we no longer need to suppose with Cross, Wackwitz, and Chandler, that Defoe was influenced by the "English Rogue" or other stories of the picaresque order. It is, further, not even necessary to suppose that he knew or used the Dutch work of Hendrik Smeeks, "Krinke Kesmes," since practically all of the details which it has been thought he borrowed from that work were open to him in the English works with which we know he was familiar. The specific sources revealed in this study indicate that Defoe (1) had a broad and intimate acquaintance with works of travel; that (2) when his memory fails him or when he is in need of further details he supplements his general reading with the latest and most reliable accounts of particular regions at hand; and that (3) he rarely consults a work in a foreign language.

Selkirk, we have seen, furnished Defoe with the abstract idea for the island story; but Knox, Dampier, and others supplied him with the concrete stuff or materials of the narrative. It is obvious, moreover, that Crusoe as a man has more resemblances to Knox than to Selkirk, and it is even possible that Defoe knew Knox and used him as the model for Crusoe.

Of the character of Defoe's invention we are prepared to say something with certainty. "Robinson Crusoe" is not a creation entirely from Defoe's imagination. He has his hero do a series of things well known in the literature of travel; suffer storm and shipwreck, endure slavery in Barbary at Turkish (or Moorish) hands, duplicate the experiences of desert island life, and participate in both commerce and travel. But in the large aspects, Defoe's genius has play in unifying in the experiences of one man these diverse elements of adventure undergone by several men. As he says in the preface to part one, "The wonders of this man's life exceed all that (he thinks) is to be found extant; the life of one man being scarce cap-

---

[366] Disregarding the religious and social and political influence which have not been included in the scope of this study.

able of a greater variety." Crusoe's character colors the whole so well that we are not aware (except for the distinct loss of interest when the island story ends) of the diversity of his sources. Especially is this true of Crusoe's life on his island; here the author has blended and unified his materials from Rogers, Knox, Dampier, and the rest, until they are scarcely distinguishable,—an artistic method that has made the search for these originals so very difficult. But even the later story has this unity of tone. We are totally unaware of the point at which Defoe ceases to depend upon Dampier and turns to Le Comte and later to Ides.

Of equal importance and interest is his invention and use of detail. With his trained eye he saw the interest awakened by the struggles of Selkirk to maintain an existence. It was not enough to relate how the unfortunate man came to be cast away, how he was rescued, and how many years intervened between those two events. Rogers and Cooke and Steele all understood the deeper interest which their readers would have in a narrative of Selkirk's adventures. And Defoe made it his business to cater almost entirely to that interest. In another of his narratives of sea life, "The New Voyage" (1724), he complains of those travellers who fill their journals[367] with such dry and unimportant matters as "how many leagues they sailed every day, where they had the winds, when it blew hard, and when softly, what latitude in every observation, what meridian distance, and what variation of the compass." Of the many things of interest which a circumnavigation of the globe offers, they give us little. "We have very little account of their landings, their diversions, the accidents which happened to them, or to others by their means. The stories of their engagements . . . . are told superficially and by halves; the storms and difficulties at sea or on shore have nowhere a full relation; and all the rest of their accounts are generally filled up with directions for sailors coming that way . . . . and how few are they?—but not at all to the purpose when we come expecting to find the history of the voyage." In "Robinson Crusoe," then, Defoe pays little attention to such matters; at least no more than is necessary to keep the reader aware of the direction and course of the journey. To the events which befall the travellers he devotes himself almost exclusively.

Where does he get those events? Does he fabricate them independently of his sources, or does he borrow them along with his geography and information about the peoples among whom his hero travels? These questions we can now answer in part, though of course it should be remembered that no one can with certainty analyze an incident and tell which elements are the product of the writer's creative imagination and which

[367] *New Voyage* (1899), p. 3.

are echoes or fugitive recollections in the back of his mind of similar happenings; both must be treated together, in most cases, as his contribution.

We have seen how Defoe transformed Dampier's account of Captain Johnson's murder by the Malayans while repairing his vessel; Crusoe purchased a ship whose captain was so murdered, but the details of the murder are subordinated to the element of piracy for which Defoe is not greatly indebted to Dampier. His more usual practice, however, is to embroider details to the suggestions afforded by his sources. When Dampier reports that the natives along Tonquin Bay are a thievish people, trading in pitch, tar, and oil, and seizing shipwrecked sailors for slaves to their king, Defoe puts these suggestions in concrete form by inventing an encounter in which these traits are manifested. He has Crusoe turn his ship upon its side on the beach to stop a leak; the natives, seeing the vessel thus, imagine it to be cast away, and thereupon proceed to plunder the ship and to take the crew captive. In defending themselves Crusoe's men make use of the chief commodities of the region, turning against the savages their native tar and pitch which, boiling in cauldrons, was waiting to pay the ship's seams.

The account of the Chinese mandarin, the "greasy don" who rode in a state of "perfect Don Quixotism," is one of the best examples of Defoe's elaborations upon suggestions from others; he embodies in vividly concrete form what in Dampier and Le Comte had been impersonal description. Likewise from the hints in Ides of the character of the Kalmuck-Tartar brigands in northwest Russia comes the detailed account of Crusoe's experiences with those brigands. Another of Crusoe's adventures in this cold region is the destruction of a hideous idol, effected by the aid of a Scotch fellow traveller. This bold exploit, in which the aged Crusoe participates as lustily as a youth, is an outbreak symbolizing the author's disgust with the filthy idols described by Dampier, Le Comte, and, especially, Ides.

"Robinson Crusoe," finally, is not so much a fictitious autobiography (as Professor Cross suggests) as it is a fictitious book of travel, the courses and geographical matters of which are based upon more or less authentic relations, but the details of which are largely invented by Defoe from suggestions contained in these relations. Defoe shifts the emphasis from matters of interest only to seamen to others which are of more general human concern, and from mere incident to characterization.

CHAPTER III

THE COMPOSITION OF "CAPTAIN SINGLETON"

I. *Preliminary Statement*

"The Life, Adventures, and Piracies of the famous Captain Singleton . . . ." appeared on June 4, 1720. In the thirteen months which had elapsed since part one of "Robinson Crusoe" was published, Defoe had issued, in addition to his usual large number of pamphlets and other works, the following longer narratives of a fictitious or semi-fictitious character: part two of "Robinson Crusoe," "The King of Pirates," "Duncan Campbell," and the "Memoirs of a Cavalier."

Like "Robinson Crusoe," "Captain Singleton" is a story of adventure in foreign regions. The action falls naturally into two parts, each distinct from the other. The first portion tells how Singleton as a small child was kidnapped in the outskirts of London, and how, after various experiences among beggars and gypsies and in parish schools, he was befriended by a shipmaster of Bussleton (near Southampton). When grown "a great sturdy boy" he was returning from his third or fourth voyage to Newfoundland in company with this master, he had the misfortune to be taken, along with the rest of the ship's men, by an Algerine rover. Being rescued and carried into Lisbon by a Portuguese vessel, and finding his patron dead, he embarked on a voyage to Goa as servant to the ship's pilot. On the return trip he was charged with conspiring to murder the captain, and as a punishment therefor was put ashore upon the island of Madagascar with a number of his fellow-conspirators. They contrived to reach the Mozambique coast, from whence they travelled overland to the coast of Guinea. With this memorable journey through the unexplored regions of Central Africa and the return of Singleton to London the first part of the story ends.

The second part is a tale of piracy. Having squandered his treasure picked up along the golden streams of Africa, Singleton soon turned pirate. He and his comrades cruised awhile in the West Indies and along the east coast of South America. Later Madagascar became his place of refuge, and the rich vessels trading to the East Indies his prey. His final voyage was a profitable cruise among the Moluccas or Spice Islands and the Philippines, from which he returned through the uncharted regions under Australia. Finding himself wealthy enough, Singleton and his chief adviser, a boldhearted Quaker named William Walters, left their trade and repented. The story ends with their cautious return to England and Singleton's marriage with William's sister.

This narrative, though inferior to parts of "Robinson Crusoe," has nevertheless been the subject of considerable discussion and speculation. The minute and seemingly accurate information manifested by Defoe of the physiography of regions little known in 1720 is one feature of the story which has occupied the attention of numerous readers. Some have conjectured that for these geographical details he drew largely upon his imagination; others have believed that he had access to unpublished notes or maps of actual travellers (probably Portuguese) with a knowledge of facts which were not to be found in print until long afterward; and still others have held that Defoe merely made good use of the best geographical information then extant. One receives the impression from reading Professor Minto's[1] essay on the African geography of "Captain Singleton," Mr. Aitken's introduction to the story, and other writings upon the subject,[2] that Defoe's knowledge of geographical matters was almost uncanny. They hold that his presentation of the physiography of Central Africa, though not strictly accurate, was in a number of striking points far in advance of what geographers of his day said about that region. They assert, for instance, that Defoe represents the Congo River as lying partly north of the equator in accordance with fact, whereas map-makers of the time believed it to flow almost directly westward from its source to the Atlantic Ocean. To explain this, these students of Defoe were compelled either to regard him as possessing an astonishing degree of skill at guessing, or as having access to information denied to the geographers of 1720. How justified their assumptions were we shall see presently.

Another question concerning "Captain Singleton" is that of its relation to previously published accounts of pirates either actual or imaginary. For the half century preceding 1720 pirates were especially numerous in many parts of the world. Is this narrative a disguised story of an actual pirate, or is it mainly fictitious? Leslie Stephen calls Singleton a repetition of Captain Kidd.[3]

Questions of a more literary character have to do with the general problems of Defoe's art and methods mentioned in the study of "Robinson Crusoe." We wish to know how Defoe proceeded in the composition of Singleton's narrative. But, as in the case of "Robinson Crusoe," we

[1] William Minto, *Macmillan's Magazine*, XXXVIII (October, 1878), p. 459ff.

[2] See references to Wilfred Whitten's life of Defoe and to Dr. Birdwood's paper in *Notes and Queries*, Series 12, VIII, p. 251.

[3] *Hours in a Library*, I, p. 23.

shall find it necessary to know what his materials were before determining what he did with them. That is to say, we must first answer the two less literary questions of the sources of Defoe's geographical knowledge and of his information about buccaneering and piracy. Then only can we speak with any certainty of the extent and character of his imagination, of his inventive faculty, of his supposed power of making what is fictitious appear actual, and of his ability to portray character. Various suggestions, to be mentioned later, have been made as to the sources of "Captain Singleton," but none of them have been supported by any convincing evidence.

In undertaking to determine the origins of the story—the published materials of various kinds which entered into its composition—we encounter a complex problem. The narrative, as has been remarked, is not one story but two; one of foreign adventure centering about the African journey, and another of piracy; and the literary influences upon them are distinct. Broadly speaking, however, it may be said that there are three traceable streams contributing to the story: (1) the general literature of travel; (2) the more or less authentic narratives of privateers, buccaneers, and pirates of the half-century preceding 1720; and (3) the reports of the more than half-mythical pirate, Captain John Avery.

The adventures of Singleton are projected against the broad background of Defoe's reading in Hakluyt and Purchas. It is only rarely, however, that minute or concrete evidence of their influence can be singled out. More specifically Defoe made use of four writers of travel and foreign adventure, namely, Mandelslo, Knox, Dampier, and Misson; and a study of their influence upon "Captain Singleton" will be the principal task in the succeeding pages of this chapter.

Though not wholly distinct from the general literature of travel, those works dealing with privateering and piracy are at least a special division of it. Pirates have, of course, existed in all ages; but at no time have they been of so much immediate popular interest as in the last quarter of the seventeenth and the first quarter of the eighteenth century. Protected by the national hatred of the English, French, and Dutch for the Spanish, buccaneers flourished in the West Indies to a degree theretofore unknown. Their raids upon the coast cities of New Spain between Vera Cruz and Cartagena and St. Martha (on the northern coast of what is now Columbia) and their expeditions over the isthmus of Darien into the South Seas, from which they frequently returned with amazing wealth to be squandered quickly in Jamaica alehouses, attracted desperate adventurers from all parts of Europe and America. Later, when it became to England's advantage to check these marauders, they refused to give up their lawless course of living, and so became pirates without any sort of official sanction.[4] For awhile they maintained their hold in the West Indies, but later made Madagascar their chief rendezvous.[5]

Narratives of the adventures of these privateers and pirates are numerous, but we are concerned with but a few of them. The best known of all is Exquemelin's "Bucaniers of America," an English version of which appeard in 1684; it dealt principally with the exploits of Sir Henry Morgan and others in the West Indies. In 1685 Basil Ringrose's journal of his experiences in the South Seas with Captains Sharp and Sawkins was published as volume two of Exquemelin's relation. A little later two other narratives of piracy were added to these, and all four were printed together at various times throughout the eighteenth and nineteenth centuries. Dampier and Lionel Wafer, who were also with Sharp and Sawkins in the South Seas, gave more or less explicit accounts of their adventures. Defoe is known to have possessed copies of the 1699 edition of the "Bucaniers" (containing all four parts) and of Wafer's "Isthmus of America."[6] It is evident from a consideration of "Robinson Crusoe," the "King of Pirates," and "Captain Singleton," that he had read them, and Dampier, too. Finally should be mentioned Captain Woodes Rogers's cruising voyage, famous for the rescue of Selkirk from Juan Fernandez.

The particular pirate of most importance to an understanding of "Captain Singleton" is not Captain Kidd, as Leslie Stephen supposed, but, as Mr. Aitken has pointed out, Captain Avery, who occupies with reference to the story a position of even more direct significance than does Selkirk to "Robinson Crusoe." Defoe knew of Avery partly through the many exaggerated rumors of his greatness circulated in Europe, and partly through the "Life" of Avery, purporting to be by Adrian Van Broeck, which appeared in 1709. Whether or not Defoe knew the romantic version of Avery's career pictured in Charles Johnson's play, "The Successful Pirate," which had a short run at the Drury Lane theatre in 1712 and which appeared in quarto, [7, 8] we cannot tell. Though Defoe frequently condemns playgoing, he also occasionally manifests a knowledge of plays which suggests at least that he did not wholly abstain from attendance at dramatic performances. As concerns "Captain Singleton," however, Defoe's knowledge of Avery came from his narrative of

---

[4] C. H. Haring, in *The Buccaneers in the West Indies,* 1910, gives the best modern version of this change from buccaneering to piracy.

[5] See Captain Charles Johnson, *General History of the Pyrates,* 1724, for a contemporary history of their exploits. The name Johnson may be an assumed one.

[6] *Athenæum,* 1 June, 1895, pp. 706-7.

[7] John Genest, *English Stage,* II (1832), pp. 505-6.

[8] David Erskine Baker, *Biographia Dramatica,* III (1812), p. 304.

that marauder's exploits, "The King of Pirates," published in December, 1719. Here as in one important instance in "Robinson Crusoe" Defoe becomes his own "source."

With this hastily sketched background, we shall at once proceed to a more detailed consideration of "Captain Singleton" and its sources. I do not pretend to have discovered them all; nor indeed is it essential to know them all. What is necessary, however, is that we have some facts with which to replace our assumptions. In cases where it seemed profitable to do so I have indulged in speculations about Defoe's procedure; but on the whole I have adhered to demonstrable facts.

II. *Singleton's Earlier Adventures*

a. *On Madagascar*

In that admirable relation of Singleton's parentage and childhood, Defoe tells us that Singleton was kidnapped while very young and sold to a beggar-woman who sold him to a gypsy. The latter, upon being hanged "for some of her worthy actions," left him a parish charge. He thought he must have been passed about from parish to parish, attending school meanwhile. Finally a master of a ship noticed him and, when he was not over twelve years of age, carried him to sea. With this master he went several voyages to Newfoundland.

This opening of the story is much like the early portions of "Colonel Jacque" and others of Defoe's narratives of criminals. It suggests that Defoe was utilizing details from the life of some criminal whom he had talked with or of whom he had read. In fact, Professor Trent cites the story[9] as evidence of Defoe's growing interest in criminals resulting from his alliance with Applebee, the publisher of confessions and dying speeches of condemned prisoners. Though, as Professor Trent himself elsewhere states, Defoe's association with Applebee did not begin until after Singleton's narrative was issued,[10] there seems to be considerable truth in the assumption that Defoe was reading at this time in the literature of criminal biography. For in "Robinson Crusoe" and later in the "Complete English Gentleman" he speaks of Captain Vratz, whose life was included in Captain Alexander Smith's "Highwaymen" (1714).[11] Other evidence that Defoe knew Smith's book will be presented later in connection with

---

[9] *Cambridge History of English Literature*, IX (1913), p. 24.

[10] *Defoe*, p. 177.

[11] Unfortunately I have not had access to Smith's *Highwaymen*; but the life of Vratz is contained in the *General History of the most famous Highwaymen* (1734), attributed to Captain Charles Johnson, which the writer on Johnson in the Dictionary of National Biography asserts to be, in so far as the highwaymen are concerned, an almost exact reproduction of Smith's book.

another part of "Captain Singleton." It may even be of significance that the only Robert Singleton (Defoe's Singleton asserts that his name was not Robert but "plain Bob") noticed by the Dictionary of National Biography was, though long before Defoe's day, hanged at Tyburn. Robert and its various corruptions, Bob and Robin, Defoe uses frequently as names of his characters. Crusoe was called Bob by his comrade on the journey from Hull to London, and Robin by his parrot; and Moll Flanders' first husband was named Robin.[12]

Sir Henry Morgan, the famous buccaneer of the West Indies, whose achievements Exquemelin portrays at length, was kidnapped very early in life; but that fact is not recorded by Exquemelin, so that Defoe probably did not have him in mind when beginning his novel. Possibly, however, he was incorporating some facts from the life of Dampier,[13] who upon the death of his parents was taken from the "Latine School" and placed with a shipmaster of Weymouth, with whom he went a voyage to Newfoundland.

Singleton's capture by the Algerine rover and his subsequent rescue by a Portuguese vessel is merely a variation of Crusoe's capture by the pirates of Salee. A number of Singleton's courses of action Defoe had considered for Crusoe, but either developed them incompletely or rejected them entirely. Crusoe was not recaptured by a Portuguese vessel, but one of his hopes was that he might be.[14] When he did finally escape he was picked up by a Portuguese ship and carried to Bahia de Todos los Santos. Singleton, delivered by the Portuguese with whom he sailed to Goa, stopped at Bahia on the way thither. Crusoe in later years was to run the risk of falling into the hands of the Inquisition at Bahia, just as Singleton did at Goa.[15]

On the return from Goa Singleton, as has been remarked earlier, was put ashore with a number of his Portuguese comrades on Madagascar. For the background of his ensuing adventures upon that island, Mr. Aitken suggested[16] Defoe's use of De Flacourt's "Histoire de Madagascar"

[12] The name Singleton (or Shingleton) was not uncommon in England. There was the Thomas Singleton of Elizabeth's time whose career Hakluyt (V, p. 266) takes notice of; another Thomas Singleton conducted in the last half of the seventeenth century a dissenting academy similar to Morton's academy at Stoke Newington, of which Defoe was a student. (*Cambridge History of English Literature,* IX, p. 438.)

[13] Dampier, *Voyage,* II, part ii, pp. 2-3.

[14] I, p. 19.

[15] Defoe, of course, knew sufficiently about the Inquisition in many parts of the world; he also owned a copy of the 1688 translation of Dellon's *History of the Inquisition as it is exercised at Goa.*

[16] Introduction to *Captain Singleton,* p. xv.

(1661). But I can find neither evidence nor need of this assumption. De Flacourt offers a large map of the island and a number of features which could have been useful to Defoe. But in the main he restricts his observations to the southern portion of Madagascar which was best known to the French; whereas Singleton's adventures center about the northern end of the island, designated on De Flacourt's map as *"Pays Incogney aux François."*[17]

Singleton's comments upon the island and its inhabitants are general rather than specific; they are such as could have been gathered from many English sources. The unknown author of the 1709 life of Avery closed that narrative with a description of the island. Dampier says little of it; but Knox, who had been there twice for slaves, may conceivably have given Defoe some first hand information. Henry Kingsley thought[18] that the adventures of Robert Everard on Madagascar formed the nucleus for Singleton's whole career. But Mr. Aitken pointed out that Everard's adventures were first published after Defoe's death,[19] and asserted that he could find nothing in them which was used by Defoe.

It seems to me, however, that much as Mr. Aitken knew about Defoe, he misjudged his literary method in one important particular. He understood that Defoe's narratives of adventure in far-away places was based upon a wide knowledge of geography; but he assumed that in "Captain Singleton," for instance, Defoe first stored his mind with information about Madagascar and its people, and then proceeded to invent a series of incidents which conform to that information. But what appears certain from what has already been said of "Robinson Crusoe" and from what will shortly be said of "Captain Singleton" is that more frequently he picks up his geographical information and the suggestions for his incidents side by side in the journals of actual travellers. Naturally he had recourse to maps and to general information outside of these narratives, but usually there is evidence of more detailed dependence upon authentic (or what passed for authentic) relations of adventure. When Defoe prepared to send Crusoe across the little known domains of Tartary and Muscovy, he turned to Ides's record of just such a journey, incorporated into his story the latter's route of travel and his remarks about the inhabitants, and upon his suggestions based the action. Ides records something of the danger from Kalmuck-Tartar brigands; in "Robinson Crusoe" the abstract statement of fact becomes concrete in the form of an elaborate account of Crusoe's encounter with these brigands.

[17] Étienne de Flacourt, *Histoire de la grand isle Madagascar*, 1661. The large folded map is at the end of the volume.

[18] See Aitken's Introduction to *Captain Singleton*, p. xvi.

[19] In the second edition (1732) of Churchill's *Voyages*.

Similarly for Singleton's youthful adventures on Madagascar, Defoe turned to two works of travel for his materials. The first of these is the "Voyages and Travels of J. Albert de Mandelslo."[20] Mandelslo, on his return from the East Indies, anchored in St. Augustine Bay on the southwest coast of Madagascar. His description of the island and of its inhabitants covers five folio pages,[21] containing just those features mentioned by Singleton. The manner of his arrival on the Madagascar coast is, furthermore, imitated by Defoe in his account of Singleton. Mandelslo's vessel, sailing from Ceylon and reaching the Cape of Good Hope (which he says was named *Cabo de bon' Speranza* by John II of Portugal), was driven by tempests back to St. Augustine Bay where within a quarter of a league of shore she "cast anchor, at 25 fathom water. . . . "[22] Likewise Singleton and his Portuguese companions, returning from Goa (just north of Ceylon on the Malabar coast) and "having been once as high as the Cape of Good Hope . . . . or Cabo de Bona Speranza, as they (the Portuguese) call it," "were driven back again by a violent storm" and "at last came to an anchor on the coast of Madagascar" where the ship "rid in twenty-six fathoms water, about half a mile from shore." Though Singleton does not name the harbor, there can be no doubt that he means St. Augustine Bay; for they were afterward[23] to sail northward along the west coast toward what is now known as Cape St. Andrew. It was at St. Augustine Bay, furthermore, that Defoe's Avery and his unnamed hero of the "New Voyage" first stopped.[24] And Singleton himself was to return there in later years.[25]

In the story of Avery the island and its inhabitants receive scant attention; they play no part, and they are not characterized. In "Robinson Crusoe" and the "New Voyage" the few references to them are in accord with what Mandelslo relates; it is more than probable that Defoe had glanced into Mandelslo for the Madagascar incident in part two of Crusoe's story, published nearly a year previously to "Captain Singleton." Crusoe does not put into St. Augustine Bay, touching instead on the east coast as was customary for European ships bound for the East Indies.[26] Defoe's Avery, however, is made to tell of being driven from the Cape of Good

[20] Part II of Adam Olearius's *Voyages & Travels of the Ambassadors* (1662). Defoe owned a copy of this work.

[21] *Ibid.*, pp. 253-8.

[22] Mandelslo, pp. 249, 253; *Singleton*, p. 11.

[23] *Singleton*, p. 35ff.

[24] *The King of Pirates*, p. 35; *New Voyage*, p. 53.

[25] *Singleton*, p. 195.

[26] *Robinson Crusoe*, II, p. 187.

Hope to St. Augustine Bay by a hurricane similar to that which drove Mandelslo thither.[27]

Singleton's intercourse with the natives is fabricated from data which Mandelslo furnished. The former found them treacherous and brutish,[28] and feared that he and his comrades would be murdered as soon as the ship from which they had been ejected left the harbor. Many travellers had dwelt upon the treacherous character of these people, so that Defoe did not need the incidents recorded by Mandelslo exemplifying that trait.[29] Of more significance is the latter's statement that their huts[30] are made of branches of trees. So Singleton remarks[31] that he "lived in a kind of tent or hut made with the boughs of trees;" and a little later he tells of receiving aid in hut construction from the natives, who perceived the "bungling" attempts of the white men.[32] Crusoe, also, at Madagascar made a "little tent or hut, of some boughs of trees."[33]

As in Mandelslo's account[34] a small party of Singleton's fellows went inland to view the country.[35] They "found the place[36] full of cattle and provisions" including fowls and goats.[37] The exploring party met natives who offered them milk;[38] "but it was evident they did not design to give it away, but to sell it. . . ." Here again Defoe is not straying far from Mandelslo who remarks that the greatest wealth of the country is "cattle,"[39] though they have also goats and fowls.[40] He states, furthermore, that men and women "brought milk to sell." Singleton does not mention women in this connection, but Crusoe does,[41] stating explicitly that "their women also brought us milk."

Singleton reports that these natives did not value gold or silver.[42] "As to our money," he says,[43] "it was mere trash to them . . . . so that we were in a fair way to be starved. Had we but some toys and trinklets, brass

[27] *The King of Pirates*, p. 35.
[28] *Singleton*, pp. 17, 24.
[29] Mandelslo, p. 257.
[30] *Ibid.*, p. 255.
[31] *Captain Singleton*, p. 17.
[32] *Ibid.*, p. 43.
[33] *Robinson Crusoe*, II, p. 188.
[34] Mandelslo, p. 253.
[35] *Captain Singleton*, p. 24.
[36] *Ibid.*, p. 25.
[37] *Ibid.*, pp. 16, 23.
[38] *Ibid.*, p. 25.
[39] Mandelslo, p.255.
[40] *Ibid.*, p. 254.
[41] *Robinson Crusoe*, II, p. 188.
[42] *Captain Singleton*, p. 26.
[43] *Ibid.*, p. 31.

chains, baubles, glass beads, or, in a word, the veriest trifles that a ship-load of would not have been worth the freight, we might have bought cattle and provisions enough for an army . . . . but for gold or silver we could get nothing." Later, however, one of the party[44] "who had been a kind of cutler" contrived tools wherewith he "takes three or four pieces of eight, and beats them out . . . . very broad and thin; then he cuts them out into the shapes of birds and beasts; he made little chains of them for bracelets and necklaces, and turned them into so many devices of his own head, that it is hardly to be expressed." Upon presenting these to the natives, the white men "were surprised to see the folly of the poor people. For a bit of silver cut in the shape of a bird, we had two cows, and, which was our loss, if it had been brass, it had been still of more value. For one of the *bracelets* . . . . we had as much provision . . . . as would fairly have been worth, in England, fifteen or sixteen pounds. . . . Thus, that which when it was in coin was not worth six pence to us, when thus con-verted into toys and trifles, was worth a hundred times its real value . . . "

The suggestion for the cutler, soon to be called a silversmith, came from other sources to be mentioned shortly; but all the rest is founded upon Mandelslo's relation. From the natives, he remarks,[45] "we bought every day four oxen for forty pair of glass *bracelets* . . . . a sheep for two, and a calf for three . . . . and for a brass ring . . . . a man might have an oxe worth here (in Europe—compare Singleton's "in England") six or seven pounds." The purchase of substantial commodities from untutored peoples for trifles is, of course, a common-place in the literature of travel; the similarity between the narratives of Singleton and Mandelslo, however, is not limited to that element. Mandelslo remarks further:[46] "They would not meddle with our money, as being so happy as not to know the value of a thing which occasions the misery of other parts of the world." Though gold and silver, he continues,[47] are said to exist in mines in the island, the inhabitants, "making no use of these metals, and valuing tinne above silver, have not yet search'd into them." His statement that the ground there yields salt and saltpetre is useful to Defoe, who has Singleton recount[48] the curing of the flesh of cattle and goats, "the salt and saltpetre being very good."

There is, finally, the most significant of all the details borrowed by Defoe from Mandelslo. Those who have read part two of "Robinson Crusoe" and "Captain Singleton" will recall several occasions upon which

[44] *Ibid.*, p. 32.
[45] Mandelslo, p. 253.
[46] *Ibid.*, p. 254.
[47] *Ibid.*, p. 255.
[48] *Captain Singleton*, p. 40.

mention is made of the use of long poles as a sign of friendship. Crusoe, stopping at Madagascar on the way to the East Indies, learned[49] that these poles are commonly used by the natives as signs of truce. This device Singleton also learned of these people; he was later, however, to try it upon the natives of Central Africa. The people of Madagascar, he is made to say,[50] once "brought one whom they showed respect to as a king with them, and they set up a long pole between them and us . . . . this, we understood afterwards, was a token of amity and friendship; and they brought us victuals in abundance, cattle, fowls . . . . " At another time[51] "one of their captains or kings, for we knew not what to call him, came down with five or six men and some women, and brought us five goats and two young fat steers, and gave them to us." Two hours later another "king or captain," with half a hundred men appeared. "We began to be afraid of him . . . . but he perceiving it, caused two men to go before him, carrying two long poles in their hands, which they held upright, as high as they could, which we presently perceived was a signal of peace; and these two poles they set up afterwards . . . . and when the king and his men came to these two poles, they struck all their lances up in the ground, and came on unarmed. . . ." The reason for this "was to satisfy us that they were come as friends."

All this is certainly an elaboration of Mandelslo's account of a lord who, with his retinue, in which there were women, came to visit the white men. A member of the retinue bestowed upon the leader of the ship's party[52] twelve goats and two fat capons. Mandelslo continues: "They planted a great pole in the ground, as a mark of alliance they made with us, promising severely to punish such as should injure us, and desiring us to take such a course, as no disorder might happen on our side." Singleton does not say that any sort of reciprocal pledge was expected of his party, but Crusoe implies it in his statement[53] that each party set up poles.

This device of the poles which Singleton tells of is precisely that described by Mandelslo; the truce or alliance, moreover, is, in both narratives, made upon the occasion (or occasions) of visits from native leaders. In both narratives it is related that the leader's retinue, whereof part are women, present the foreigners with provisions of the same sort: Mandelslo's party receive twelve goats and two "fat capons"; Singleton's receive five goats and two "fat steers." The gifts, capons and steers, are not identical, but they have in common at least one important characteristic.

[49] *Robinson Crusoe,* II, p. 188.
[50] *Captain Singleton,* p. 31.
[51] *Ibid.,* p. 43.
[52] Mandelslo, p. 254.
[53] *Robinson Crusoe,* II. p. 188.

The use of poles as signs of friendship, I find mentioned neither in De Flacourt's "Madagascar" nor in any other account of any region whatsoever.

But Mandelslo is not the only writer contributing to the fabrication of Singleton's adventures on Madagascar. Another, whose influence is upon the action more than upon the description of the natives, is Maximilien Misson. I have previously cited some important similarities of "Robinson Crusoe" to Misson's "New Voyage of François Leguat" (1707). But regardless of whether or not Defoe used that narrative in composing "Robinson Crusoe" it is certain that he did so in fabricating parts of "Captain Singleton." According to Misson's story, long regarded as authentic but recently shown by Mr. Geoffroy Atkinson to be fictitious,[54] Leguat with seven companions was left on Rodriguez, an uninhabited island of the Mascarene group, not far east of Madagascar. These eight Frenchmen were Huguenot refugees sent out by Du Quesne to colonize Bourbon (now Reunion), another of the Mascarene Islands; but, finding that island already occupied, the ship's captain, a man cruel and unjust, put them ashore on Rodriguez, where they maintained themselves something as Crusoe was later to do on his island. After two years they escaped in a bark of their own contrivance to the Dutch on Mauritius, a third island of the same group. There they were mistreated by Diodati, the governor, who spitefully imprisoned them in a barren region and refused even to allow them proper care during sickness. After the peace of Ryswick, however, the survivors were released and permitted to return to Europe.

Between their adventures and those of the boy Singleton and his Portuguese comrades on Madagascar there is considerable similarity. Both parties are put ashore against their wishes, though for different reasons; the French refugees are placed upon Rodriguez by a villainous captain, whereas Singleton and his fellows are mutinous members of the ship's crew who are allowed to go ashore on Madagascar as an alternative to hanging. Both parties are given ammunition and other provisions.[55] One of Singleton's fellows, in despair at the prospect, rashly swam off to the vessel, and, after circling it for several hours, obtained the mercy of being picked up and pardoned.[56] Similarly Misson's story relates the efforts of a companion of Leguat to escape from Mauritius by swimming to a Dutch

[54] Geoffroy Atkinson, *The Extraordinary Voyage in French Literature from 1700 to 1720* (1922). See also an article entitled *A French Desert Island Novel of 1708*, in *Publications of the Modern Language Association*, XXXVI (1921), p. 509ff.

[55] *Captain Singleton*, p. 16; *Leguat*, p. 55.

[56] *Captain Singleton*, p. 17.

vessel moored off shore.[57]   Though taken aboard, the Frenchman, less
fortunate than Singleton's Portuguese seaman, was sent back to captivity
with his companions.

Singleton[58] and his fellows, moreover, built a camp on the banks of a
stream, precisely as the Frenchmen on Rodriguez did.[59]   In each case there
are a number of huts for individual men, besides those designated especially
for the general kitchen and for the assembly of the colony.[60]

These likenesses, being of a general character, are not sufficient in
themselves to constitute proof of Defoe's use of Misson's narrative; it is,
therefore, of importance that one episode common to the two stories
furnishes definitely the proof insufficiently established by the previously
considered resemblances.   Singleton's account of the sloop which he and
his comrades constructed for their voyage to the mainland of Africa betrays conclusive evidence of having been based upon Leguat's relation of
the construction of a craft by the Frenchmen to carry them to Mauritius.
This evidence consists of (1) similarity of general procedure, (2) similarity
of details, (3) similarity in the order of recording those details, and (4)
similarity of diction.

Having introduced the matter of building a vessel, Leguat remarks:[61]
"This enterprize appear'd *very difficult* . . . . we had . . . . *few tools;*
we had neither pitch nor tar, nor *cordage,* nor anchor, nor compass, nor a
hundred other necessaries . . . . and all eight of us without serving any
apprenticeship, became carpenters, *smiths, rope-makers* . . . . and generally everything that was necessary for us to be . . . . *necessity was a law to
us,* it supply'd all our defects."   Singleton opens his account in like manner:[62] "When we came to set close to this work we found it *very laborious
and difficult,* having but *few tools,* no ironwork, *no cordage,* no sails; so
that, in short . . . . we were obliged to be our own *smiths, rope-makers,*
sail-makers, and indeed to practice twenty trades that we knew little or
nothing of.   However, *necessity was the spur to invention. . . .*"

Leguat continues to tell of the work of construction,[63] speaking of the
craft's dimensions and remarking that one of their number, a silversmith
named John de la Haye, added to the supply of nails.   Similarly Singleton[64] next alludes to the dimensions of his vessel, and in the paragraph fol-

[57] *Leguat,* p. 166ff.
[58] *Captain Singleton,* p. 39.
[59] *Leguat,* p. 55ff.
[60] *Captain Singleton,* p. 39; *Leguat,* p. 55ff.
[61] P. 106.
[62] P. 47.
[63] P. 107.
[64] P. 48.

lowing says that "our artist, of whom I have spoken already, who was now grown a very dextrous smith, made us nails, and . . . . spikes such as we wanted." Defoe began[65] by calling this "artist" a "kind of cutler, or worker in iron," but very soon remarked[66] that "ever after we called (him) silversmith."

But Singleton's cutler or silversmith is not wholly based upon Leguat's; instead he has two prototypes, both distinctly recognizable. Leguat's silversmith is one; the other is a cutler (or more correctly, a series of cutlers, a different man, apparently, being detailed each day for that work) mentioned by Dampier. The latter relates[67] that at the Bashi Islands his shipmates purchased provisions of the natives with such trifles as nails and spikes. "It was," he continues, "one man's work to be all day cutting out bars of iron into small pieces with a coal chisel; and these were for the purchase of hogs and goats, which they would not sell for nails. . . ." It will be recalled that Singleton's cutler, having contrived several sorts of tools from a cold-chisel, hammered out pieces of eight and other coins and cut them into trinkets with which to barter for provisions. This scheme was worked successfully not only in Madagascar but also throughout the journey across Africa. What Defoe did was to personify the "office" of cutler as suggested by Dampier and to merge it into the character of Leguat's silversmith; or, possibly, to endow the latter with the duties suggested by Dampier.

After recording the making of nails by their silversmiths, both Singleton and Leguat next concern themselves with pitch for the seams, ropes, and anchors, though Singleton treats these subjects in the reverse order. The Frenchman states[68] that as a substitute for pitch and tar they used certain "gums which we found on the trees in plenty, and temper'd it with oil. . . . " Ropes they made of the fibres of plantain leaves, and, in lieu of an anchor, they procured a heavy rock.

Singleton's party contrived no substitute for an anchor[69] as one was useless without cable; instead they contented themselves with making some ropes "of such stuff as they (the natives) make their mats of," and with these they secured their vessel to objects on shore. For tar and pitch they did what they could, "with tallow and oil,[70] to make a mixture to supply that part," but were unsuccessful. Later a native showed them a tree which furnishes "a liquid that is . . . . almost as strong as tar"; that

[65] P. 32.
[66] *Captain Singleton*, p. 33.
[67] Dampier, I, p. 435.
[68] *Leguat*, p. 107.
[69] P. 48.
[70] Pp. 48-9.

they boiled and so made "a sort of stuff which served us for pitch." This
secret thus borrowed from Misson, who in turn had it from some one else,
stood Singleton "in good stead" upon many subsequent occasions. Leguat's
party did not, apparently, boil the gum which they took from the tree;
instead they tempered it with turtle oil when it had been mixed with
bitumen. Probably Defoe's idea of having the gum boiled is another contribution of Dampier, whose "Voyage" I shall presently show to be an important source for a considerable portion of Singleton's subsequent adventures. Dampier, in the account of his first voyage to the East Indies,—
the account which Defoe used,— tells[71] of a tree on Condore Island (at
the mouth of the Mekong River in Cambodia), "from whence is drawn a
sort of clammy juice, which being boiled a little becomes perfect tar; and
if you boil it much it will become hard as pitch." He states that his
partners used it for both tar and pitch "and found it very serviceable."[72]

A few other details of Singleton's and Leguat's accounts are significantly similar. Closing his report of the building of the bark, the latter
remarks:[73] " . . . . and we made a sail *as well as we could.*" So Singleton says[74] that they fitted sails *"as well as we could."* He next speaks[75]
of making a rudder and a tiller; Leguat mentions them only after describing the launching of the vessel.[76] Singleton then remarks[77] that they stored
their craft with victuals and "put as much fresh water on board as we
. . . . knew how to stow (for we were yet without casks)." These pre-
cautions, obvious as they are, are nevertheless in part due to Leguat's
mention of providing sustenance;[78] he adds, " . . . . we fill'd the barrels
we had for that use with fresh water." Each party, finally, is without a
compass, and each remedies that deficiency partially through the discovery that one member of the group has a cheap substitute. The Frenchman observes:[79] " . . . . we began the building our boat knowing we had
no compass . . . . but . . . . one of us found a little solar quadrant. . . .
which cost him three pence at Amsterdam; and tho' 'twas not good we were

---

[71] I, p. 390.

[72] It should be remarked that Robert Knox, in his autobiographical notes first
published in 1911, describes (p. 350) a tree on Sumatra which gives off a gum or
rosen; this rosen is boiled with oil and used for "all their ships in India as we doe
pitch." De Flacourt (p. 137) mentions a Madagascar tree the gum of which is
excellent for paying the seams of vessels.

[73] P. 108.

[74] P. 49.

[75] P. 49.

[76] P. 109.

[77] P. 49.

[78] P. 108.

[79] P. 108.

glad he had found it . . . . " Singleton briefly states:[80] " . . . . we had no compass with us but a little brass pocket compass, which one of our men had more by accident than otherwise. . . ."

b. *The Journey across Africa*

Equipped with their newly completed bark, Singleton and his comrades sailed from Madagascar toward the mainland of Africa and in time reached the Mozambique coast in 12 degrees 35 minutes south latitude.[81] At this point the party[82] "took one of the rashest, and wildest, and most desperate resolutions that ever was taken by man, or any number of men, in the world; this was, to travel overland through the heart of the country, from the coast of Mozambique . . . . to the coast of Angola or Guinea . . . . a continent of land of at least 1800 miles. . . ." As their avowed purpose was to secure passage back to Europe, this was indeed a rash project; they might instead have gone a very few miles to the strong Portuguese settlement at Mozambique where they, all Portuguese except Singleton, would have been welcomed and aided in getting to their native land. For the ordinary reader, however, this inconsistency, being unobserved, impairs in no way his interest in what is usually considered the most striking feature of the story, namely, the journey across Africa.

For this journey I have discovered no specific source; that is to say, no account of a previous journey through that region which Defoe followed. There were extant in 1720 many records of similar overland expeditions. One of them, that of Ides's travels from Peking through Tartary and Muscovy to Moscow, Defoe had actually used in part two of "Robinson Crusoe." Many such are given by Hakluyt and Purchas; the latter has a number relating to Africa. There are, for instance, Alvarez's journey from the Red Sea to the court of Prester John in Abyssinia, and[83] Richard Jobson's 900 mile voyage up the Gambia River —the very route once contemplated by Singleton for passing to Cape Verde. But none of these offers any very definite help to Defoe, who sends Singleton straight west from Mozambique, allowing him to work northward gradually until even with the Guinea coast.

There is, however, no reason for supposing that Defoe could not have invented Singleton's journey without aid from the records of actual travellers. His principal need would have been a few concrete suggestions as to the character of the inhabitants, the kinds of animals, the vegetable and mineral products, and the physiography of the country.

[80] P. 51.
[81] Pp. 56-7.
[82] P. 54.
[83] Purchas, VI, pp. 234ff., 517ff.

In spite of all that has been said about the vividness of detail of this journey, the fact remains that Singleton's remarks concerning the people and the country are cautiously general. That is to say, they deal mainly with the large features, and, though seldom actually in error, they infrequently reveal any extended acquaintance with the interior regions. Whenever they do appear to make such a revelation, they can in nearly every case be found to have warrant in published works of geography and travel available to Defoe and to every other Englishman of his day.

Take, for instance, Singleton's descriptions of the African natives. Those on the Mozambique coast who met the wanderers as they arrived from Madagascar have one striking characteristic: "both sexes" are "stark naked."[84] Defoe, as any one may observe from reading of Crusoe's voyage from Salee to Cape Verde,[85] was in the habit of describing native Africans of both sexes as stark naked; he does so, also, on three other occasions in "Captain Singleton."[86] But Singleton's comment upon the natives of Mozambique was no idle fancy of Defoe's; for a writer in Purchas[87] had long before this said that the people of Mozambique "go all naked," and Ogilby had described them with the same phrase that Defoe was to use.[88] In all other respects these people, as portrayed by Singleton, are in no way different from those of Madagascar. They respond to the sign of peace (the long pole), and they eagerly trade provisions for the trinkets made by the cutler.[89]

The natives of regions inland are variously described as treacherous or friendly; some responded to the sign of the long pole, and some did not; all were astounded at the firing of weapons, as were those encountered by Crusoe north of Cape Verde. Those who were forced to accompany the party as slaves and burdenbearers proved devoted and faithful; in fact, they are very much like Crusoe's Friday. Upon one occasion Singleton calls them Indians,[90] a term which he was to apply later to the natives about Australia.

Evidently in this we have no special information about the peoples. The same is true of Singleton's account of the animals. The principal ones mentioned by him are elephants, buffaloes, deer, lions, leopards, crocodiles,

[84] *Captain Singleton*, p. 53.

[85] *Robinson Crusoe*, I, p. 31ff.

[86] *Captain Singleton*, pp. 88, 122, 134.

[87] Purchas, VI, p. 509.

[88] John Ogilby, *Africa* (1670), p. 610. Mr. Aitken (*Captain Singleton*, p. xv), rightly thought it possible that Defoe had studied Ogilby's book—a very large folio volume—before writing Singleton's African adventures.

[89] *Captain Singleton*, pp. 53-4.

[90] See Professor Trent's comment, *Robinson Crusoe* (1916), p. 344 (note to p. 91).

hyenas, tigers, and civet cats.   There is nothing here beyond the most elementary facts about Central Africa.   We now know that tigers are exclusively an Asiatic animal, but Defoe is following the geographers of his day in asserting their presence in Africa.   Morden reported[91] that the rivers of Africa are full of crocodiles, and that Ethiopia (meaning the central and southern portion of Africa given the special name of Ethiopia by early writers) abounds[92] in elephants, lions, tigers, wolves, hyenas, civet cats,[93] and other beasts.   Such was common knowledge.   Singleton tells[94] of being advised by the natives of Mozambique to ward off dangerous beasts by kindling fires; Ogilby[95] reports this as one of the customs of the Mozambique peoples.   Later, in a severe encounter with beasts in Central Africa, Singleton killed[96] what "seemed to be an ill-gendered kind, between a tiger and a leopard."   This is as far as Defoe goes in adopting the fabulous reports accepted by Heylin and other seventeenth century geographers.   In Morden[97] we read that the African deserts have many monsters; for "creatures of several species couple and engender at the watring places, where they often meet."

Singleton's geography likewise does not differ greatly from that given by the maps and records extant in 1720.   Remembering how little was actually known of Central Africa until late in the nineteenth century, the casual reader finds Defoe's narrative a startling anticipation of the discoveries of those men who but yesterday brought to light the true courses of the Nile and the Congo and the location of Lakes Nyasa, Tanganyika, Victoria Nyanza, and Albert Nyanza.   In the century preceding the explorations of Livingstone, Stanley, Speke, and others, the maps of Africa discreetly left this interior region blank, in acknowledgment of the lack of information about it.   Under such circumstances it was not strange that some readers of a few decades ago hailed Defoe's as an unusual feat of the imagination; or that others believed him to have had access to the maps and notes of some actual traveller (presumably Portuguese) who had penetrated those unknown regions. Professor Saintsbury,[98] apparently, is still of that opinion.

A little investigation, however, reveals to more careful readers two things: (1) that Central Africa as Defoe portrayed it in Singleton's story

[91] Robert Morden, *Geography Rectified* (2nd edition), p. 446.
[92] *Ibid.*, p. 494.
[93] *Ibid.*, p. 446.
[94] *Captain Singleton*, p. 56.
[95] John Ogilby, *Africa*, p. 610.
[96] *Captain Singleton*, p. 116.
[97] Morden, p. 446.
[98] George Saintsbury, *The English Novel*, p. 68.

has only a superficial resemblance to that region as it is actually known to be; and (2) that, unlike their late eighteenth and early nineteenth century successors, the seventeenth and early eighteenth century map-makers boldly set forth mountains, rivers, and lakes in Central Africa, agreeably to the imaginary Singleton's report. Two large lakes appear in practically the same position on all their drawings of Africa, namely, Lake Zafflan or Zaflan (a little north of where Lake Nyasa is now known to be, and about where Tanganyika is), and Lake Zaire or Zembre, directly west of Zafflan and half way between it and the Atlantic coast. It was from Lake Zaire that the Nile and Congo were thought to flow, though other branches of the Nile were represented as flowing from Lake Zafflan and from various parts of Abyssinia. This representation of Africa was general throughout the seventeenth century. One finds these features on the map of Africa drawn by Hondius,[99] and on the world map by Blaeu probably made in 1605.[100] Peter Heylin's "Little Description of the great World" represents it so in the editions of 1639, 1670, and 1703. Morden[101] in 1688 stated that the headwaters of the Nile, "now well-known, are in Æthiopia." His map agrees with those just mentioned concerning the positions of lakes and rivers. The maps in Ogilby's "Africa" and in Dampier's "Voyage" likewise repeat those features. It is, then, possible that Defoe relied neither upon his imagination nor upon maps and notes of Portuguese travellers, but upon the published maps and accounts of Africa current in his day.

To test the truth of this possibility, the late Professor Minto[102] made a detailed comparison of Singleton's path through Africa with both present day maps and a few current in Defoe's day. But in spite of his painstaking endeavor to clear up this matter, he has made a number of serious blunders which vitiate much of his report and make necessary going over the whole matter again.

Opening his paper with the remark[103] that a "close tracing of the course that Captain Singleton followed across Africa dissipates the idea that Defoe might have had access to the notes of some real seventeenth century traveller," Professor Minto soon admits that there is nothing violently improbable in supposing that Defoe (who the writer says knew the Portuguese language) had procured from some Portuguese adventurer notes of an actual journey and used them as a basis, and finally con-

[99] Purchas, V, p. 304.

[100] Edward Luther Stevenson, *William Janszoon Blaeu* (1914), p. 52.

[101] Morden, pp. 441, 443.

[102] William Minto, *Through the Dark Continent in 1720* in *Macmillan's Magazine*, XXXVIII (October, 1878), p. 459ff.

[103] *Ibid.*, p. 460.

cludes, after a survey of the whole, that[104] Defoe probably got his information from unpublished Portuguese sources. The gunner (who having maps was the guide of Singleton's party), says Professor Minto, was Portuguese and would use Portuguese maps. Just how this gunner's imaginary maps could have helped Defoe is not made very clear. Professor Minto's study, then, ends by accepting as probable what in the beginning he had asserted to be unfounded, namely, that Defoe had access to information of actual adventurers who had explored the coast, at least, of Africa.

In the body of his discussion Professor Minto's position is more consistent, though not free from gross error. He asserts with justice[105] that, "though Defoe set forth with inimitable vividness the best knowledge of his time . . . . it falls considerably short of modern knowledge in point of minute accuracy."

Singleton's description of the Quilloa River (upon which he started westward from Mozambique), he thinks,[106] contains much guess-work, though having an element of truth in the account of the cataracts; there are such cataracts on the East African rivers. "His lower cataract with its sheer descent," continues Professor Minto, "might pass for the Victoria falls of the Zambesi, and the succession of cataracts higher up the river have a resemblance in character to the falls on the river Shiré. It may have been some rumour of these waterfalls that he thus boldly localized. Still, while the Rufiji (the river, apparently, which Singleton called the Quilloa) is unexplored, it would be rash to say that Defoe has drawn upon his imagination for the most remarkable feature of his great river."

The implication here that Defoe was probably using Portuguese information (presumably unpublished) of the Zambesi and the Shiré must not pass unchallenged. Singleton's party encountered waterfalls twice on the Quilloa. Of the first one[107] Singleton thought "the whole body of water fell at once perpendicularly down a precipice above sixty foot high, which made noise enough to deprive men of their hearing." It was audible for ten miles before he reached it. The second falls was really[108] a series of cataracts, making a "noise confused and frightful."

It is not impossible, of course, that Defoe took these details from Portuguese rumors of the Shiré and the Zambesi, as Professor Minto suggests, but it is improbable. For reports of waterfalls on African rivers

[104] *Ibid.,* p. 465.
[105] William Minto, p. 460.
[106] *Ibid.,* p. 462.
[107] *Captain Singleton,* p. 74.
[108] *Ibid.,* p. 82.

were common in published accounts of Africa. Andrew Battell tells[109] of seeing a "great fall of water" of the river Coanza on the Angola coast. There the water "falleth right downe, and maketh a mightie noyse, that is heard thirtie miles." Another account given by Purchas[110] states that at one point the Congo flows through "a certain straight between the rockes, where it falleth with such a horrible noyse, that it may be heard almost eight miles." This the Portuguese called "Cachuiuera, that is to say, a fall, or cataract, like to the cataracts of Nilus." The latter were sufficiently well-known. In its course towards Egypt, said Heylin,[111] the Nile "divers times meeting with lower valleys, falleth downe headlong with such force and furie, that the continuance of the noyse deafeth all the neighbouring inhabitants." Ogilby reported[112] of the Senegal River that in many places it is not navigable because of great rocks which make cataracts like those of the Nile. Defoe needed no other suggestions than such as these.

The first great lake which Singleton encountered (about where Lake Tanganyika is), Professor Minto rightly says[113] was the Lake Zafflan of the seventeenth century maps; but here again he implies Defoe's use of Portuguese sources by remarking that Portuguese traders had gone so far westward from Mozambique and that beyond this "Defoe's geography becomes indisputably wild and fabulous." Such are the terms which Professor Minto applies to Singleton's second lake, a vast body of water from which his guide, the gunner, thought the Nile arises, and to the third lake nearby stretching across the equator. As Professor Minto warns us,[114] these lakes are far from the true position of the Victoria Nyanza and the Albert Nyanza, which even a well informed reader might think them to be. Singleton travelled 1,300 miles due west from 12 degrees south latitude on the Zanzibar coast; this lands him 1,000 miles from the Victoria Nyanza, but "as nearly as possible to the Lake Zaire of the seventeenth century map-makers."

The third lake, which Singleton found lying just northeast of Lake Zaire and which forced him north of the equator, Professor Minto has not seen on any map, new or old. The inference is that for this lake Defoe had no other warrant than his imagination, or perhaps Portuguese rumors.

[109] Purchas, VI, p. 382.

[110] Ibid., VI, p. 420.

[111] Peter Heylin, Little Description of the Great World (ed. 1639), p. 725.

[112] Africa, p. 343.

[113] William Minto, p. 463.

[114] Ibid., p. 465.

It is true that no such lake has been discovered; but that none like it appeared on any seventeenth century maps is not quite true. For strangely enough, Moll's world map in the front of the first volume of Dampier's "Voyage,"—a work consulted by Defoe in the composition of both "Robinson Crusoe" and "Captain Singleton,"—shows a lake lying as nearly as we can determine in the very position given by Singleton. I grant that most of the map-makers of that day placed this lake farther north, and represented the Niger River as rising from it. It was, therefore, called Lake Niger by Hondius, Ogilby, and others. This inaccuracy is not strange in a day when the Niger was thought to have its origin near that of the Nile, to run due north until even with Cape Verde, and then to turn and run straight west for that cape. Singleton's reason for urging his comrades to go northeast, instead of southwest to the Congo as the gunner advised, was that they might take advantage of the opportunity of floating down the Niger to Cape Verde. A glance at modern maps reveals that Singleton's conception of the Niger's course, though in precise accord with that of the maps of his day, was wrong in every particular. For the source of the Niger is not in Central Africa at all; instead it is but a little way southeast of Cape Verde (near Sierra Leona), from whence it flows northeast (not west), later making a sharp turn to the southwest and running into the gulf of Guinea.

This "Niger Lacus" of Ogilby and Hondius Moll, on the above-mentioned map, brought a few degrees to the southward and allowed its southern end to protrude plainly across the equator. It is, therefore, certain that in this matter of Singleton's lake lying across the equator Defoe is hanging to the skirt of what passed then for geographical knowledge, and not venturing any wild guesses of his own.

The greatest error in Professor Minto's study is in regard to what Singleton says of the course of the Congo River; this he understands to be as follows. After the adventurers had passed around the north end of the lake lying across the equator, the gunner advised them that they should *turn a little to the south* (Professor Minto's words, not Singleton's) *to strike the Congo.* One is tempted, says Professor Minto,[115] to conclude hastily "that Defoe was writing from the information of . . . . some traveller on the Congo who had traced its course north of the equator." Singleton did not, we are told, reach the Congo because a great desert intervened. "Still the gunner's geography would have been verified had the desert not intervened; his chart marked the true course of the Congo in one great particular at least, as it has been ascertained by Mr. Stanley . . . . " Again, Professor Minto reiterates[116] that Defoe was right about

[115] William Minto, p. 464.
[116] *Ibid.*, p. 465.

the course of the Congo when English, Dutch, and French map-makers were wrong. Into these conclusions Mr. Aitken has followed him,[117] and has thus given rise to the commonly accepted opinion on the subject.

There are, however, two startling errors in Professor Minto's procedure. In the first place he is mistaken in thinking that upon the seventeenth century maps the Congo was normally shown as flowing directly west from its source to the Atlantic. Had he consulted any considerable number of maps of that period he must have observed that on many of them the course of the Congo was represented as making a distinct curve northward toward the equator. There is, for example, Morden's map of 1688[118] upon which the Congo is made to flow almost directly north from its origin in Lake Zaire; when approximately three degrees from the equator, it is made to turn sharply to the southwest in its way to the Atlantic. So Ogilby has shown it on his large folio map of 1670.[119] Upon other maps the Congo's approach to the equator was even more pronounced. Notable among these was the "Map of the World, on which is delineated the Voyages of Robinson Cruso," appended to the "Farther Adventures" of August, 1719,—ten months before "Captain Singleton" was published; thereon the Congo, in its northward sweep, is shown actually touching the equator, from which it recoils sharply to the southwest. Presumably Defoe did not himself draw this map, but undoubtedly he saw it. One of the most prominent London map-makers of Defoe's day was Herman Moll, a native of Holland, who furnished maps for the later volumes of Defoe's "Tour." I have already referred to his map of the world in the first volume of Dampier's "Voyage." On that map the Congo is represented as making only a broad and gentle sweep toward the equator; but one of its branches is laid down as flowing from the Niger Lake, which, as has been said previously, was placed across the equator by Moll. Another of Moll's maps of the world, the original date of publication of which I have not been able to determine,[120] represents the Congo as having its source *north* of the equator, and as flowing southwest to the ocean in a fairly straight course.

It is clear, then, that the majority of maps of the half century preceding 1720 represented the Congo as making a considerable curve north-

[117] Introduction to *Captain Singleton*, p. xiv.

[118] Morden, p. 441.

[119] John Ogilby, *Africa*, p. 1. See also various sectional maps scattered through the volume.

[120] Herman Moll, *Atlas Minor*, map No. 1. This oblong quarto volume is undated; the Dictionary of National Biography (article on Moll), however, lists it as of the year 1732. Practically all of the maps had been published earlier in separate form.

ward toward the equator before turning southwest to the Atlantic, and that a few at least represented it as touching and even flowing across the equator. Had Defoe manifested a belief that the Congo lay partly north of the equator (as both Professor Minto and Mr. Aitken assert that he did), he would have been doing nothing for which he was without the authority of reputable map-makers.

The astounding thing, however, is that Professor Minto has read "Captain Singleton" to so little purpose as to misunderstand what Defoe actually says therein about the Congo's course. It is hardly less incredible that Mr. Aitken and others have not recognized the blunder. For nothing whatsoever in "Captain Singleton" gives ground for thinking that Defoe believed any part of the Congo to lie north of the equator. Here is what Defoe really says. Singleton's party[121] has passed to the north both of the great lake from which the river, thought to be the Nile, flowed, and of the nearby lake stretching across the equator; they are then in north latitude. Singleton proposed[122] continuing northward to the "Rio Grande . . . . for I knew that at last it would bring us down to the Cape de Verd where we were sure of relief . . . ." Singleton, however, was an inexperienced youth and had to submit to the Portuguese gunner who[123] "advised us that, as soon as we had passed this lake (the one lying across the equator), *we should proceed W. S. W., that is to say, a little inclining to the south, and that in time we should meet with the great river Congo. . . .* " Singleton does not say how far north of the equator they are, nor how far southwest they must travel to reach the Congo; all that he says is that if they incline a little to the south of west they will "in time" meet the Congo. One does not have to be a Euclid to discern that no specific relationship of the position of the Congo to that of the equator is here predicated. The phrase "a little inclining to the south" determines not the length of their movement but its direction. By carelessly reading this one sentence Professor Minto has misunderstood Defoe's whole meaning.

That my interpretation of the point is the right one is borne out by the succeeding narrative of the attempt of the adventurers to find the Congo. Turning southwest, as the gunner suggested, they reached[124] a "vast howling wilderness" which finally caused them to abandon the Congo region as their goal and to adopt Singleton's plan of going northward. It is this wilderness which Professor Minto and Mr. Aitken assert prevented the party from discovering the Congo north of the equator. But, as I

---

[121] *Captain Singleton*, pp. 118-123.

[122] *Ibid.*, p. 124.

[123] *Ibid.*

[124] *Captain Singleton*, p. 127.

have shown, the fact that they are north of the line when they decide to turn southwest towards the Congo is no evidence that they did not expect to recross the line to the south before reaching that river. And that was precisely what they did. For, in a paragraph which Professor Minto and Mr. Aitken appear to have overlooked entirely, Defoe actually states that they reached the equator (if indeed they did not cross it) without finding the Congo. From the lake which forced them north of the line, they marched four days southwest;[125] by that time they found a wild desert which they penetrated for five more days.[126] But their progress was slow "for it was excessively hot; and *we were much about the very equinoctial line, we hardly knew whether to the south or the north of it.*"

There can be no doubt of the meaning. Their course southwest, pursued for nine days, had brought them to the equator, but it had not brought them to the Congo which lay still beyond the "vast howling wilderness." At this point, as has been said, the gunner of necessity yielded to Singleton's plan; the party turned northward[127] again, and in time reached the Guinea coast.[128]

By failing to find warrant on maps accessible to Defoe for the lake lying across the equator, and by misunderstanding what Defoe really says about the course of the Congo, Professor Minto has led students of Defoe into two errors, namely, into supposing (1) that he boldly invented that lake, and (2) that he made an important anticipation of modern discoveries concerning the true course of the Congo. But, as has just been demonstrated, Defoe is in both cases following the maps at hand. For at least one map placed Niger Lake across the equator just where Singleton discovered his; and, though there were not lacking maps showing the Congo flowing north of the equator, Defoe follows the majority by representing it as lying south of that line.

What should be emphasized is that Defoe did not need to go elsewhere than to books printed in English for Singleton's journey through Africa. The statement of Professor Minto that near the two coasts Singleton's geography has a considerable degree of accuracy, whereas in the interior it is "indisputably wild and fabulous," is not, as he supposes, evidence that

[125] *Ibid.*, p. 125.

[126] *Ibid.*, p. 126.

[127] *Ibid.*, p. 130.

[128] In about a month the party is in latitude 8 degrees 5 minutes, presumably north. This statement does not, however, hang very well with one made a little later (p. 132) to the effect that having gone 4 degrees further north they were in latitude 3 degrees 16 minutes. The contradiction may be removed by assuming that both statements mean south latitude, but in that case the whole narrative becomes hopeless as far as locating its path is concerned.

Defoe was indebted to Portuguese sources (who had settlements on both coasts and who presumably had penetrated inland a considerable distance from them) for his knowledge of those coasts.   Heylin, Ogilby, and Morden, also, knew the coasts better than they knew the interior, where their geography became indisputably wild and fabulous.   Defoe possessed no knowledge either of the country, its people, or its products which could not have been culled from printed works accessible to any Londoner of 1720.

We have already seen that the island lakes and rivers mentioned by Singleton were, broadly speaking, those shown on the maps of that day. They are the large features which every map supplied.   But for great stretches in between Defoe had no recourse except his imagination.   On the whole, however, he used that faculty with judgment and restraint. The smaller ranges of mountains, rivers, and deserts, he attempts to set forth conformably to the knowledge or surmises of reputable geographers. This attempt is well illustrated in the case of the small rivers encountered by Singleton as he travelled north along the east side of the great lake from which it was conjectured that the Nile arose.[129]   To his left is an inland body of water, to his right a ridge of mountains (mountains which show plainly on Moll's map of the world in Dampier) ; the rainy season has just closed.   Given these conditions, the invention of rivers to carry the enormous quantities of water from the mountains to the lake is both easy and safe.

A word should be said here of Defoe's method of determining the limits of the rainy season in the tropics.   His rule briefly is this : the rainy season comes and goes with the run in its yearly swing between the tropics of Cancer and Capricorn.   He may have taken this from Dampier, who remarks that,[130] within the torrid zone, the sky grows cloudy and the atmosphere moist as the sun comes nearer : "for the rains follow the sun and begin on either side of the equator, within a little while after the sun has crost the equinox, and so continue till after his return back again." But no matter where Defoe got it, he used this scheme for Central Africa[131] and for Crusoe's island.[132]   It is, then, no evidence of especial knowledge that he speaks so confidently of the seasonal changes of a particular place in the tropics.   All he required to know is the approximate latitude of the place ; then with his knowledge of the sun's movements and with this rule to guide him he calculated with sufficient accuracy the wet and the dry periods.

[129] *Captain Singleton,* p. 119.
[130] Dampier, II, part iii, p. 77.
[131] *Captain Singleton,* p. 112.
[132] *Robinson Crusoe,* I, p. 117.

After turning northeast toward Guinea, Singleton's party found a river which later sank into the sand and so disappeared.[133] Such a river Morden had reported[134] to be in the region. Their finding of gold between Lakes Zafflan and Zaire is not surprising to one who has read anything of the products of that part of Africa; Morden[135] says that it abounds in gold "which is found in the shallows of rivers" in one place, and "upon the superficies of the earth" in another. The later stop of Singleton's comrades for gold as they neared the Guinea coast is to be expected; everyone in Defoe's day knew that Guinea was famous for its gold, for which one of its sections was called the Gold Coast.

Another part of Guinea was for an analogous reason known as the Ivory Coast. Singleton's report of elephant teeth is in agreement with many which Defoe probably had read. He states that in the region around the old Lake Zaire[136] the "ground was scattered with elephants' teeth in such a number as is incredible." Several there were "so heavy as the strongest man among us could not lift." One monstrous head was the largest Singleton ever saw; of it he remarks: " . . . . the flesh was consumed, to be sure, many hundred years before, and all the other bones; but three or four of our strongest men could not lift this skull and teeth; the great tooth, I believe, weighed at least three hundredweight . . . . I observed the whole skull was as good ivory as the teeth, and, I believe, altogether weighed at least six hundredweight. . . . " Purchas, similarly, reported an account[137] of elephants' teeth from Ethiopia weighing two hundred pounds each; and Hakluyt described[138] an elephant's head brought from the coast of Guinea, "of such huge bignesse, that only the bones or cranew thereof, besides the nether jaw and great tusks, weighed about two hundred weight, and was as much as I could well lift from the ground: insomuch that considering also herewith the weight of two such great teeth, the nether jaw with lesse teeth . . . . with all the other parts . . . . in my judgment it could weight little less than five hundred weight. This head divers have seene in the house of the worthy marchant sir Andrew Judde. . . . "

Several echoes of "Robinson Crusoe" are heard during the relation of this journey. The incident of the killing of a leopard is very like Crusoe's killing of a leopard on the west coast of Africa during his flight from Salee. In both stories the native Africans are terrified by the report

[133] *Captain Singleton*, p. 135.
[134] Morden, p. 492.
[135] *Ibid.*, p. 492.
[136] *Captain Singleton*, p. 99.
[137] Purchas, VI, p. 445.
[138] Hakluyt, VI, p. 164.

of the gun, in both the leopard is large and "admirably spotted all over," in both the natives remove the skin with sharp wooden instruments, and in both the hero (Crusoe and Singleton, respectively) keeps the skin for his own purposes.[139]

I have already commented upon the fact that both Crusoe and Singleton found the natives naked and afraid of fire arms, and upon the resemblance of Singleton's negro captives to Crusoe's Friday. On one occasion the chief of these captives (who, having been a king's son, was called "the Prince") had an encounter with wild beasts which recalls distinctly Friday's adventure with the bear in the Pyrenees;[140] the Prince not only acted like Friday, but talked like him as well. Finally, the palisade[141] about Singleton's camp, and his clothing of animal skins[142] are reminiscent of similar devices of the island portion of Crusoe's story.

In concluding this section of the study of "Captain Singleton," I wish to reemphasize these facts. (1) There is no evidence for the belief that Defoe utilized either the records of a real African traveller or information received privately from Portuguese or other sources. For (2) all the acquaintance he betrays with the people, products, and physiography of the African continent lay open before him in geographies and books of travel. More specifically it may be said that Defoe did not depart from the practice of map-makers of his day in designating the course of the Congo, nor in placing a lake across the equator toward the west coast of Africa.

It is to be repeated that in considering this African journey I have not attempted to show what particular geographies or books of travel were actually used by Defoe; but I have endeavored to make clear that he manifests no information of Africa which necessitates assuming with Professors Minto and Saintsbury and others that Defoe had access to special material denied to the general public of the day.

III. *Singleton as a Pirate*

a. *Elaboration of Avery's career*

The rest of Singleton's story deals with his career as a pirate. After he and his Portuguese comrades accomplished their journey from Mozambique to Guinea, they separated, some going one way and some another. Singleton himself got back to England with considerable wealth in the form of golddust picked up along the African rivers. This he soon squandered, and setting out to sea again turned pirate.

[139] *Robinson Crusoe*, I, pp. 32-3; *Captain Singleton*, pp. 75-6.
[140] *Robinson Crusoe*, I, p. 328ff.
[141] *Captain Singleton*, p. 103.
[142] *Ibid.*, p. 140.

The narrative of his piracies is largely an elaboration of the story of Avery which Defoe himself had written, entitled "The King of Pirates," and published in December, 1719, six months previously to the issuing of "Captain Singleton." I do not mean that Singleton is Avery under a new name, but that his career is modelled after Avery's. Such is the opinion of Mr. Aitken[143] and such will, I think, be the opinion of any one who compares a little the two narratives. The only evidence for this cited by Mr. Aitken is the fact that "Quaker William (in Singleton's story) is foreshadowed (in the "King of Pirates") by a Quaker captain who would not hesitate to use the cannon-ball."[144] But other similarities are not lacking. Both Singleton and Avery, after a short period of cruising about in American waters, sail for Madagascar and the East. In the East Indies both gain inestimable wealth plundering the ships of the Great Mogul and others, with Madagascar as their rendezvous. Both, finally, tire of piracy after having amassed enough wealth, and set out for England by way of the Persian Gulf and Busra and the Arabian desert,— the route which, we have seen, Dampier suggested to Defoe for Crusoe, but which Defoe rejected. Avery, moreover, figures in "Captain Singleton," joining Singleton with men and ships at Madagascar. Certain other events in Avery's career as related by Defoe, furthermore, creep into Singleton's adventures.

The gossipy "Life and Adventures of Captain John Avery" (1709) has already been mentioned. It purported to have been the work of one Adrian Van Broeck,[145] a Dutch gentleman who had escaped from Avery's colony on Madagascar. But the judicious reader will accept such a statement with caution; for not only does this account freely incorporate much of the contemporary exaggerations of Avery's greatness,—his setting up as a king on Madagascar, with unlimited plunder got in the Indies and a powerful body of men behind him, and his marriage with the daughter of the Great Mogul, captured by him,—but it also betrays no actual acquaintance with the real life of Avery.

Defoe's "King of Pirates" comprises two letters purporting to be from Avery himself, who, angered at the impudence of the writer of the "Life and Adventures," took the opportunity of telling his own story. Just where Defoe got his information of Avery for these letters is not fully known. Sir John Knox Laughton asserts[146] that both "The Life and Adventures" and "The King of Pirates" are fiction "with scarcely a

[143] Introduction to *King of Pirates,* p. x. See also the similar statement of Mr. G. H. Maynadier in his introduction to the *King of Pirates* (1903), p. x.

[144] *The King of Pirates,* p. x.

[145] Such is the statement of the preface.

[146] *Dictionary of National Biography,* article on Avery.

substratum of fact." Defoe appears to have taken some suggestions both from the anonymous "Life" and from common rumor; but these he handles with his customary restraint, rejecting what is obviously fanciful, and striving to make the exploits credible. One portion of the "King of Pirates," however, is based upon Dampier's voyages. Our business here is not to investigate Avery's career as Defoe gives it, but Singleton's; but since the latter is so greatly indebted to the former it will be of material assistance to us in discovering how Defoe worked to know something of the character of the "King of Pirates." The portion of that work which Defoe fabricated with the aid of Dampier is the voyage of Avery from the West Indies around Cape Horn to Juan Fernandez, and the subsequent piracies in the South Sea; but as this adventure is not reproduced in "Captain Singleton," the detailed proof of the assertion is here omitted.[147]

Sir John Laughton's statement that the "King of Pirates" is almost wholly fictitious is, I think, true. It should be remarked, however, that in one important particular, a particular not recorded, so far as I can discover, by any other writer previously to 1724, it agrees with the account of Avery in Captain Charles Johnson's "General History of the Pyrates" of the year 1724. That particular is the incident of the stealing of a merchant vessel at the Groyne (Corunna.) According to Defoe's version this was when Avery was endeavoring to return to his comrades on Madagascar; but Johnson records it as being at the outset of his career.

The latter's relation of it is as follows.[148] Avery was first mate of a vessel commanded to sail for Corunna, or the Groyne, in company with a second vessel. It is reported that "he insinuated himself into the good will of several of the boldest fellows on board the other ship . . . . finding them ripe for his design, he at length propos'd to them to run away with the ship. . . ." The plan was speedily carried out. The conspirators from the other vessel came aboard in the night when the captain was in bed, and joining with Avery and others weighed anchor and stood out to sea. Later when the captain awoke, he and five or six of the crew who refused the opportunity of becoming pirates were set ashore. Thereupon the rogues sailed for Madagascar.

[147] Compare *The King of Pirates*, pp. 20-30, and Dampier, I, pp. 80-150.

[148] Johnson's account of Avery is reprinted in Howard Pyle's *Buccaneers and Marooners of America* (1897), pp. 385-403, from which I have taken it. I have not examined the *General History of the Pyrates*, but have read the portions of it reprinted in Captain Charles Johnson's *History of the Lives and Adventures of the most famous Highwaymen* . . . (1734). Whether this Captain Charles Johnson is the same as the one who wrote the history of the pirates, or whether there really existed a Captain Charles Johnson at all, we do not certainly know.

Four years earlier than Johnson Defoe had written the story in essentially the same way, though with details which Johnson omits. In the first place, Defoe's Avery pretends that in things so modern he must not mention[149] names of persons or places, because to do so might lead to his apprehension. He nevertheless states that having an opportunity "to go chief mate on board a stout ship bound from London to —," and being through stress of weather at anchor on the coast of Spain, he, with ten followers among the crew, "took up arms in the middle of the night, secured the Captain . . . . and . . . . the rest of the men," and declared his intention. "The captain and nine men," he continues, "refused to come into our projected roguery . . . . so we set them on shore. . . ." Following this Defoe gives some details unmentioned by Johnson. He speaks of there being a small quantity[150] of baled goods on board the stolen vessel, and of taking in "beef and fish at —, where we lay fifteen days, but out of reach of the castle or fort," and of sailing to the Canary Islands on the way to Madagascar.

A second version of this event (Johnson's is really the third in point of time) Defoe gives us in "Captain Singleton."[151] Singleton, having in the approved fashion of pirates wasted "in all kinds of folly and wickedness" his store of gold gathered along the banks of African streams, shipped himself "in an evil hour to be sure, on a voyage to Cadiz, in a ship called the——. . . . and being on the coast of Spain, was obliged to put into the Groyn by a strong southwest wind." There he and a young villain of the crew, named Harris, became warm friends, and conspired to stir up a mutiny and to seize the ship. Another scoundrel on board a second English vessel in the harbor was attempting, in correspondence with them, to carry out a similar scheme with respect to his vessel. Finding but eleven of their men to be trusted, Singleton and Harris failed in their part; so they ran away in the ship's boat to join their fellow-conspirator, Wilmot, who had met with greater success. The rogues first put in at Cadiz where they traded some bales of English goods for ammunition and sustenance, and then sailed for the Canary Islands and the West Indies.

Where Defoe got this incident which he thus incorporates into Singleton's story, I am unable to determine. Apparently it was not mentioned in the "Avery" of 1709 nor the play of 1712. Nor does Sir John Laughton regard it as sufficiently authenticated to be listed among those scanty facts about Avery which are known. That Johnson, who in his "Highwaymen" of 1734 was to record the adventures of Colonel Jacque along with those of Jonathan Wild and other actual rogues, did not take the incident from

[149] *King of Pirates*, p. 43ff.
[150] *Ibid.*, p. 44.
[151] *Captain Singleton*, p. 157ff.

Defoe's pamphlet on Avery is clear. It is, therefore, certain that both Defoe and Johnson were depending upon actual reports (probably unwritten) of Avery's exploits.

In "Captain Singleton" the incident, though obviously based upon Defoe's own previous relation of it in the "King of Pirates," is elaborated according to his usual method. The circumstances of the forming of the conspiracy and of the securing of provisions at Cadiz are given with greater attention to detail. This, it seems to me, is Defoe's essential contribution to the realistic novel. The scene must be realized, not hurried through as is frequently done in romances. The incident is not a means to an end altogether; to a certain extent it becomes an end in itself. There are two distinct gains which this method affords to Defoe. In the first place, the narrative takes on the atmosphere of actual experience, and, in the second, it gives opportunity for the characterization of individuals.

From the Groyne and Cadiz Singleton and Harris, under the leadership of Wilmot, did not sail to Madagascar, but to the West Indies. Their cruising adventures thereabouts for two years do not differ essentially from those recorded by Exquemelin, Dampier, and other writers of accounts of piracy in those waters. They capture[152] a Spanish sloop at Cartagena, the scene of many attacks by English buccaneers (Dampier,[153] also, tells of capturing a Spanish vessel there) ; they haunt Campeachy Bay; they plunder vessels from New England and Pennsylvania. Pursued by English men-of-war, they escaped toward Cartagena, and continued along the north coast of South America past St. Martha and the Dutch island of Curaçoa (the island sought by Pitman and Whicker in their escape from Barbados—see the discussion of their adventures in the preceding chapter) to Tobago, thus going over a course which Dampier and his fellows had taken and which Dampier described in considerable detail.[154] They haunted Tobago and Trinidad (the region of Crusoe's island), and captured a Portuguese vessel entering All Saints Bay (Bahia de Todos los Santos), the scene of events in the life of Crusoe and in the earlier career of Singleton. After cruising in the region of Buenos Ayres and the De la Plata, they followed in the wake of Avery, Kidd, and actual pirates of the very year of 1720 (when the West Indies were no longer safe for pirates), by sailing away to Madagascar.

Defoe's Avery had cruised a brief period among the West Indies before venturing into the South Sea and to Madagascar. Some of his experiences in the West Indies Defoe reutilized in fabricating Singleton's adventures. Such a one is the securing of William Walters, better known as Quaker

---

[152] *Captain Singleton*, p. 161.
[153] Dampier, I, pp. 44-5.
[154] *Ibid.*, pp. 44-64.

William, who thereafter becomes the most important character of Singleton's story. This bold Quaker was taken from a Pennsylvania sloop[155]
and forced, though not against his will, to serve the pirate crew in the
capacity of surgeon; later he became the shrewdest pirate of them all.
Defoe had, as Mr. Aitken pointed out, drawn a first sketch of this Quaker
in the "King of Pirates," in the person of a Quaker commander of an
Irish vessel captured by Avery[156] in the West Indies. ". . . . had he
been equal to us in force," Avery is made to say, "it appeared by his
countenance he would not have been afraid of his flesh, or have baulked
using the carnal weapon of offense, viz., the cannon-ball." Unlike William
Walters, however, this Quaker grimly, and (one imagines) somewhat
reluctantly declined the opportunity of turning pirate; he was, therefore,
set ashore.

In connection with William Walters and his prototype in the "King of
Pirates," it should be observed that the interrelation of Defoe and the
contemporary writers of criminal lives is but little understood. It is
assumed that he turned to their records for much of his materials in such
works as "Moll Flanders," but more precise knowledge we do not possess.
Professor Chandler's erroneous supposition that Defoe himself served
an apprenticeship in the writing of actual criminal biographies before
turning to his fictions about criminal characters has been commented upon
in my opening chapter. Here it is sufficient to point out a few traces of
the criminal biographies upon "Captain Singleton."

A Quaker highwayman whose adventures were related by Captain
Alexander Smith in his "Highwaymen" of 1714 probably furnished
Defoe with the chief features for his two Quaker seamen. That merry
bandit,[157] Jacob Halsey by name, robbed his victims "in the formal language of the worst of British schismaticks." Like the Irish captain who
would not "have baulked using the carnal weapon of offense, viz., the
cannon-ball," Halsey punished undocile victims "with the temporal
weapons of sword and pistol." Defoe's allusion to the captain as a
"Quaking Skipper" is reminiscent of the term "Quaking Highwayman"
applied to Halsey. Precisely that of Quaker William is Halsey's manner
of speaking. "Dearly beloved," said the latter to a man whom he was
robbing, "be not surpriz'd at what I am going to say to thee; for 'tis . . . .
only to borrow what money thou hast about thee. . . ." Upon another
occasion he said, "Look thee, friend, I am not like one of the prophane
ones, who spoil men in the terrifying words . . . . but an Israelite that

---

[155] *Captain Singleton*, p. 163.

[156] *King of Pirates*, pp. 14-5.

[157] I regret having to rely upon the reprint of this highwayman's story in Johnson's *History of the Highwaymen* of 1734, pp. 140-144.

spoils an Egyptian with all the good humour . . . . in the world; so open thy purse strings strait. . . . " Quaker William's euphemistic circumlocutions and his sense of humor are too well known to require lengthy comparison with these traits in Halsey; one example is sufficient. "Hark thee friend," says William to Singleton,[158] "thou hast made a fine piece of work of it now . . . . to borrow thy neighbor's ship here just at thy neighbor's door and never ask him leave. Now, dost thou not think there are some men-of-war in the port? . . . . thou wilt have them upon thy back before night . . . . to ask thee wherefore thou didst so." The account of Halsey's career, however, furnished Defoe with but the bare outlines for Quaker William, and emphasizes thereby Defoe's power of characterization.[159]

A second detail of "Captain Singleton" which may have come from the criminal biographies is the name of Singleton's comrade, Wilmot. Thomas Wilmot, hanged in 1670, was another of the highwaymen whose life Smith records.[160]

Returning to the features of Singleton's West India adventures which came from the "King of Pirates," we may notice that both Singleton and Avery went to Cuba to secure beef;[161] Defoe knew from his reading in Dampier that Cuba was well stocked with cattle.[162] But Singleton does not follow Avery around Cape Horn to the South Sea; that region had been pretty thoroughly worked by Defoe in Avery's story and by the actual pirates of the "Bucaniers of America." Instead Singleton follows Avery's subsequent course to Madagascar and the East Indies where piracy was both more profitable and more interesting.

One other incident of Singleton's career on the coast of South America remains to be mentioned, namely, the finding of a vessel drifting at sea.[163] The occupants proved to be negro slaves who had found a way to kill all the officers of the ship and members of the crew, intending to return to their native land. Ignorant of navigation, however, they could do nothing but drift at the mercy of the waves; when rescued by Singleton they were upon the point of being wrecked upon the shore of South America. Defoe is here utilizing an incident recorded by Exquemelin in the "Bucaniers of

[158] *Captain Singleton*, p. 169.
[159] The suggestion of Mr. James Ryan, editor of the works of Robert Knox, that Knox is the prototype of Quaker William need not be taken too seriously. For, as I have pointed out in the preceding chapter, Knox lacked not only the clear vision and tact of Defoe's Quaker, but also his humor and native shrewdness of speech.
[160] See Johnson's *Highwaymen*, p. 108ff.
[161] *King of Pirates*, p. 11; *Captain Singleton*, p. 162.
[162] Dampier, II, part ii, pp. 33, 98.
[163] *Captain Singleton*, p. 177ff.

America."[164] The natives of Cape Gracias á Dios, says Exquemelin, "have among them a few negro slaves, who happened to arrive there, swimming after shipwreck made on that coast: for being bound for Terra Firma, in a ship that carried them to be sold there, they killed the captain and mariners, with the design to return to their country; but being ignorant of navigation, they stranded their vessel hereabouts." The principal changes made in the incident by Defoe are the shifting of the scene of the action, the rescuing of the vessel before it is driven ashore, and the giving of an additional reason for the killing of the ship's men; that additional reason is the mistreatment of the female slaves.

What to do with the 600 negroes Singleton did not know. Finally he consented to Quaker William's taking them to the coast of Brazil; there by stealth he sold them to Crusoe's whilom neighbors, the Portuguese sugar planters about Bahia de Todos los Santos, and thus rendered the service which shipwreck and twenty-eight years of solitude had prevented Crusoe's performing.

Singleton's journey to Madagascar was the usual one about the Cape of Good Hope to St. Augustine Bay, the scene of his first landing on the island, when as a mere lad he was put ashore on a charge of mutiny. One event of the journey occurring at Good Hope is of interest because it almost certainly is based upon an experience in the life of Robert Knox, an experience not recorded in Knox's published work, the "Ceylon." It, therefore, strengthens the presumption advanced in the preceding chapter that Defoe knew Knox personally. Singleton's report of the affair follows. The "case, in short, was this:[165] Captain — (I forbear his name at present, for a particular reason), captain of an East India merchant-ship, bound afterwards for China, had found some reason to be very severe with his men, and had handled some of them very roughly at St. Helena; insomuch that they threatened among themselves to leave the ship the first opportunity. . . ." Finding that Singleton's men were pirates, a number of them escaped to his vessel and turned pirate also. The experience of Knox's to which this incident is very similar occurred at St. Helena where he was at anchor after his voyage to Madagascar. Alleging ill-treatment,[166] his men mutinied and actually ran away with his vessel, the *Tonqueene Merchant*. Both before and afterward Knox made voyages to the East Indies and China. Defoe changes the scene and the details somewhat, but mentions practically every circumstance connected with Knox's trouble. The men, says Defoe, had been harshly treated at St. Helena, the Captain made voyages to the East Indies and to China,

[164] I (1771), p. 215.
[165] *Captain Singleton*, p. 193.
[166] Robert Knox, *Ceylon*, p. 233.

and there was "a particular reason" why the captain's name and ship should not be mentioned. Defoe may, of course, have pleaded the last in order to escape the trouble of inventing names; but more probably he did so out of deference to Knox who was still alive when the story appeared.

With headquarters at Madagascar Singleton, still in company with Wilmot, imitated the exploits of Avery as recorded in Defoe's "King of Pirates." Like Avery he captured a rich vessel belonging to the Great Mogul.[167] At this point Avery himself enters the story, having[168] just taken "one ship with the Great Mogul's daughter, and an immense treasure in money and jewels." The last incident had been related in detail in the "King of Pirates,"[169] though the shipwreck which Singleton says befell Avery on his return to Madagascar is a feature invented after the "King of Pirates" was written; the latter work says specifically[170] that the return to Madagascar was free from disaster. Singleton repeats those circumstances of which rumor had made so much in Europe, namely, that Avery planned building a strong city and establishing a place of retirement for himself and his men.

Singleton and Wilmot about this time quarreled and separated. Afterward Singleton cruised in the East Indies with Quaker William as his chief counsellor. Wilmot, on the other hand, became a confederate of Avery, and so passes out of the story. Except for his scheme of returning finally to England through the desert of Arabia, Avery's career contributes nothing further to Singleton's.

b. *The Voyage to the Spice Islands*

Singleton's final cruise led him around Ceylon and along the Coromandel coast to Bengal Bay, from whence he passed to Sumatra for provisions; then, sailing under Sumatra and Java, he steered for the Moluccas or Spice Islands. Having secured a rich cargo of spices by plundering there and around the Philippines, he sold his cloves and nutmegs to Chinese merchants. This transaction brought to him and his men immense wealth, so that they feared to return by either the Malacca or Sunda straits. Hence they steered southward, keeping to the east of the Philippines and Australia, and later sailed west under the little known island of Australia, turning northward finally to Java and Ceylon.

This extensive voyage is another of the undeveloped schemes suggested in "Robinson Crusoe." While trading back and forth from Bengal Crusoe

[167] *Captain Singleton*, p. 201.
[168] *Ibid.*, p. 205.
[169] *King of Pirates*, p. 57ff.
[170] *Ibid.*, p. 62.

apparently made several such voyages; one of them is delineated on the map prefixed to the "Farther Adventures," but in the narrative[171] they are barely mentioned. Later, when on the coast of China,[172] he contemplated such a voyage, but gave it over.

Dampier had visited the Moluccas. He had, in fact, on one occasion[173] traversed approximately Singleton's very course, though going in the opposite direction. At the time he was abroad the *Cygnet;* an entertaining account of her fortunes and disasters may be found in Mr. Masefield's "A Mainsail Haul." After the *Cygnet's* crew had run away with her, leaving their captain at Mindanao, they returned to Madagascar (where, as Captain Knox told Dampier, the *Cygnet* sank in St. Augustine Bay) by travelling east of the Philippines, through the Moluccas, under Java and Sumatra to the Coromandel coast. They did not then, as Singleton did on the outward voyage, pass between Gilolo and New Guinea; instead they passed north of Gilolo. But upon the occasion of his voyage of exploration to New Holland (Australia) in 1699, Dampier went and returned through the passage between Gilolo and New Guinea.

Whether or not Defoe was directly indebted to other writers than Dampier for the action and the geographical facts of Singleton's adventures in the Moluccas I am unable to determine. Numerous other accounts of East India voyages were available in 1720. Magellan, Drake, Keeling, and others had explored[174] that region in part. Nieuhoff, especially, had described, with numerous illustrations, the Spice Islands.[175]

Many Englishmen of the seventeenth century knew of the Spice Islands because of the charges of extreme cruelty to English merchants there in 1622 preferred against the Dutch. During the war between England and Holland a half century later, Dryden seized the opportunity of reviving the affair and introduced it on the stage in "Amboyna, or the Cruelties of the Dutch to the English Merchants."[176] Defoe shows that the charges of cruelty were well known; for he makes Singleton say,[177] when his men captured an Amboyna vessel and in anger desired to slay the crew, "the reason, I suppose, any one will guess."

Defoe's own library contained several works describing the Moluccas, among them Mandelslo's journal which, as has already been shown, was

---

[171] *Robinson Crusoe*, II, pp. 214, 217.

[172] *Ibid.*, p. 249.

[173] Dampier, I, pp. 305-470. See also Dampier's map, I, p. 282.

[174] Purchas, II, pp. 116, 134ff.; 523ff. Magellan himself died in the Philippines, but his men sailed southwest through the Moluccas.

[175] John Nieuhoff, *Brazil and the East Indies* (1703?), p. 195ff.

[176] Genest, I, p. 147.

[177] *Captain Singleton*, p. 218.

used in the fabrication of Singleton's earlier adventures on Madagascar. But in none of these have I been able to discover any concrete incidents or facts which Defoe certainly used.

Practically all the knowledge Defoe possessed (or manifests possessing in "Captain Singleton") of the East Indies and the little explored region about New Holland (Australia) is contained in the "Voyage" of Dampier. Defoe, moreover, leaves here and there a trace of his dependence upon Dampier; it is not presumptuous, therefore, to assert that in Dampier we have the most important external influence upon this portion of Singleton's story.

Setting out from the Bay of Bengal, Singleton, as has been stated, put in at a Sumatra town for provisions: principally[178] "a large quantity of pork, pickled up and well salted," and "forty hogs alive." In addition thereto he mentions securing rice, guams (yams) and potatoes, and *"ducks, and cocks and hens."* All of these Dampier in his account of the East Indies mentions frequently—more frequently perhaps, than any other products; and he usually groups them as does Defoe. Of the south coast of China he states that rice and hogs are plentiful,[179] and that "the tame fowls are *ducks, and cocks and hens."* He reports[180] that in the Nicobar Islands (just northwest of Sumatra) there were "no yams, potatoes, rice . . . . yet they have a few small hogs, and a very few cocks and hens like ours." "Yames and potatoes" he twice speaks of as products of the Bashi Islands.[181]

Dampier's account of these islands (off the north coast of Luzon, the most northerly of the Philippines) Defoe must have read with interest; for he again and again incorporates into his narratives suggestions from its twenty pages.[182] I have contended previously that Crusoe's selection of a site for his dwelling and his construction of that dwelling are based upon Dampier's description of the practice of these Bashians in building their domiciles. It was from this part of Dampier's narrative, moreover, that Defoe got his idea for the cutler or worker in iron whom he combined with Leguat's silversmith to form Singleton's "artist." From this account we now find Defoe taking the suggestions for Singleton's yams and potatoes.

Here also Defoe got his idea for Singleton's hogs. Dampier tells of buying them in large quantities, both to eat fresh[183] and to put in salt.

[178] *Ibid.*, p. 217.
[179] Dampier, I, p. 406.
[180] *Ibid.*, I, p. 480.
[181] *Ibid.*, I, p. 433.
[182] *Ibid.*, I, pp. 420-440.
[183] *Ibid.*, I, p. 435.

Before leaving the islands his men had "salted 70 or 80 good fat hogs, and bought yams and potatoes good store to eat at sea." Other details which Defoe took from Dampier's account of the Bashi Islands will be mentioned later.

As a route to the Philippines Dampier personally preferred[184] sailing by way of Cape Horn and the Pacific Ocean (as he had just done) ; but he speaks of three openings from the west, namely, "the streights of Mallaca or Sundy, or else some other streights east of Java." Singleton rejected the two former,[185] in favor of the last; "leaving the straits of Sunda and the isle of Java on the east," he approached the Spice Islands from the south, and "steered directly through a large outlet, which they called a strait," to the east of Java.

Being then in the region of Banda, Singleton[186] captured a Dutch vessel loaded with nutmegs. From trading with the natives for more nutmegs he was prevented by the Dutch[187] "who made themselves masters of those islands," and "forbade the people dealing with us, or any other strangers whatever, and kept them so in awe that they durst not do it." It was resolved, therefore, to go to Ternate, another of the Spice Islands, and complete the cargo with a lading of cloves.

Dampier had said[188] that Banda was famous for its nutmegs and Ternate for its cloves (though Defoe may have learned this from other sources) ; he had, furthermore, stated that the Dutch monopolized the spice trade.[189] "For," said he, "the Dutch being seated among the Spice Islands . . . . will not suffer any of the natives to dispose of it (spice), but to themselves alone. Nay, they . . . . will not suffer the spice to grow in the uninhabited islands, but send soldiers to cut the trees down."

Singleton's vessel, springing a leak some time later, was compelled to anchor "upon a small island not far from Banda." There the Dutch had no representatives, and Singleton[190] "found ways to trade with the natives (for spice), without the knowledge of . . . . the Dutch." Dampier relates[191] being told "that near the island of Banda there is an island" where spices were literally rotting on the ground, and "that it would not be a hard matter for an English vessel to purchase a ships cargo of spice of the natives" there.

[184] Dampier, I, p. 351.
[185] Captain Singleton, pp. 216, 7, 8.
[186] Ibid., pp. 218, 9.
[187] Ibid., p. 219.
[188] Dampier, I, p. 447.
[189] Ibid., I, pp. 316-7.
[190] Captain Singleton, p. 220.
[191] Dampier, I, p. 317.

North of Banda Singleton's ship[192] fell among some rocks. Dampier repeatedly encountered shoals in the East Indies, particularly on one occasion when passing beneath Mindanao, slightly north of the scene of Singleton's mishap. Both Singleton and Dampier escaped shipwreck, though their rudders were damaged. Here we find Defoe echoing Dampier's very words. The latter reports:[193] *"We struck off a great piece of our rudder. . . ."* And Singleton, likewise, found that the rocks had *"split a great piece off the rudder."*

The *Cygnet* was otherwise unhurt, but Singleton's vessel had to be laid aground upon the shore of an island for repairs. The men lived ashore in tents while the ship's bottom was repaired and cleaned.[194] Dampier twice reports living ashore in tents while the *Cygnet* was being overhauled and cleaned; once at the Bashi Islands[195] and once on the northwest coast of Australia.[196] Upon the latter occasion, his fellows, like Singleton, ran their vessel as close on shore as possible where *"at low water she was left dry."* Singleton, less successful, says that at *"low water she lay almost dry."*

Singleton's next venture[197] was to steer through the passage between Gilolo and New Guinea, as Dampier had done both in going to and returning from New Holland in 1699,[198] and to sail northward past the Philippines. There he fell in with Chinese vessels trading to and from Manila, where they purchased both spices and European goods brought across the Pacific by the Manila-Acupulco ships. These Chinese junks he plundered to such purpose that, as Singleton says,[199] "our men began to be of my opinion,—that we were rich enough." He pursued his way to Formosa, where by stealth he disposed of his cargo to Chinese merchants; the latter, being thus saved a tedious voyage to Manila, were glad to purchase even though from people whom they knew to be pirates. The latter, having acquired 50,000 ounces of gold by the transaction, were at the end of their cruise and ready for the return.

The action of this part of the narrative is mainly Defoe's own invention; but all the suggestions for it lay before him in Dampier's book. That is to say, Defoe having familiarized himself with such facts as Dampier

[192] *Captain Singleton*, p. 219.
[193] Dampier, I, p. 381.
[194] *Captain Singleton*, pp. 220-1.
[195] Dampier, I, p. 436.
[196] *Ibid.*, I, p. 469.
[197] *Captain Singleton*, p. 224.
[198] Dampier, IV, p. 102ff. See also the maps in the fronts of volumes III and IV.
[199] *Captain Singleton*, p. 225.

records of his cruising about the Philippines, fabricated upon the basis of these data Singleton's adventures.

Dampier tells[200] of the arrival of the Spanish fleet which made regularly appointed journeys between Acupulco and Manila; in fact, the *Cygnet's* crew had made more than one attempt to capture the fleet on the way across the Pacific. That crew, like Singleton, lay in wait for prey about Manila,[201] but, unlike him, did not execute their plan very successfully. Finding themselves too early for the Acupulco ships, they left the Philippines for the coast of China, and later returned by way of Formosa (near which Singleton traded with the Chinese merchants) to the Bashi Islands where they delayed too long. In the autumn they decided to sail away for Cape Cormorin—Singleton's destination.

For the return both Dampier's comrades of the *Cygnet* and Singleton wait for the October monsoons to bring favorable winds,[202] both avoid the Dutch[203] at the Strait of Sunda by keeping to the southward, and both sail south along the east coast of the Philippines, each encountering thereby and island not set down in the charts.[204] But whereas the *Cygnet* picked her way through the Spice Islands much as Singleton had done in the outward voyage, the latter chose the novel and sensational route around New Holland, or Australia, finally coming up under Java on the way to Ceylon.

Dampier never sailed completely around Australia. Schouten and Le Maire[205] had been along the northeast coast early in the seventeenth century. Toward the middle of that century their countryman, Abel Tasman, had been far south of it, discovering what he named Van Dieman's land but what we now call Tasmania. A casual glance at the mid-eighteenth century maps reveals that even then the southeast coast of Australia was still almost entirely undetermined. An English writer of 1744[206] expressed the belief that the Dutch purposely concealed what knowledge they possessed of that region, and discouraged further explorations there, that they might keep unchallenged their hold.

In Defoe's day the north and west coasts were but imperfectly known, and the south and east coasts were not defined at all. Dampier in 1697 had expressed the belief[207] that it was owing to the neglect of the Pacific

---

[200] Dampier, I, pp. 303, 7, 384-9.
[201] *Ibid.*, I, pp. 387-9.
[202] Dampier, I, p. 437; *Captain Singleton*, p. 226.
[203] Dampier, I, p. 440; *Captain Singleton*, p. 232.
[204] Dampier, I, p. 443; *Captain Singleton*, p. 233.
[205] Purchas, II, p. 230ff.
[206] Harris, *Navigantium atque Itinerantium Bibliotheca*, I (1744), p. 325ff.
[207] Dampier, I, pp. 351-2.

as the easiest and quickest way to the East Indies that the "vast tract of *Terra Australis* which bounds the South Sea is yet undiscovered." Two years later he set out in charge of an expedition to New Holland to see what discoveries he could make there. Then it was that he passed over Singleton's route through the Moluccas and through the passage between Gilolo and New Guinea, explored the northeast coast of the latter for some distance, and later returned by the same path.[208] At that time it was thought that New Guinea was joined to New Holland, as Japan was believed by many to be connected with the mainland of Asia. Dampier suspected, however, what we now know to be true, namely, that a passage existed between the two; he was prevented from verifying this, and long after his death the existence of Torres strait was unknown.

This voyage Dampier recounted in two thin quarto volumes published in 1703 and 1709, respectively.[209] That Defoe was acquainted with these two later volumes of Dampier's and got from them facts about Brazil and its chief port, Bahia, is a probability which I have emphasized in considering "Robinson Crusoe." That Defoe's "New Voyage" of 1724 is, in those parts dealing with the Moluccas and Australia, largely an ill-disguised imitation of Dampier's report of his Australian voyage must, I think, be evident to any one who compares them. Mr. Masefield, to whose admirable edition of Dampier I have more than once alluded, remarked briefly[210] that, unlike "Robinson Crusoe" and "Colonel Jacque," the "New Voyage" shows its derivation; "it smacks strongly of the Voyages of Narborough, Dampier, and Shelvocke." The leader of the imaginary expedition recounted in the "New Voyage" not only follows Dampier through the Gilolo passage and along the New Guinea coast, but also harps upon the importance of making discoveries thereabouts as he proceeds.

It was from this account by Dampier that Defoe got all the data he needed for Singleton's extraordinary voyage around New Holland, though he may have read one of the English translations of Tasman's explorations. Like Dampier, Defoe calls the natives of New Holland and of the neighboring regions Indians.[211] The two agree, moreover, in the character of those natives. Both speak of hostile[212] natives, of uncommunicative

---

[208] *Ibid.*, IV, p. 102ff.

[209] I shall follow the method already used in the preceding chapter, and designate these as volumes three and four of Dampier's *Voyage*. To this Dampier himself gave sanction by calling the 1703 quarto volume three; the later one he called simply a continuation of three.

[210] John Masefield, Introduction to *Defoe* (1909), p. xixff.

[211] Dampier, I, pp. 387, 487; IV, pp. 65, 75; *Captain Singleton*, pp. 235-6.

[212] Dampier, IV, p. 139; *Captain Singleton*, p. 236ff.

natives,[213] of natives who flee[214] and drive their herds with them, and of natives who crowd the shore to see them.[215] Both describe natives armed with lances and bows and arrows, and ornamented about the head with feathers.[216] Both find water hard to get,[217] and both get roots and hogs on shore.[218]

The incident of most interest and importance in this voyage of Singleton's around Australia is, beyond doubt, the hollow-tree fight with the natives of the region of the southeast coast of that island. But precisely where that event occurred has, I think, never been pointed out. Nor has it been noticed that Defoe here manifests a belief that Tasmania is an island.

When "Captain Singleton" was written, Tasmania, then known as Van Dieman's Land, was assumed to be part of southern Australia, just as New Guinea was thought to be part of northeastern Australia. Abel Tasman, the most famous of the Dutch explorers of the seventeenth century, had in 1642 discovered the island and sailed along its southern coast without suspecting that it was an island. His chart of Australia and the surrounding regions was followed by all the better map-makers and seamen of Defoe's day. Dampier mentions using it as his guide, and Captain Bowrey, an Englishman, is now known to have made one of the most exact copies of it.[219] Where Tasman's data failed them, Moll and other reputable hydrographers stopped their coast lines, thus leaving a total blank. We find, therefore, on the later seventeenth and early eighteenth century maps, that though western Australia was placed in fairly accurate outline, the southeast coast was not even attempted; on the east there was no line at all, and on the south the line from the west stopped short near the center of what is called now the Great Australian Bight. Off to the south of this undefined region, a shaded line horseshoe shaped indicated the southern extremity of Van Dieman's Land (now Tasmania), which was thought to be the southern extremity of Australia. After its discovery Tasmania was not again visited,[220] apparently, until 1772. It was not known to be an island until 1798 (sixty-seven years after Defoe's death) when Bass sailed through the strait which bears his name.

[213] Dampier, IV, pp. 96-7, 137ff.; *Captain Singleton*, p. 234.

[214] Dampier, IV, p. 138; *Captain Singleton*, p. 234, 5.

[215] Dampier, IV, pp. 118-19, 123; *Captain Singleton*, p. 235.

[216] Dampier, IV, p. 137; *Captain Singleton*, p. 234-5. Schouten's account (Purchas, II, 230ff.), however, mentions feathers as a part of the dress of these peoples.

[217] Dampier, III, 145, 749; IV, 15. *Captain Singleton*, p. 235.

[218] Dampier, IV, pp. 96-7, 137; *Captain Singleton*, p. 233.

[219] Dampier, III, p. 135. Article on Tasman in the *Encyclopædia Britannica* (11th edition).

[220] See the article on Tasmania in the *Encyclopædia Britannica*.

Notwithstanding these facts, Defoe has Singleton sail directly through Bass Strait and anchor on the north coast of Tasmania, thus indicating that he regarded Tasmania to be an island. He does not say this in so many words; but, after careful comparison of his text with many maps current in 1720, I am convinced that this is his plain meaning.

Singleton "stood southward[221] . . . . leaving Gilolo on the starboard side . . . . coasted the country they call New Guinea, where, in the latitude of eight degrees south" he stopped for provisions. Farther than this the maps of 1720 did not go. Defoe (showing thereby that he was keeping in touch with the maps) remarks that from thence Singleton left behind him[222] all "that any of our charts and maps took any notice of," and went on southward "to the latitude of seventeen degrees (south)," where he "made land to the westward." He was then about even with Cooktown, though far east of it; Defoe is assuming, of course, that the coast line of New Guinea and that of Australia is continuous. Following the shore for four leagues, "at length[223] we found the land break off, and go trending away to the west sea." This was not meant to be the southeast point of Australia, however, for Singleton continued his "course a little west of south" until below the tropic of Capricorn. Then, he says, "we stood away fair west, and held it out for about twenty days, when we discovered land right ahead on our larboard bow." This land, which I believe to be an attempt at localizing the northern shore of Tasmania, is the scene of the hollow-tree fight.

Singleton is made to say that he turned west just after crossing the tropic of Capricorn (23½ degrees south latitude); had he actually done so he would have encountered the east coast of Australia a little north of Brisbane. A little later, however, he states that his westward course was between the 31 and 35 parallels[224] or about even with the Cape of Good Hope. As Good Hope is in approximately latitude 35 degrees south, this calculation would place him about even with Sidney—still a little too far north to pass under Australia.

With due allowance for the apparent contradictions just mentioned, it is evident that Singleton's course westward along the south coast of Australia lay between the tropic of Capricorn (or 23 degrees and 30 minutes) and the 35 parallel. He passed, then, between Australia and Tasmania (the southern boundary of which was laid down in approximately 42 degrees south latitude), and anchored on the north coast of the latter which lay "on our larboard bow." It is apparent that Defoe

[221] P. 233-4.
[222] P. 234.
[223] P. 234.
[224] PP. 244-5.

places the south coast of Australia too far north, and that he extends
the north coast of Tasmania both too far north and too far east; but it is
equally apparent that he has Singleton sail through what the geographers
of the day mistakenly regarded as an area of dry land.

Whether in thus anticipating by seventy-eight years the finding of Bass
Strait, and the discovery that Tasman had happened upon an island and
not the mainland of Australia,—whether in this Defoe was merely taking
a license pardonable in a writer of fiction dealing with distant lands, or
whether he shrewdly surmised that Tasmania is an island, we cannot determine. When it is remembered, however that he was keenly interested in
geographical problems, such as the possibility of the northern routes to
the Orient, and that he more than once speaks of the errors of "our hydrographers," it appears highly probable that he actually believed later search
would prove Tasmania to be without connection with the mainland of
Australia.

It was, then, upon the north shore of Tasmania (the extent of which
was somewhat erroneously conceived) that the hollow-tree fight occurred.
For this thrilling encounter I have no definite source to offer; I have,
however, a number of suggestions which may lead to a better understanding of the event. In the first place, the general setting including the
character, dress, and behavior of the natives, is almost identical with that
pictured by Dampier apropos of an encounter with the natives along the
southeast coast of New Guinea.

Singleton found when he landed that the people whom he had seen on
the shore "fled up the country,[225] nor would they hold any correspondence
with us, nor come near us. . . . We set up white flags for a truce, but they
either did not or would not understand it. . . . We found[226] good water
here . . . . the people, if they had any cattle, drove them all away, and
showed us nothing but themselves, and that sometimes in a threatening
posture" and in great numbers. Their arms were long lances, half pikes,
and bows and arrows. Though they had some clothing about the lower
parts of their body, the distinctive feature of their dress was the "great
high things on their heads, made . . . . of feathers, and which looked
something like our grenadiers' caps in England."

"When we saw them so shy," Singleton continues, ". . . . our men
began to range over the island, if it was such, . . . to search for cattle,
and for any of the Indian plantations, for fruit or plants." Thus it was
that his men were beset by a shower of arrows from the trees and that
the hollow-tree encounter began.

[225] P. 234.
[226] P. 235.

Dampier's experience was very similar. His boats were ashore for water,[227] and "if possible to get some hogs, goats, yams, and other roots[228]. . . ." Upon trying to communicate with the natives, he found them "sly and roguish."[229] His description of them is suggestive of Singleton's. The women were clothed about the waist and thighs, and the men, like those which Singleton saw, were "finely deck'd with feathers of divers colours about their heads." Their weapons were lances.

Like Singleton's followers, his men found as they approached the shore that "the natives in great companies stood to resist them; shaking their lances and threatening them." His men made "signs of friendship" to no purpose;[230] "for the natives waved them off," and would not "be prevailed upon to a friendly commerce." Dampier tells[231] of visiting their villages; he found "all the houses abandon'd by the inhabitants, who (like those Singleton speaks of) had carried with them all their hogs, &c." Later his men hunted about on shore for provisions[232] as Singleton's men did, and actually had a slight brush with the natives. In each narrative shots are fired more to terrify than to kill the savages, and in each it is supposed that some had been wounded by the firing.

Thus far Defoe clearly is following Dampier; but for the eleven day siege of the tree trunk which immediately ensues Dampier offers no parallel. Returning to their vessel after being attacked from ambush by the natives, Singleton's men were a second time fired at from the top of "a prodigious great trunk of a great tree." Eight pages[233] are devoted to recounting the siege and destruction of the tree, through the hollow trunk of which the natives had an entrance into an underground cave with a second entrance concealed in the side of a nearby hill. After unsuccessful attempts at smoking out the besieged and at burning the tree, it was proposed to cut the tree down—a performance which would have required two days. This was rejected in favor of Quaker William's plan of blowing the tree to splinters with powder. When that was accomplished, two barrels of powder were placed in the cave itself; the opening was rammed shut and the powder ignited. The force of the explosion "burst its way out among some bushes on the other side of the little hill . . . . roaring out there as out of the mouth of a cannon." The native garrison suffered ghastly mutilation; "some of them had no arms, some no legs, some no

[227] Dampier, IV, p. 136.
[228] Ibid., p. 137.
[229] Ibid., p. 138.
[230] Ibid., p. 140.
[231] Ibid., p. 139.
[232] Ibid., pp. 139-140.
[233] Captain Singleton, pp. 236-244.

head; some lay half buried in the rubbish of the mine . . . . and, in short, there was a miserable havoc made in them all; for we had good reason to believe not one of them . . . . could escape, but rather were shot out of the mouth of the cave, like a bullet out of a gun."[234]

This account of the explosion is very much like a report of an incident which seven years later Defoe was to incorporate in the third volume of his "Tour thro' the Whole Island of Great Britain."[235] This event was a "melancholy accident" happening in or near Lumley Park. Some miners digging into a cavity released therefrom the pent up air which exploded "like a mine of a thousand barrels of powder, and getting vent at the shaft of the pit, burst out with . . . . a terrible noise. . . . There were near three score poor people lost their lives in the pit, and one or two, as we were told, who were at the bottom of the shaft, were blown quite out . . . . and were found dead upon the ground."

Whether or not Defoe knew of this mine disaster when he wrote "Captain Singleton" it is impossible now to determine; but it is my opinion that he did, and that he made use of it there. Many of the incidents related in the three volumes of the "Tour" Defoe had heard about much earlier. Particularly in the months preceding the Scottish Union he had been back and forth to Edinburgh, and probably got much of his information of the northern countries at that time. We know so little of his life, however, that it is exceedingly dangerous to assert more positively just when he may have visited a specific place. Powder explosions seem to have had an unusual interest for Defoe; several mentioned in volume one of the "Tour" will be considered in connection with an episode of the "Memoirs of Captain Carleton."

Of the suggestion for the hollow tree, there is little to be said. Another such tree figures in the boyhood experiences of Colonel Jacque. Many narratives of travel speak of hollow trees. Knox and his comrade concealed themselves in one in their escape from the Sinhalese,[236] and Lionel Wafer[237] took refuge in one during a sudden rainstorm and flood which overtook him on the isthmus of Darien. Both these accounts Defoe had read. It may be of significance, however, that Dampier tells of finding a great tree on one of the Spice Islands.[238] Six lusty men who had been log-cutters at Campeachy Bay required a day and a half to fell it. Though

---

[234] *Captain Singleton*, p. 244.

[235] The incident related in the *Tour* may be found reprinted in *Reprints of Rare Tracts* . . . (Newcastle, 1849), p. 10. Each section of the book has separate pagination.

[236] *Ceylon*, p. 263. Defoe later in *Captain Singleton* (p. 282) mentions this very circumstance.

[237] *The Isthmus of America*, p. 14.

[238] Dampier, I, p. 450.

this lusty tree was "very green and flourishing . . . . it was perisht at the heart."

Having revenged themselves sufficiently on these natives of Tasmania, Singleton and his men[239] sailed west for ten days, and then turned northward expecting to go directly to Ceylon. But through an error in their calculations they met with the west coast of Australia, approximately where Dampier first touched land in his outward journey.[240] Singleton then turned northwest to the south coast of Java; there he anchored in "seven fathom water" and took in provisions. There also he "spied a large ship" bearing directly toward him; when she was within a league he stood ready to defend himself. It transpired that she was a Dutch vessel and that she had mistaken Singleton's for another of her own fleet.

Defoe is here following again in Dampier's course. The latter, upon returning from New Holland, came up under the Java coast,[241] anchored in "twenty four fathom water," and took in provisions.[242] Like Singleton, he saw[243] a Dutch vessel about two miles away which came after him "with all the sail she could make," though she had no intention of attacking him.

From Java Singleton[244] "went merrily on for the coast of Ceylon," and had an elaborately described encounter with the natives, obviously based upon Knox's account of his relations with the Sinhalese. Singleton's experiences agree in every particular with what one might expect from reading Knox's narrative. At the end, however, Defoe boldly tells the reader[245] that the treatment Singleton met with "agreed so well with . . . . what happened to one Mr. Knox . . . . that it could not but be very much to my satisfaction to think what mischief we had all escaped; and I think it cannot but be very profitable to record the other story (too) . . . . to show whoever reads this what it was I avoided, and prevent their falling into the like, if they have to do with the perfidious people of Ceylon." Thereupon he launches into an extended narrative of Knox's story. He thus skilfully calls our attention from the fact that he may be fabricating upon the basis of the earlier work, by citing that work in corroboration of the truth of his own report.

Like Knox, Singleton was compelled to anchor on the Ceylon coast because of storm,[246] though Knox's vessel was damaged by storm elsewhere

[239] *Captain Singleton*, p. 244 ff.
[240] Dampier, III, p. 117 ff.
[241] Dampier, IV, p. 179.
[242] *Ibid.*, p. 180.
[243] *Ibid.*, p. 182.
[244] *Captain Singleton*, p. 248.
[245] *Ibid.*, p. 271.
[246] *Ceylon*, p. 189. *Captain Singleton*, p. 252.

and was brought to Ceylon merely for repairs, whereas Singleton's vessel was driven ashore there. Singleton, like Knox again, received a warm invitation from the king to pay him a visit. Warned by Quaker William, who had heard of Knox's fate, Singleton was too wary to fall into that trap. There ensued long dialogues between William and a Dutch prisoner among the natives who represented the king's general.

Finding the Englishmen unwilling to accept the invitation of their king, the Sinhalese army, marshalled on the shore about the ship, suddenly let loose a volley of "fire-arrows"; whereupon the pirates fired their cannon with deadly accuracy several times into the native ranks. The latter immediately ceased firing, and sent the Dutchman forward again with the information that the native general was "much mollified by the slaughter of his men, and that now he (William, acting as interpreter) could have anything of him (the general)."

" 'Anything!' says William; 'what have we to do with him? Let him go about his business, and carry his men out of gunshot, can't he?'

" 'Why,' says the Dutchman, 'but he dares not stir, nor see the king's face; unless some of your men come on shore, he will certainly put him to death.' " And that, of course, was the point of the whole trouble.

After further fruitless arguing the Dutchman consented to be rescued by Singleton's men, and the pirates sailed away leaving the general to make whatever explanations to the king he thought best. That the Sinhalese made prisoners of the Dutchmen, as well as of Englishmen (and Portuguese), Defoe knew from his reading of Knox,[247] who also tells of the unenviable fate of the king's favorites when they disobeyed or displeased him.[248]

Singleton was then ready to retire; but how to get back to England in safety he did not know. After sailing up past Goa and the Malabar coast and selling the last of their cargo to English merchants at Surat, he and Quaker William elected to take the route considered by Crusoe when at Bengal, namely, the way of the Persian Gulf and Busra and the caravans over the Arabian desert to Aleppo and Scanderoon (Alexandretta), and from thence through the Mediterranean to Europe. In Crusoe's case Defoe got the idea from reading Dampier. But before writing "Captain Singleton" Defoe had already sent Avery home by a modification of that route; at Bagdad, Avery shifted his course to Ispahan and Constantinople. Singleton and William, however, dressed as Armenian merchants and passed over the route now followed by the Bagdad railway to Alexandretta, and in time reached England.

[247] *Ceylon*, p. 293.
[248] *Ibid.*, pp. 216-7.

IV. *Preliminary Conclusions*

The materials used in "Captain Singleton" were, as we have seen, taken from a number of sources. The earlier adventures on Madagascar are based upon Mandelslo's account of his visit there, and upon Misson's fictitious narrative of the experiences of Leguat and his companions in the Mascarene Islands. For the journey across Africa no specific source has been discovered. It has been demonstrated, however, that geographies and maps printed in English and extant in 1720 contain all the information of the region which Defoe needed for that journey. We have seen, furthermore, that Defoe agreed with map-makers of his day in the placing of lakes and rivers in Central Africa, anticipating in no way later discoveries nor indulging in striking guesses of his own. It is, therefore, unnecessary to suppose, with Professors Minto and Saintsbury, that Defoe had access to unpublished maps and notes of Portuguese travellers, or with Mr. Aitken[249] and a recent writer in "Notes and Queries,"[250] respectively, that his knowledge of Africa may have been gained from rare old sixteenth century works, such as "a Spanish globe of 1530 or 1540" or Adam Ortelius's atlas published at Antwerp in 1574.

Singleton's career of piracy is on the whole modelled after that of Avery as set forth in Defoe's own "King of Pirates," but has additional features imitative of parts of Exquemelin and Dampier. The closing voyage to the East Indies and the return around Australia is indebted principally to Dampier.

The action of the story is, as is the case in "Robinson Crusoe," based upon that of other adventurers. Defoe sends his hero over a series of routes described by previous writers, and from their suggestions about the physiography of the regions, and about their peoples and products, fabricates Singleton's activity. An exception to this should be noted in the case of the African journey for which Defoe appears to have been indebted to no previous traveller across Africa. But for that journey Defoe got many suggestions from written sources.

But the use of sources by Defoe in "Captain Singleton" is not that of the plagiarist. Singleton's adventures are not slavish imitations of those of other men. The elements derived from the various narratives are unified. The reader does not observe when Defoe ceases to depend upon Mandelslo and turns to Misson; in fact, he is not aware that Defoe has been depending upon Mandelslo or any one else. The story is not a mosaic or a patchwork, but Singleton's story.

[249] Introduction to *Captain Singleton*, p. xiv.
[250] Series 12, VIII (26 March, 1921), p. 251.

Nor is "Captain Singleton" a mere series of interesting episodes; for, though it breaks into two parts, each part is a distinct unit. The earlier division centers around the adventure across Africa. That was a stupendous undertaking, and its working out required somewhat the same attention to minutiæ that Crusoe's island life called forth. The path lay through an unexplored region, vast in extent and inhabited by uncivilized peoples. There were neither roads nor the ordinary means of conveyance. These handicaps Singleton's party surmounted with foresight and perseverance. Natives were captured and enslaved for guides and servants; buffaloes were harnessed to carry shelter and provisions; and routes were determined with the aid of maps.

Many readers of "Robinson Crusoe" must have speculated upon whether or not the island story was an original part of Defoe's plan in writing Crusoe's life, or whether its possibilities were seen only after he had wrecked Crusoe upon his island. This African journey of Singleton raises a similar query. Defoe apparently set out to write a story of piracy with Singleton as its hero; he has him as a boy become a thief and villain, showing an inclination to piracy which amazed his Portuguese comrades, bad as they were. But the sensational scheme of traversing the unexplored regions of Africa lured him away from what thus appears to have been his original plan, and itself became the center of interest. The story of piracy followed, but not till the African adventures were brought to a distinct close. For these reasons, it appears likely that the portions of greatest interest in the two novels, namely, Crusoe's island life and Singleton's African adventures, were afterthoughts with Defoe, the value of which he did not understand until he began to work them out.

Specific instances of Defoe's method of working are observable in "Captain Singleton." We have seen how he combined suggestions from Dampier and Misson for Singleton's "artist," the cutler or silversmith. A more important character, Quaker William, appears to have been modelled after a Quaker highwayman whose career was delineated in the criminal biographies. For the incident of Singleton's turning pirate at the Groyne Defoe elaborated without changing essentially an event which he had already described in the "King of Pirates."

Significant as an illustration of Defoe's inventive faculty is the account of the encounter with the Tasmanian natives. From Dampier Defoe got suggestions of the treacherous character of the people around Australia, and with these suggestions as a basis invented a detailed account of the siege of the hollow tree which those natives had occupied as a citadel. To the action he brings his interest in powder explosions, his love of heroic action, and his power of realizing a situation.

Some traits of Singleton's character as Defoe portrays it are of importance. The boy Singleton manifests slightly, as Crusoe does not, one trait of the picaro, namely, a half-cynical delight in his dishonesty. Though disgusted by the debauchery of the Portuguese seamen, he had become an "arrant thief," finding ways of diverting gold into his own pocket from the pockets of the pilot, his master, and the captain, who trusted him. Thus in a measure he follows in the footsteps of Lazarillo and his successors who cheat their masters. The particular phase of this which seems to indicate picaresque influence is the tone in which it is related. Though Defoe is usually severe in his condemnation of the delinquencies of his characters, Singleton, in such remarks as the following, betrays a note of cynical levity:[251] " . . . . they thought me honest, which, by the way, was their very great mistake." Shortly afterward in Madagascar Singleton leads his older comrades into projects of piracy with more readiness than Defoe's characters usually manifest in turning to an evil course, and with something of the boldness and zest for wickedness of the picaros. These traces are slight, however, and are quickly replaced by greater moral seriousness.

A criticism of the opposite sort comes from Sir Leslie Stephen, who remarks[252] that, though Defoe's villains do detestable things, they always speak like respectable Englishmen with an eye to the main chance. This Sir Leslie advances as proof of Defoe's inability to see inside his characters and to discern that their souls may differ from his own. The observation has truth in it, but it is not wholly true in the case of Singleton. There Defoe is attributing to his hero the very traits manifested by such actual pirates as had published their journals. That is to say, Defoe was imitating authentic records, and the faithfulness of that imitation shows both in the speeches and the actions of the characters. Sharp and his historian, Ringrose, were pirates. Even Dampier, called by Coleridge "a man of exquisite refinement of mind,"[253] cannot be wholly cleared of the charge of having been a pirate. Yet, like Singleton, these men denounce needless acts of cruelty; nay, they even show traces of piety. Dampier repented in the course of an East India storm and prayed for deliverance. The following from Ringrose's journal is not without significance:[254] "Sunday, January the 9th. This was the first Sunday that ever we kept by command and common consent, since the loss and death of our valiant commander Captain Sawkins, who would throw the dice

[251] *Captain Singleton*, p. 6.
[252] *Hours in a Library*, I, p. 20ff.
[253] John Masefield, Introduction to Dampier's *Voyages* (1906), p. 10.
[254] *The Bucaniers of America*, II (1771), p. 22.

overboard, if he found them in use on that day." Not all pirates are like Israel Hands and John Silver; and Defoe's are fashioned after the variety with which their creator was familiar.

Another feature of "Captain Singleton" and others of Defoe's stories which has been repeatedly commented upon is his frequent mention of sums of money. He has Avery plunder a ship of so many thousands of pieces of eight, and Singleton amass prodigious wealth in pieces of eight, in uncoined gold, and in precious commodities such as pearls and diamonds. Defoe undeniably does frequently employ these terms. But the inference derived from this fact is, it seems to me, overemphasized. It is inferred that Defoe's was a crass materialistic soul whose god was merchandise. There can be no doubt that he was deeply interested in commerce, or that in parts of "Colonel Jacque," for instance, he manifests unusual pleasure in mentioning large amounts of money. But in "Captain Singleton" he was doing nothing that is not conventional in the literature which he was imitating. Pirates have always hunted for treasure; that is why they are pirates. Gold was the inspiration of most of the early settlers in the new world. Raleigh's golden dreams of an Eldorado infected many seventeenth century men of good repute. One may observe by a very casual glance into the volumes of Hakluyt and Purchas that their pages mention sums of money quite as often as do Defoe's.

Defoe had his material interests. Perhaps it would be fairer to say that he preferred concreteness to abstraction. But altogether too little is said of the other side of his nature; of his interest in music, in the welfare of women, and in humane treatment for the insane as shown in his "Essay on Projects" (1697) and in his "Augusta Triumphans" (1728). Professor Trent believes that there is good reason to think that, in addition to his fondness for music and his taste for good literature, Defoe "knew something about pictures" and that "he was much interested in architecture and landscape gardening." Traces of such interests as these, however, one would scarcely look for in a tale of piracy like "Captain Singleton."

CHAPTER IV

The Authorship and Composition of the "Memoirs of Captain Carleton"

I. *History of the George Carleton Problem*[1]

The Carleton memoirs were published May 16, 1728, (O. S.),[2] with the following title page:

THE MEMOIRS OF AN English Officer, Who serv'd in the Dutch War in 1672. to the Peace of Utrecht, in 1713. Containing several Remarkable TRANS-ACTIONS both by Sea and Land, and in divers countries, but chiefly those wherein the Author was personally concerned. Together with A DESCRIPTION of many Cities, Towns, and Countries, in which he resided; their Manners and Customs, as well Religious as Civil, interspers'd with many curious OBSERVATIONS on their Monasteries and Nunneries, more particularly of the famous one at Montserat. On the BULL-FEASTS, and other publick Diversions; as also on the Genius of the Spanish People, amongst whom he continued several Years a Prisoner of War. No Part of which has before been made publick. By Capt. GEORGE CARLETON, LONDON, Printed for E. Symon, over against the Royal Exchange, Cornhill. MDCCXXVIII.

Within ten days a second title page was substituted, and the book was reissued as "The Military Memoirs of Captain George Carleton . . . . " with a few other minor changes in the title, and in the dedication and the preface. The date of this reissue has heretofore been assumed to be July 25, 1728,[3] on which day an advertisement of it appeared in the "Evening Post." But identically the same advertisement was carried in the "Post Boy" (no. 6063) of May 25, 1728, approximately nine days after the first issue was placed on sale. A third and a fourth issue from the original impression appeared in 1741 and 1743, respectively.[4] During the first half of the nineteenth century no less than four editions of the book appeared.

As the title suggests, these memoirs purport to recount the military career of one George Carleton from 1672, when a young gentleman of

[1] This introduction is a condensation of the opening portion of my thesis submitted in 1920 for the degree of Master of Arts. Taken from that source, likewise, are the various remarks throughout this chapter relating to the Solebay engagement.

[2] G. A. Aitken, *Academy*, XLIII (3 June, 1893), p. 438.

[3] *Notes and Queries*, 2nd Series, VII, pp. 150-1.

[4] C. E. Doble, *Academy*, XLIII (6 May, 1893), p. 393.

about twenty years he took part as a volunteer under the Duke of York in the famous naval battle of Solebay, to the close of the War of the Spanish Succession with the treaty of Utrecht in 1713. Two years after Solebay Carleton enlisted under the standards of the Prince of Orange in the Lowlands where he fought steadily till the temporary lull ·in 1678, his bravery winning him a place as ensign in the regiment of Sir John Fenwick. Upon being sent to England with his regiment at the time of the Monmouth rebellion (1685), Carleton left the service of the Prince and accepted a lieutenantcy in the newly raised regiment commanded by Colonel Tufton. Upon the accession of William and Mary he first served in Scotland with Tufton's, but as a reward for an unusual feat at the capture of Lethindy Castle he was not long after offered a captaincy in the regiment of Brigadier Tiffin with which in 1692 he returned to fight in the continental wars until the peace of Ryswick in 1697.

The war being over, Tiffin's regiment was sent to Ireland and from thence to the West Indies; Carleton, however, exchanged places with a half-pay captain, and so escaped going to the Indies. When the War of the Succession opened he was recommended by Lord Cutts to the Earl of Peterborough and was appointed to a place on Peterborough's staff, accompanying the expedition to Spain in 1705. He participated in the famous capture of Barcelona and in several other important actions, until wounded and taken prisoner at Denia in 1708. The closing portions of the "Memoirs" tell of his fortunes as a prisoner, commenting at length upon the character and customs of the Spanish people, describing many interesting places, and relating numerous anecdotes. At the close of the war (1713) he received his freedom and leisurely travelled back to England. At this point the account ends.

The book, though very readable, appears to have excited little notice until in 1784 it fell into the hands of Dr. Johnson, "who told Sir Joshua Reynolds that he was going to bed when it came, but was so pleased with it, that he sat up till he had read it through, and found in it such an air of truth, that he could not doubt of its authenticity. . . ."[5] As a probable result of Dr. Johnson's remarks, the "Memoirs" soon attracted the attention of Sir Walter Scott. Sir Walter, likewise, had no doubt of the genuineness of the narrative, and reissued it (1809) as authentic history. In his preface he commented upon the strain of "grave manly reflection" and the "plain and soldierlike" style which pervaded the work.

New fortunes, however, were in store for the book. When in 1830 Walter Wilson published his "Memoirs of the Life and Times of Daniel Defoe," he included it among the works of that author, finding in it a

[5] James Boswell, *Life of Johnson*, IV (1887), p. 333.

general resemblance to the "Memoirs of a Cavalier" and to other acknowledged works of Defoe.[6] This entirely novel position was supported by
Lockhart, when seven years later he brought out his life of Scott.[7]
But, he thought, Defoe must have "had before him the rude journal of
some officer who had fought and bled in the campaigns described with
such an inimitable air of truth." Further support came to the growing
Defoe tradition from Tegg and Hazlitt who in 1840 and 1841, respectively,
incorporated the Carleton story in their editions of Defoe's writings, and
from Lowndes and G. L. Craik who unhesitatingly ascribed it to Defoe.[8]

Meanwhile Lord Stanhope had discovered the name "Captain Carl-
tone" in a manuscript list of the English prisoners taken at Denia in 1708.
This was immediately seized upon as sufficent proof of the authenticity
of the "Memoirs," upon which Lord Stanhope did not hesitate to rely
fully in his history of the war in Spain.[9] But Lord Stanhope's credulity
in no way surpassed that of a small group of investigators who discussed
the Carleton puzzle in "Notes and Queries" in 1858 and 1859, and continued a scattering fire on the subject until about 1890. Their most important contribution to our knowledge of the book was the discovery of
the fact that in February, 1704/5, there actually was a Captain George
Carleton on the Irish half-pay list,[10]—a fact in perfect agreement with the
statements of the "Memoirs."

Not long after a Captain Percival Carleton, carrying on an extensive
investigation preparatory to writing a history of the Carletons, discovered
a copy of the royal warrant of October 28, 1700, placing "Captain George
Carleton of Tiffin's Regiment" on half-pay, and an entry in Betham's
"List of Wills" showing that "administration of the goods and effects of
'Captain George Carleton, of Tiffin's Regiment,' was granted at Dublin,
3rd Sept., 1730, to a Margaret Westmoreland,"—an error for Mary Toms
of St. Margaret's Parish, Westminster.[11] The citation of the warrant
placing Carleton on half-pay is, like the similar one referred to previously,
in strict accord with the "Memoirs"; while the account of his will,
with the correction given, is a valuable addition to our slender store of

[6] Walter Wilson, *Memoirs of the Life and Times of Daniel Defoe*, III (1830),
pp. 589-591.

[7] J. G. Lockhart, *Life of Scott*, III (1902), p. 74.

[8] W. T. Lowndes, *Bibliographers Manual*, I (1857), p. 614; G. L. Craik, *History
of English Literature and the English Language*, II (1866), pp. 272-3.

[9] Philip Henry, Earl of Stanhope, *History of the War of Succession in Spain*
(1832), 135.

[10] *Notes and Queries*, 3rd Series, VI, p. 375.

[11] Captain P. A. Carleton, *Memorials of the Carletons*, p. viii; Colonel Arthur
Parnell, *English Historical Review*, VI (1891), p. 109.

facts concerning the soldier's life. Beyond doubt Carleton was a flesh and blood person, and no more figment of Defoe's imagination.

In line with these considerations we find William Lee in 1869 declaring himself unable to find any evidence, internal or external, for attributing the "Memoirs" to Defoe. He added, moreover, that he found Carleton to have been a real person and the writer of his own memoirs. With this decision Mr. James Crossley, an eminent nineteenth century student of Defoe, agreed.[12]

The revival of belief in the genuineness of the Carleton story was presently emphasized by a number of historians who placed full reliance in its statements.[13] Influenced no doubt by the opinion of his fellow-countryman, Sir Walter Scott, John Hill Burton dismissed the case for Defoe in these sarcastic terms: "The reasons for Defoe's authorship are a curious instance of illogicality in the conditions. The work is so exactly what a plain intelligent man, who had seen and taken part in all that he narrates, would have made it, that it must be the work of the cleverest imitators." It was impossible, Burton further declares, that Defoe could "have discovered the fundamental facts of the narrative without access to documents jealously guarded in the private repositories of those who held them as confidential."[14] These arguments were all summed up in the article on Carleton in the Dictionary of National Biography (1887); for Sir Leslie Stephen had become convinced of the authenticity of the "Memoirs" and had enrolled its hero among the worthies of the realm.[15]

And thus the matter stood until Colonel Arthur Parnell published his "History of the War of the Succession in Spain" in 1888. Previous to that time, as Colonel Parnell has pointed out,[16] practically every nineteenth century history of the Peninsular campaigns used the "Memoirs" as authentic,—that was the easy procedure with the scarcity of other materials and with the opinions of Dr. Johnson and Sir Walter Scott favoring it,— and at the same time practically all the nineteenth century editions of Defoe's works included the "Memoirs." And strangely enough both the historians and the students of Defoe were content to let matters rest in

[12] William Lee, *Daniel Defoe,* I (1869), pp. 438-9.

[13] Philip Henry, Earl of Stanhope, *History of England comprising the Reign of Queen Anne,* I (1872), p. 217, note 7; John Hill Burton, *Reign of Queen Anne* II (1880), p. 173; F. W. Wyon, *History of Great Britain during the Reign of Queen Anne,* I (1876), pp. 352, 357. Mr. Wyon, though denying the genuineness of the Carleton narrative which he found to be a composition of Defoe, makes the curious blunder of relying upon Lord Stanhope, who had swallowed it whole.

[14] *Reign of Queen Anne,* II, pp. 173-4.

[15] Leslie Stephen, *Hours in a library,* I (1907), p. 4.

[16] *English Historical Review,* VI, p. 106.

this contradictory state. That the truth might be discovered by further investigation seems to have occurred to neither group.

The earlier students of the problem believed the authenticity of the memoirs depended upon whether Carleton was a real or a fictitious person; that accounts for their complacency upon finding a historical Captain George Carleton whose career in some points at least paralleled the account given in the "Memoirs." Here, they said, is a flesh and blood man perfectly capable of writing his own story: why mention Defoe in connection with what is obviously a true and genuine record? But Colonel Parnell, though he does much more than his predecessors toward identifying the historical Carleton, at the same time reveals the book to be in part a collection of plagiarisms from the "Memoirs" of Sir William Temple, the "Account of Peterborow's Conduct in Spain" by Freind, and the letters of the Countess D'Aulnoy.[17]

Having demonstrated the presence of fictitious passages in the Carleton narrative, Colonel Parnell gave a decidedly new turn to the situation by arguing ably that the real author was neither Carleton nor Defoe, but Dean Swift. A number of circumstances make this conclusion plausible. The author was beyond doubt a warm admirer of Peterborough; he had, moreover, based his relation of that nobleman's career upon the "Account" compiled from Peterborough's own papers by Dr. Freind. Both Swift and Dr. Freind were close associates of Peterborough. To this should be added the facts that in 1728 both Carleton, a needy veteran of seventy-six, and Swift were living in Dublin, and that on one other occasion Swift is known to have aided an old soldier to publish his memoirs.[18] The supposition is that having picked up some notes or jottings from his needy fellow-townsman, Swift carried them to Peterborough in London, who added further materials from his own papers, and, in the summer of 1728, fabricated with aid from the works of Freind, Temple, D'Aulnoy, and others the narrative which has for nearly two centuries misled historians.

Colonel Parnell, moreover, found in the "Memoirs" a satiric vein; a general stylistic resemblance to "Gulliver's Travels" and to other prose works of Swift; a sneering attitude toward the Irish; and a classical tone beyond Defoe,—all suggestive of Swift. Against the authorship of Defoe, he pleaded his illiteracy, his sturdy manly honesty, his sincere and earnest religious views, and the absence of any known connection between Defoe and Peterborough, Defoe and Carleton, or Defoe and many of those whom

[17] Parnell, *Dean Swift and the Memoirs of Captain Carleton*, in the *English Historical Review*, VI, p. 97 ff.

[18] *The Memoirs of Captain Creichton,* 1731.

Parnell thinks were maligned in the "Memoirs." More significant is Parnell's attempt to prove that Carleton himself could not have written the
book.

Several years elapsed before Mr. C. E. Doble took up the challenge
given by Colonel Parnell and came to the support of the Defoe faction.
Accepting Parnell's account of Carleton's life and of the plagiarisms as
correct, Mr. Doble concerned himself only with the contention that Swift
was the author of the "Memoirs."[19] He pointed out a number of reasons
why it is highly improbable that Swift could have at the time participated
in such a fabrication. He then proceeded to examine minutely the substance of the "Memoirs," and from his wide intimacy with the multifarious
writings of Defoe developed a strong case for Defoe's authorship. As
the larger features at least it was in harmony with the account given in the
well be omitted here.

About this time were unearthed a few documents throwing light on
the earlier career of the historical Carleton and showing that as regards
the larger features at least it was in harmony with the account given in the
"Memoirs." The first of these was a memorandum inclosed in a letter of
1685 written in Carleton's behalf by Dr. John Covel. It reads thus.[20]

> Mr. Carlton hath been tenn yeares in the service of the Prince, 7 yeares as a
> voluntier, 3 years an Ensigne in Sr Hen Bellasis his regiment. He was at the
> Battel of Seneife, and the Seidge of Mastricht, where he was wounded. . . . He
> hath been at sea with Sr Edw. Spragg.

Here is a useful sketch of Carleton's life from 1672 at which time the
"Memoirs" opens to 1685; and excepting slight discrepancies in the matter
of dates, concerning which the "Memoirs" is usually rather vague, it dis-
agrees with the "Memoirs" only in giving Bellasis's instead of Fenwick's
as the regiment in which Carleton was ensign.

The other documents filled the gap in our knowledge of the career of
the historical Carleton between 1685, when Covel's letter was written, and
1697, the date of the earliest traces of him which Parnell was able to find.
According to the memoirs, Carleton soon after the Monmouth rebellion
(1685) was made a lieutenant in Tufton's regiment, and about 1690
promoted to a captaincy in Tiffin's. Though unable to find any record
of a Lieutenant George Carleton, Colonel Parnell did, however, find a
Villar Carleton who had been made an ensign in Tufton's within a few
years of the date suggested in the "Memoirs." This Villar (or Viller)
Carleton he supposed to have been a relative of George Carleton and to
have furnished information used in that portion of the "Memoirs." But

---

[19] C. E. Doble, *The Memoirs of Captain Carleton; Swift or Defoe?* in the
Academy, XLIII, pp. 393 ff., 438 ff., 461 ff., and 482 ff.

[20] *Academy*, 6 July, 1889, p. 10.

Mr. Charles Dalton in 1894 produced copies of commissions showing that not only were George and Viller Carleton the same individual, but also that the account in the memoirs is substantially true. According to these records, Viller Carleton was made ensign in Tufton's January 1, 1687/8. On March 1, 1689/90,——Carleton was appointed lieutenant in Sir James Leslie's (late Tufton's) regiment of foot. This, Dalton rightly thought, was Viller Carleton promoted in the regular course. The next commission reads : "Commission to Villiers Carleton, esq., to be Capt. of the company of which David Rindes was late Capt. in the regiment of foot commanded by Zacharia Tiffin, dated at Whitehall, 21 March, 1691/2." To cap it all, a manuscript army list of 1694 contains among the names of the officers of Tiffin's regiment that of "Captain George Villars Carleton, March 21, 1691/2." Mr. Dalton, irritated by the efforts of Colonel Parnell and Mr. Doble to prove the Carleton story fictitious, concluded in triumph, "On the principle that the devil is not so black as he has been painted, I believe that Captain George Villiers Carleton was not such a consummate liar as has been represented."[21] No matter how unwarranted Mr. Dalton may have been in believing the "Memoirs" genuine, there is no doubt that he supplied the last piece of evidence needed to connect the "Mr. Carlton" who had "been at sea with Sr Edw. Spragg" and "tenn yeares in the service of the Prince," with the Captain George Carleton of Tiffin's regiment who was placed on half-pay in 1700 and who accompanied Peterborough's army to Spain in 1705.

Since the exposures of Colonel Parnell, historians have on the whole taken a conservative attitude toward the "Memoirs." A biographer of Peterborough is inclined to believe they may be genuine. "Probably," says he, "the share of the editor who put the materials into shape was rather less, and the share of the old officer who lent his name rather more than it has become of late the fashion to concede."[22] Professedly following this biographer, the Honorable J. W. Fortescue, in his history of the Britsh army, actually makes use of some episodes from the Carleton narrative.[23] More conservative histories, such as the "Political History of England" and the "Cambridge Modern History," have either ignored the "Memoirs" entirely or have mentioned them as untrustworthy.

While careful historians have been rejecting the book as unauthentic, writers on Defoe, on the other hand, have been diffident of attributing it to him. Thomas Wright, following Mr. Lee, omits it from his list of Defoe's works, and Mr. G. A. Aitken omits it from his edition of Defoe's

[21] Charles Dalton, *Academy*, XLVI (11 August, 1894), p. 104.

[22] William Stebbing, *Peterborough* (1890), p. 55.

[23] *History of the British Army*, I (1899), pp. 460, 461, 489.

narratives, feeling that "the only safe course is to . . . . reject everything which does not bear convincing proof of genuineness."[24] Professor
Saintsbury, judging from the point of style only, thinks it more probable
that Swift rather than Defoe was the author.[25] According to Mr. Arundell
Esdaile, the attribution of the work to Defoe is questionable; Mr. E. A.
Baker thinks it is "probably authentic"; and Mr. Michael Barrington
asserts definitely that the book is a genuine memoir and quotes from it in
his beautifully printed "Grahame of Claverhouse."[26] The Defoe theory,
meanwhile, has been championed by the eminent authority on Defoe, Professor Trent.[27]

Such for nearly two centuries have been the fortunes of the "Memoirs
of Captain Carleton." Its authenticity has been asserted by Dr. Johnson,
Sir Walter Scott, Lord Stanhope, William Lee, James Crossley, J. H.
Burton, J. Ormsby, Sir Leslie Stephen, Charles Dalton, E. A. Baker, and
Michael Barrington. Colonel Parnell, with some slight comfort from
Professor Saintsbury, has supported the cause of Dean Swift. The
chief supporters of the Defoe claim have been Walter Wilson, Lockhart,
Lowndes, Craik, and many other mid-nineteenth century historians of
English literature, Mr. Doble, and Professor Trent. Such investigators
as Thomas Wright and Mr. Aitken have remained neutral.

From this mass of conflicting evidence and conjecture two facts appear to me to be obvious. First, that practically every new fact discovered concerning the career of the historical Carleton tends to confirm
the approximate correctness of the account of that career given in the
"Memoirs." And, secondly, that the closer the contents of that narrative
are analyzed the more untrustworthy they appear, and the more they
point to Defoe as their author.

The importance of the question at issue becomes apparent when
we recall that in spite of all that has been done to discredit the genuineness
of the book and to prove that Defoe was its author, most students have
remained unconvinced. Between the fear of historians that it may be
fictitious and the fear of literary investigators that it may be genuine, the
"Memoirs" is being generally neglected. Many readers who are familiar
with "Colonel Jacque," the "Memoirs of a Cavalier," and "Duncan Camp-

<hr/>

[24] Thomas Wright, *Life of Defoe* (1894), p. 405ff.; G. A. Aitken, Preface to
Romances and Narratives of Defoe, I, p. x.

[25] Article on Defoe in the *Encyclopædia Britannica*, VII (9th ed.), p. 29.

[26] Arundell Esdaile, *English Tales and Prose Romances* (1912), pp. 208-9. E. A.
Baker, *Guide to the best Fiction in English* (ed. 1913), p. 13. Michael Barrington,
Grahame of Claverhouse (1911), p. 24.

[27] W. P. Trent, *Daniel Defoe* (1916), pp. 210, 262-3-4. See also the *Cambridge
History of English Literature*, IX (1913), p. 25.

bell," are wholly unacquainted with the Carleton story. This is owing entirely to the fact that the only two recent editions of Defoe's narratives have through an excess of caution omitted it, though including a number of works of far less worth.[28] It is manifestly not sufficient to show that portions of the "Memoirs" were fabricated. The whole must be reinvestigated and fact sifted from fiction. The Carleton myth, if it is a myth, must be annihilated, and the question of authorship definitely settled. That Defoe fabricated the whole story from the slightest suggestions of Carleton's activity I have not the slightest doubt, and I shall attempt to set forth more clearly than has yet been done the proof of that fact.

When the question of authorship is proved then—and only then—may we proceed safely with a consideration of the "Memoirs" as illustrative of Defoe's method of composition. Fortunately, not all the labor expended in demonstrating the authorship will be lost; for the character of the work and the materials which went into its fabrication will be set forth in the process of determining who wrote it.

II. *Did Carleton write the "Memoirs"?*

Although, as has been said, the main purpose of this study of the "Memoirs of Captain Carleton" is to arrive at a better understanding of Defoe's method of composition, it is necessary first to remove any lingering doubts that Defoe actually wrote the major portion of the book. The situation as to the question of authorship is this.

We have a work purporting to be the genuine memoirs of an old soldier whom we know from external evidence to have had a career closely paralleling that set forth in the narrative. It has been shown, however, (1) that portions of the work are not true, for in one or two notable instances at least it has distorted the facts of Carleton's life, and (2) that other portions large in extent are borrowed from, or based upon, previously published histories and works of travel. The fact that the "Memoirs" is in part spurious (or at least fabricated) has led to the setting up of Swift and Defoe as rival claimants with Carleton for the authorship. The arguments advanced in favor of the Defoe claim, though more plausible than those favoring Swift, have failed to convince such scholars as Mr. Aitken and Thomas Wright. Recent writers, notably E. A. Baker and Michael Barrington, have reasserted a belief that the work may be genuine. Professor Trent alone has continued to champion the cause of Defoe.

[28] G. A. Aitken, *Romances and Narratives of Defoe*, 1895; G. H. Maynadier, *The Works of Daniel Defoe*, 1903.

With all possible deference to Professor Trent's opinion, with which I am in perfect agreement, I still regard it as unsafe to proceed without more convincing evidence that Defoe wrote the Carleton story. Like Professor Trent, I believe Colonel Parnell's exposure of the untrustworthy character of the "Memoirs," though not exhaustive nor always accurate, owing to lack of information, to be sufficient to establish the fact that Carleton himself did not write it. And like him, I consider Mr. Doble's arguments for Defoe as convincing. The fact remains, however, that these opinions have not prevailed generally among students. Whether or not the weight of Professor Trent's authority is sufficient to make them ultimately victorious is uncertain. Meanwhile there is further proof of the total worthlessness of the "Memoirs" as history, of the slenderness of Carleton's contribution to it, and of the fact that Defoe was the chief instrument in its fabrication.

That Carleton himself wrote any considerable portion of the book is absolutely untrue. For, although it does actually follow in a general way his course as a soldier through the various. campaigns from 1672 until 1713, it departs from that course at certain points and distorts it at others, showing thereby that the real author was in many respects either ignorant of, or indifferent to, the career of his hero; the narrative of Carleton's conduct in those campaigns may, wherever we are able to test them, be shown to be fictitious; and, finally, investigation reveals that the book has little to offer that was not current in published works available to any Londoner of 1728, and that, in fact, the account of every battle and every campaign was based upon those published records. It should be added, furthermore, that the contents of the work in other respects are not at all such as we have a right to look for from the historical Carleton.

The narrative is, on the whole, a sort of history of the times. It is not a complete nor wholly reliable history; that is to say, though it gives a slight thread of running narrative of the wars, it records only such events as are striking or diverting. There is, in fact, very little indication of the writer's having a more intimate knowledge of these scenes which concern Carleton personally than he has of those with which he had no connection. He writes with the same interest and assurance of the later as of the former.

There is, to be sure, a thread of activity credited to Carleton which runs through the whole narrative giving it a sort of unity. That thread, moreover, approximates his career as we now know it to have been. But upon closer examination it is evident that the author pays little attention to Carleton's actions, ignoring or distorting them in numerous cases; whether this is owing to a lack of information or a desire to make the story more interesting we cannot always tell. In some instances, however, it is plainly the result of ignorance, or, what amounts to the same thing, indifference.

Consider, for example, the statement in the "Memoirs"[29] that Carleton's bravery at the siege of Mastricht, where he was wounded, won for him a commission as ensign in Sir John Fenwick's regiment (1676). Carleton, we know, was actually wounded at that siege, but he never held a commission of any sort in Fenwick's. Four or five years after the operation before Mastricht he was, however, made an ensign in Sir Henry Bellasis's regiment.[30]

A similar misstatement of the "Memoirs" informs us that shortly after his arrival in England in 1685 Carleton received from King James a lieutenant's commission in a "new rais'd regiment" commanded by Colonel Tufton, and that "under this commission" he witnessed the maneuvres on Hounslow Heath and the mock siege of Buda.[31] Carleton was indeed given a post in Tufton's, but not until January 1, 1687/8, after the maneuvres referred to were over. His commission, moreover, gave him not the rank of lieutenant, but that of ensign only. Just when he left Bellasis's, or why, or what he did in the meantime, we do not know. Two years more were to elapse before his promotion to a lieutenancy. Further disregard for fact appears in the statement of the "Memoirs" that for bravery at the capture of Lethindy Castle (1690) Carleton was soon after advanced to a captaincy in Tiffin's. Among other reasons (to be considered later) for believing that the account of Carleton's bravery upon this occasion was the invention of the author is the fact that Carleton remained with Leslie's two years after the affair at Lethindy Castle before receiving his commission in Tiffin's.[32]

Absolutely false is the assertion attributed to Carleton that, after participating with Tiffin's in the secret expedition of the Duke of Leinster during the summer of 1692, he arrived in Flanders in time to take part in the battle of Steenkerke. All the records agree in stating that Tiffin's arrived in Flanders just after, not just before, that engagement.[33] The "Memoirs," however, recounts the events of that battle with the same assurance and acquaintance with details as it does those battles in which Carleton is known to have engaged.

[29] P. 25. All references are to the first edition.
[30] See the memorandum to Dr. Covel's letter of 1685 quoted *supra*.
[31] *Memoirs,* pp. 38-9.
[32] Carleton, p. 45.
[33] Carleton, pp. 46-49; Boyer, *William III,* II, p. 339.

An outline comparison of the military career of the historical Captain George Carleton with the account of that career as set forth in the "Memoirs." Asterisks indicate the points where the "Memoirs" ignores or distorts the facts.

Carleton's career as shown by historical documents	Carleton's career as set forth in the "Memoirs"

1672

| Served at sea under Spragge in 1672 or 1673 | Served under Spragge in battle of Solebay |

1674-1685

| Served under Prince of Orange in Flanders | Served under Prince of Orange in Flanders |

1674

| Battle of Seneffe | Battle of Seneffe |

1676

| Wounded at Mastricht | Wounded at Mastricht *Made ensign in Fenwick's |

1680-1681

| *Ensign in Bellasis's | |

1685

| Came to England with regiment to help suppress Monmouth | Came to England with regiment to help suppress Monmouth *Soon made lieutenant in Tufton's |

1685-1688

| | Stationed near London |

1688

| *Ensign in Tufton's Stationed at Berwick | Stationed at Berwick |

1689-1690

| Served in Scotland *Lieutenant in Leslie's (formerly Tufton's) | Served in Scotland |

1692

| Captain in Tiffin's Secret expedition of Duke of Leinster *Landed at Ostend after battle of Steenkerke Fortified Dixmude | Captain in Tiffin's (no date) Secret expedition of Duke of Leinster *Landed at Ostend in time to participate in Steenkerke Fortified Dixmude |

1693

| Spent in or near London *November—returned to Lowlands | Spent with Tiffin's on duty in the tower of London |

1694
*Returned to Lowlands

1695
*Attack on Kenoque

*Vaudemont's retreat from Arseel
*Bombardment of Brussels
*Siege of Namur

1696

Returned to England at time of the conspiracy	Aided Lord Cutts in the capture of the conspirators against William III
Returned to Flanders	Returned to Flanders

1697

End of war—returned with Tiffins' to England and then to Dublin	End of war—returned with Tiffin's to England and then to Dublin

1697-1705

*Cashiered for duelling (1700)	*Changed places with half-pay captain
Placed on half-pay on account of wife and three children	to avoid going to West Indies with Tiffin's

1705

*Went to Spain with Peterborough as a free lance	*Through the courtesy of Lord Cutts, he went to Spain as a member of Peterborough's staff

1705-1708

Engineer at Barcelona, Requena, Cuenca, Alicante, and Denia	Engineer at Barcelona, *Tortosa, Requena, Cuenca, Alicante, and Denia
Captured at Denia	Captured at Denia

1708-1713

Prisoner in Spain	Prisoner in Spain

1713

Liberated and allowed to return—later lived in Dublin	Liberated and allowed to return—later lived in Dublin

The historical documents upon which rests our knowledge of Carleton's career are these. The memorandum to Dr. Covel's letter mentioned *supra* covers the period from 1672 to 1685. The Calendar of State Papers records his various commissions during the years from 1688 to 1692 inclusive (all quoted in the *Academy,* XLVI, p. 104). His being stationed at Berwick in 1688-9 is indicated by a paragraph in the C. of S. P. (Dom. Ser., 1689-1690, p. 17). For his activity between 1689 and 1697 we are dependent upon various records of the movements of his regiment, Tiffin's. The documents relating to the circumstances under which he was cashiered and placed upon the half-pay pension list, and under which he went to Spain, are cited by Colonel Parnell (*English Historical Review,* VI, p. 108). A brief sketch of his services in Spain may be found in the Calendar of Treasury Papers (1720-1728, vol. CCXLI, 1722, Pt. I, p. 177); for fuller details of these services see again the *English Historical Review* (VI, pp. 108-9).

Statements equally false were to follow in connection with the famous campaign of 1695. The "Memoirs" omits all mention of the desperate attack on Fort Kenoque in which Tiffin's bore the brunt of the fighting,[84] and centers its attention upon the better known events, namely, the retreat of Vaudemont from Arseel, the bombardment of Brussels, and the storming of the Namur citadel. In all of these last Carleton is made to tell of taking a distinguished part. The closest search, however, reveals not the slightest evidence that any part of Tiffin's had a share in these operations. The "London Gazette" mentions regiment after regiment which participated in the several assaults upon Namur, but we look in vain for any mention of Tiffin's in that connection.[85] The "Memoirs," nevertheless, relates with full particulars Carleton's part in those assaults wherein he attracted the attention of Lord Cutts, thus opening the way for later fabrications.

The most marked of all the inventions of the "Memoirs" center about the years from 1697 to 1705. In them Carleton's activity is set forth as follows. The peace of Ryswick having put a stop to the war, he found himself stationed in Dublin. He had occasion, however, to be in London on regimental business at the particular moment when Tiffin's was ordered to embark for the West Indies. Having no mind to go thither, and finding it impossble to reach Dublin in time for the voyage, he secured permission to exchange places with a half-pay captain, who went in his stead. No dates are given for these transactions, nor for those which follow. Unable to endure the state of inactivity in which he was thus left, Carleton happened upon his old friend of the siege of Namur, Lord Cutts. The latter, who had just been appointed to office in Ireland, asked Carleton's advice about a Dublin residence. Carleton replied that hē himself had a Dublin house suitable to his lordship's tastes, to which his lordship was welcome. In return for this generosity Cutts recommended his benefactor to the Earl of Peterborough, who appointed the half-pay captain to his staff and took him along on the expedition to Spain in 1705.[86]

Such is the account given in the "Memoirs." How far from the truth it is Colonel Parnell has pointed out.[87] Here are the facts. In May of 1700 Carleton was tried by court martial and found guilty of bullying an inferior officer and of fighting a duel with him, for which he was cashiered on October 14 of that year. Through the kindness of Lord Galway, who wrote to the War Secretary in London that Carleton had

[84] Luttrell, *Brief Relation*, III, p. 491; *London Gazette*, No. 3088, 13-17 June, 1695.

[85] *London Gazette*, No. 3100; *English Historical Review*, VI, p. 116; Carleton, pp. 53-60.

[86] Carleton, pp. 70-75.

[87] *English Historical Review*, VI, pp. 107, 8, 9.

"une femme" and three children with no other means of support than the captain's salary, the broken officer was granted a half-pay pension of 3s. a day. This was upon October 28, 1700,—two years before Tiffin's left for the West Indies. Obviously an half-pay captain with a dependent family was not likely to have under his ownership a Dublin house which would have attracted the fastidious tastes of Lord Cutts. We have seen, moreover, that Carleton did not take part in the siege of Namur, and, therefore, had no reason to be acquainted with Cutts. Just where Cutts lived in Dublin we do not know, but it appears to have been in Kerry House, the family residence of the Fitzmaurices, where he died less than two years later.

Further proof that this bargain with Lord Cutts was fabricated is that Carleton had no post on Peterborough's staff. Instead he went as a volunteer without a particular post. This fact is well authenticated. Besides a positive statement to that effect in the Treasury Papers, there is indication that he lived from hand to mouth during the years of his service, dependent upon the bounty of any one whom he might serve. Certain it is that as late as 1722 he was still petitioning the government for remuneration for his service in Spain. And, moreover, for all the years from 1700 to 1728 he drew his half-pay pension. Had he been a member of Peterborough's staff, his name would have been stricken from the pension list, and he would have had no difficulty in securing remuneration for his work in Spain.[88]

Here, as Colonel Parnell has argued, we see the methods of the writer of fiction. The actual service of Carleton at Kenoque was replaced with an invented report of his bravery at Namur, in order that Carleton might be introduced to Lord Cutts and the way paved for the elevation to Peterborough's staff.

Such are the distortions in the "Memoirs" of the external facts of Carleton's life in so far as we can check them with more or less official records. They are, briefly, (1) placing him in Fenwick's regiment as an ensign in 1676, whereas his commission came in Bellasis's in 1680 or 1681; (2) the promotion to a lieutenantcy in Tufton's shortly after Carleton's arrival in England in 1685, whereas he did not join Tufton's (indeed Tufton's was not organized) until 1688, and then only as an ensign,—the lieutenancy followed after a delay of two years, namely, in 1690; (3) the implication that his captaincy in Tiffin's came in 1690 instead of 1692, and the assigning of a false reason (as will abundantly appear later) for the promotion; (4) the statement that Carleton participated in the battle of Steenkerke which he is made to describe at length, although that engagement was already over when Carleton landed in Flanders; (5) the failure to mention the desperate assault on Fort Kenoque, the only fighting which Carleton saw in the campaign of 1695, and the recounting instead of fictitious adventures about Arseel, Brussels, and Namur; (6) the complete invention of the reasons for Carleton's being placed on half-pay and the distortion of the circumstances under which he went to Spain in 1705.

This comparison of the slender thread of Carleton's activity as related in the "Memoirs" with independent records concerning him reveals (1) that whoever wrote the "Memoirs" had before him (either upon paper or in his mind) at least a bare outline of Carleton's whole career from 1672 to 1713; (2) that that outline was either inaccurate or incomplete; and (3) that whenever the interest of the narrative called for it the facts stated in the outline were ignored or distorted.

Lest the reader, however, should think from what I have just said that the "Memoirs" as a whole is, with these few exceptions, a fairly accurate record of the military performances and experiences of George Carleton, it is necessary to remind ourselves again of the slenderness of this thread relating to Carleton's conduct. It forms an almost negligible part of the narrative, answering such questions only as, what battles did he take part in, and what was his rank at the time? It is barely sufficient to prove that the George Carleton who gave the title to the book was identical with the historical George Carleton. The vastly greater portions of the narrative, purporting to deal with what Carleton actually did and saw in those engagements, I have not yet touched upon. And it is in them that we shall see that the author of the "Memoirs" had extremely few data furnished him by Carleton personally, or that he is indifferent to the data he possessed.

The book, of course, does not pretend to be a biography, but, as the title suggests, a book of reminiscences. That allows room for the introduction of many interestng observations, incidents, and anecdotes of which he may have heard or read only. Certainly as a subordinate officer who participated in most of the events which he is made to describe, Carleton must have had a perspective far different from that of a mere onlooker; that is to say, the men and events of his own company and regiment would have loomed larger in his mental view than those with which he had no connection. What is indisputable, however, is that whoever wrote the "Memoirs" had no such view. The author writes as a general or a historian who sees the campaign as a whole, with the various elements in their proper proportion and not distorted by a more intimate knowledge of, and interest in, one part than another.

It is significant that there is in the narrative not a mention of a fellow ensign, lieutenant, or captain who can be traced through army commission

records. In the account of the siege of Mastricht, Carleton is made to state
that Captain Barnwell was his captain; but that follows the false statement
that Carleton had been made an ensign in Fenwick's. As Barnwell was a
captain in Fenwick's, to which Carleton never belonged, he could not have
been Carleton's captain. Barnwell, however, was mentioned in the "London Gazette's" report of the siege, which, as I shall later prove, the author
of the Carleton story used as his principal source. We know from authentic
records that Tankred was Carleton's major in Leslie's; that David Rindes
preceded him as commander of his company in Tiffin's; that Abraham
Griffin was appointed ensign to him in 1693; that in 1700 he fought a
duel with Ensign Alexander Cory. But no such names appear in the
memoirs. The author concerns himself chiefly with well-known characters
whose actions were recorded in histories and newspaper accounts. Whenever lesser persons are referred to, there is always some vagueness in the
statement which prevents identification.

There is extremely little in the book which deals with Carleton personally. Many events he is made to say that he witnessed. Many others
he is connected with in some manner or other. But in nearly every case,
it may be shown that the event is borrowed from history and the connection with Carleton made by the author, or else that it is fictitious.

Consider the first episode of the narrative, the sea fight at Solebay.
Little attention has been paid by previous investigators to this engagement. The account of it, however, being complete in itself and standing
apart from the later story represents, or may represent, in miniature the
character of the whole work, and may, therefore, furnish us with a key
to its composition.[39]

According to the "Memoirs," Carleton, then a young gentleman of
twenty years, was a volunteer on board the *London* commanded by Sir
Edward Spragge, vice-admiral of the Red Squadron. Under such circumstances we have a right to expect a memoir, if it is genuine, to concern
itself chiefly with those events happening on or near the *London.* That is
to say, the *London* would be the center both of the narrator's interest and
of his knowledge, and that in general other events would suffer in both
in direct proportion to their remoteness from that center. A hasty survey
of the episode, however, reveals that we get nothing of the sort. The
account is a very general summary of the battle such as a history might
give, without the slightest mention of Carleton's duties or actions during
the fighting. The battle itself is summarized in a single paragraph. Of
the remaining ten paragraphs, one relates the conduct of the admiral, the
Duke of York; another, the fate of the *Royal James* and of the Earl of

[39] Carleton, pp. 1-10.

Sandwich; a third, the fortunes of the *Catherine;* three tell of the losses on both sides; another brief one tells of some notable men who gained experience in the battle; and the remaining three narrate anecdotes which are not of an historical character. Every one of these, except the information as to the Duke of York's conduct and two of the anecdotes, relates not to the *London* and the Red Squadron, but to Sandwich and the Blue.

The closest scrutiny reveals few elements which have the appearance of being the personal experiences or recollections of George Carleton—facts concerning himself and his own vessel. Making the most generous allowances, there are but eight of such items to be found. It is to be emphasized that the majority of these relate to Carleton only in the sense that they are said to have been witnessed by him, and not that he participated in them. The following arrangement of the data is in the order in which they are recounted.

1. 1672, George Carleton (not named, as the history is related in the first person), about 20 years old, a gentleman volunteer with Sir Edward Spragge aboard the *London* (p. 1).

2. Incident of the Duke of York's taking refuge on the *London; his bravery attested* (pp. 3, 4).

3. Incident of the finding of the Earl of Sandwich's body (p. 4 ff.).

4. Anecdote of a man who, though a brave duellist, was so terrified by the fire of battle that he asked his comrades to tie him fast that he might not run away (pp. 6, 7).

5. Sir George Rooke mentioned as lieutenant to Spragge (p. 8).

6. Carleton reported to have seen the wreck of an enemy ship standing out of water (p. 8).

7. The anecdote of Spragge's pigeons which instinctively change ship with their master (pp. 9, 10).

8. Carleton leaves the fleet soon after the battle (p. 10).

Of these eight items, only the first and the last, briefly relating his entrance into and his exit from the fleet, concern Carleton personally. The second, describing the conduct of the Duke of York, may or may not be true. The bravery of the Duke on this occasion is well-known;[40] but the particulars mentioned in the "Memoirs" are scarcely susceptible of proof. It may be remarked, however, that it is unlikely that the conduct of the admiral of the fleet in a great battle, especially when that admiral is the son of one king, brother to a second, and destined to be king himself, should wait fifty-six years to be made known through the memoir of an obscure old soldier.

The third item, relating to the discovery of the body of the Earl of Sandwich, is, fortunately, capable of being tested. First of all it must

[40] Bishop Parker, *History of my own Times* (1727), pp. 150-4.

be recalled that two years after the battle of Solebay Carleton is said in the "Memoirs" to have gone to serve under William of Orange in the Lowlands. This journey the author of the "Memoirs" seems unquestionably to have had in mind when he composed the account of the incident under consideration. It was a well-known fact (reported in the "London Gazette," no. 685) that over a week later the body of the Earl, who was lost in the engagement at Solebay, was discovered floating at sea, and was brought to shore at Harwich. In the "Memoirs" it is pretended that in his passage from Harwich to Rotterdam two years later, Carleton learned of the fact from the master of the packet boat on which he was travelling, this master being none other than the discoverer of the body. On the surface this appears plausible enough; but upon closer examination it becomes evident that the author has fallen into a significant discrepancy through his hasty and careless method of composition. For when the Solebay episode is finished and Carleton is ready in the summer of 1674 to go to the Lowlands, he does not go by way of Harwich and Rotterdam. On the contrary his route is by way of Dover, Calais, Dunkirk, and Brussels.[41] Which of these two routes Carleton actually travelled will in all likelihood never be known; probably the author of the "Memoirs" did not know. But that he did go to Flanders before August, 1674, is quite certain from external evidence.[42] If so, his most direct route would be the second one given in the "Memoirs"; for the Prince's army was stationed then at Nivelles, about twenty miles southwest of Brussels. Had Carleton gone through Harwich and Rotterdam, he must have travelled considerably out of his way.

The manner in which this discrepancy occurred is obvious. The author of the "Memoirs," seeking to connect his hero with an event so interesting as the discovery of the Earl's body, noticed in the "Gazette" (as I shall show later) that the body was found somewhere near Harwich, recalled that Harwich is the usual place for taking passage to Holland, and so happened on this future journey of Carleton's as a scheme for the connection. It was only when he came to write of Carleton's career in the Lowlands that he discovered through Boyers "History of William III"[43] that the Prince's army was not in Holland at all, but at Nivelles in Belgium, as has been stated. By that time, however, he had either forgotten about, or lost interest in the incident of the Earl's body.

This explanation becomes the more certain when it is shown on other grounds that the episode as related in the "Memoirs" is full of fictitious

[41] Carleton, pp. 4, 11.
[42] *Academy*, 6 July, 1889, p. 9.
[43] I (1702), p. 49.

statements. For the detailed reports in the Calendar of State Papers[44] of the finding of the body of Sandwich make clear that the body was not discovered by the crew of a packet boat as the "Memoirs" states, but by some seamen from the *Gloucester*, a war vessel, who were out in a ketch trying to recover some of the *Gloucester's* equipment which had been lost on a place called the Sunk,—apparently a sandbar off the coast. Other statements in the "Memoirs" are equally far from the truth. It is related there that this master of the packet boat was led to his discovery through seeing a great flock of gulls hovering over the body, which came nearly being returned to the waves "as the corpse of a Dutch man"; and that there was "found about him between twenty and thirty guineas, some silver, and his gold watch." The fact is that the body was not discovered by the presence of gulls; the ketch was "sweeping and labouring" to recover some anchors, and happened on the body. None of the authentic reports mentions the presence of fowls. It is, furthermore, well attested that the Earl was in his clothes, and decorated with the Order of the Garter. So dressed he would certainly not pass long for a Hollander, though his corpulent figure might favor the misapprehension.

There appears to have been some basis for the statement about the gold watch; a gold watch is actually mentioned among the articles so found. But beyond that the whole Carleton account seems to be fictitious. A correspondent of Sir Joseph Williamson, then a secretary in the naval department, mentions seeing, besides the watch, three elaborately jewelled rings, and his George, the jewelled pendant to the collar of the Order of the Garter.[45] Thus the whole incident connected with this journey of Carleton from Harwich to Rotterdam turns out to be a fabrication with no more basis than the generally known fact that the body of Sandwich had been found at sea and brought to Harwich.

Authority for the sixth item, Carleton's claiming to have seen the wreck of a ship of the enemy which had been sunk, is likewise found in the "Gazette" (no. 684), which asserts that the whole fleet saw it. Omitting the fourth item, the anecdote of the cowardly duellist, we find in the fifth the statement that Sir George Rooke (who, of course, was not Sir George till later) was youngest lieutenant to Spragge. As the young George Rooke and George Carleton were thus shipmates, the statement at first glance gives promise of some special knowledge on the part of Carleton, but that promise is dissipated when the author proceeds in the same sentence to tell of other men who held various posts throughout the fleet, indicating that his acquaintance with the *London* is no more intimate than it is with a number of other vessels.

[44] Dom. Ser., May 18 to Sept. 30, 1672 (1899), pp. 191, 194, 205, 207.
[45] C. of S. P., Dom. Ser., May-Sept., 1672, pp. 205.

There remain still to be considered the fourth and seventh items in the list; one relating to the cowardly duellist, the other to Spragge's interesting pigeons. Neither, however, throws any light on Carleton's conduct, being merely impersonal anecdotes of curious events which he is said to have witnessed.

This completes the survey of the personal touches in the first episode of the "Memoirs." What is the result? There are eight passages which promise something in the nature of personal knowledge or experience, but in every case except two the promise is belied. Two of those passages may have been (and as a matter of fact were) based upon reports in the "London Gazette"; another is more than likely taken from a similar source; a fourth is given casually in company with other items far removed from the pretended author; and two others are merely anecdotes that anyone might relate and attribute to the occasion. The personal element in a ten page narrative simmers down to the two statements that (1) Carleton, a young man of about twenty, was a volunteer aboard the London with Sir Edward Spragge, at the battle of Solebay in 1672, and that (2) shortly after the engagement he left the fleet. It is evident, therefore, that this part of the "Memoirs" could have been fabricated with no more knowledge of what George Carleton did or saw on the 28th of May, 1672, or for that matter in his whole life, than is contained in the memorandum to Dr. Covel's letter, "He hath been at sea with Sr Edw. Spragg." The author, then, would place him aboard Sir Edward's ship, the London, in one of the most famous events of Spragge's career; estimate his age and rank from general circumstances and from his later career; and assume that he left the fleet soon after the battle, as a volunteer would be quite likely to do when the crisis was past.

But did not Carleton see anything worth recording besides the bravery of the Duke, the cowardice of the duellist, and the pigeons of Sir Edward? Was he exposed to danger? Was he frightened? Was he wounded? What was the nature of his duties? We search in vain for traces of any such matters. The author knows what a strenuous fight the Royal James put up before sinking; he knows about the Catherine; that she was captured, that her men recovered her, and even that in later times she was commanded by the Earl of Mulgrave, who had a painting of her made in his house in St. James Park; further still, he remembers the name of a "very fine gentleman" aboard her who was devoured in the hold by hogs. But does he know anything about the London? He gives a long list of persons who "as I remember" lost their lives in the engagement; is it not significant that not one of those men was aboard his own ship?

Of the Dutch losses the "Memoirs" mentions but one ship, the account of which, as will be shown in its place, is apparently a garbled version of what the "Gazette" reported of two ships. But other accounts tell of a half-dozen enemy ships being sunk, one by the *London*,—a statement confirmed by Spragge in his official report of the battle.[46] Strangely the author of the "Memoirs" says nothing of all this. One would imagine, did he not know otherwise, that Sir Edward kept the *London* out of the fighting, so little is said of her share in the fray.

But whether or not the *London* sank a Dutch vessel, there is no doubt that she bore a prominent part in the fighting, and one naturally wishes to know why the "Memoirs" tells nothing of it; why the author mentions so few events which occurred aboard his own ship in proportion to those he relates as happening on other ships; why, though he gives a long list from memory of those killed elsewhere, he records no casualties among his own shipmates; and why he mentions not a single act performed by himself, or a single incident in which he was actively or passively a participant. The answer is obvious: the author was not at Solebay, and had to make use of such materials as were at hand when fabricating the story.

What is true of the Solebay episode can likewise be shown to be true of subsequent portions of the story, namely, that the narrative reveals scarcely a trace of genuine first hand knowledge on the part of the writer, and that when knowledge is presented as such it can usually be demonstrated to be fabulous. Not all parts of the "Memoirs" are capable of being tested as is the account of Solebay. Others of importance, however, are.

Such a one is the report of Carleton's bravery at the capture of Lethindy Castle in Scotland, which is said to have won for him a captaincy in Tiffin's. The "Memoirs" states explicitly that the commander, Sir Thomas Levingston, wrote to court "a full account of the whole action. In which being pleas'd to make mention of my behaviour, with some particularities, I had soon after a commission order'd me for a company in the regiment under the command of Brigadier Tiffin."[47] Long ago a credulous writer in "Notes and Queries" expressed the opinion that if this "account" could be discovered it would solve the whole question of authorship.[48] But now that it has been found, the only light it throws on the question is to confirm the opinion of skeptical readers that the "Memoirs" is a fiction. For Carleton is not mentioned therein, nor any such incident as that described by the "Memoirs" of the use of grenades in the capture.[49]

[46] *London Gazette*, no. 684; *Dartmouth Mss.*, III, pp. 15-17; C. of S. P., Dom. Ser. May-Sept., 1672, pp. 163-5.

[47] P. 45.

[48] *Notes and Queries*, 2d Series, VII (19 February, 1859), p. 150.

[49] Doble, *Academy*, XLIII, p. 461.

Of the errors and distortion of facts in the account of Carleton's conduct in Spain, Colonel Parnell has remarked that to correct them would necessitate the introduction of his whole history of the war of the succession in Spain.[50] I shall point out but one instance. In the detailed account of the capture of Montjuic and Barcelona, the "Memoirs" pretends that it was Carleton who saw the danger of a cowardly retreat following the death of Prince George and who hurried away to warn Peterborough. The danger was a real one, mentioned in Freind's "Account of Peterborow's Conduct" and in Boyer's "Queen Anne."[51] But the officer who carried the message to Peterborough was not Carleton; instead it was Colonel Rieutort.[52]

The most sweeping evidence, however, that the book does not consist to any considerable extent of the genuine reminiscences of Carleton is the fact that it is almost wholly based upon written records. Colonel Parnell demonstrated this to be true for large sections of the work; but how completely borrowed is the story even he failed to recognize. The main part of the narrative of Carleton's experiences between the years 1674-1678 Parnell traced to their origin in the "Memoirs" of Sir William Temple.[53] Some later events such as Carleton's part in the Arseel retreat (1695) and in the apprehending of the conspirators of 1696, he believed were concocted from other historical accounts. For Carleton's subsequent career in Spain, Parnell found the chief borrowing to be from Freind's "Account" and the letters of the Countess D'Aulnoy, with minor assistance from such works as Temple's "Miscellanea," and Swift's "Conduct of the Allies." Although his arguments for the use of these minor works are not very convincing, there can be no doubt of the debt to Temple, Freind, and D'Aulnoy,—an obligation which can hardly be overstated. For a fuller understanding of the way in which the "Memoirs" was composed, however, it is necessary to point out a significant error in Colonel Parnell's treatment of the sources of the story, and to add other important sources to his list. One of the surprising things is the discovery of how painstakingly the materials for the narrative were gathered.

In the first place, it should be said that for the account of Carleton's earlier years in the wars in Flanders, Temple's "Memoirs" is the ultimate, not the immediate source. Close investigation reveals the fact that the plagiarisms which Parnell supposed to have been taken from Temple were

[50] English Historical Review, VI, p. 119.

[51] John Freind, Account of the Earl of Peterborow's Conduct in Spain (1707), p. 35; Abel Boyer, Queen Anne, I (1721), p. 322. I have not had access to issues of the London Gazette after 1700.

[52] Parnell, War in Spain (1888), p. 133.

[53] English Historical Review, VI, p. 131ff.

in fact taken indirectly from Temple through Abel Boyer's "William III" which appeared in 1702.[54]   In that history Boyer borrowed copiously from Temple, whose works he was later to reissue.   The portion of Temple's "Memoirs" which he found most to his purpose in writing the life of William III is the same as that from which Parnell thought the author of the Carleton story took his materials.   The hastiest comparison of Temple's "Memoirs" and Boyer's "William III" reveals that the latter has done little more in the earlier portion than to reproduce Temple verbatim.   Occasionally he omits or changes the wording of a phrase, and sometimes he puts in an additional paragraph of his own, or omits one of Temple's.   Had Boyer copied from Temple without alteration, it would, of course, be impossible to determine which of the two writers the author of the Carleton story was following.   But a careful comparison of the three accounts, with especial attention to Boyer's variations from Temple, makes clear that it was Boyer and not Temple whose history is used as a basis for parts of the "Memoirs of Carleton."

The proof for this assertion, no matter how positive it may be, is obtained only after studying the whole period from 1674-1679.[55]   To 1678, there is little to judge from; here and there are to be found minor items mentioned in both Boyer and the Carleton story but not in Temple, though (with one notable exception to be dealt with later) never any mentioned by Temple and Carleton but not by Boyer.   That is to say, whenever Boyer differs from or supplements Temple, Carleton agrees with Boyer rather than with Temple.[56]   It may be noted that all three of the passages quoted by Parnell to show that the author of the Carleton narrative had borrowed from Temple appear verbatim in Boyer.[57]

Not, however, till the very end of the period in question does the evidence become conclusive, that is, with the account of the battle of St. Denis in 1678.   To this encounter Temple devotes but a sentence or two, mentioning that "upon the 14th of August" the Prince of Orange attacked the enemy with resolution, and that night put an end to the fighting.[58]   Boyer, however, treats the battle in detail.   He relates that the Duke of Monmouth joined the Prince just before the fight began, that the Earl of Ossory led the English and the Scotch regiments, that Monsieur Auverquerque shot a French officer who was aiming his pistol

[54] The final volume, the third, did not appear until 1703.

[55] Carleton, pp. 11-37; Boyer, I, p. 49-115; Temple, *Works*, I (1720), pp. 388-470.

[56] See the mention of Sir Walter Vane and the Marquis of Assentar among the slain by Boyer (I, p. 50) and Carleton (pp. 14, 18).

[57] Carleton, p. 14; Temple, I, p. 388; Boyer, I, p. 51; *English Historical Review*, VI, p. 131.

[58] Temple, *Works*, I (1720), p. 470.

at the Prince, and many other facts, none of which Temple has touched.[59]
He, furthermore, differs from Temple as to the date, giving it not as
August 14, but as Sunday, August 17. The Carleton narrative, likewise,
gives the date as Sunday, August 17, and relates practically all the details
which Boyer gives and which Temple omits.[60]

There is, as has been mentioned, one noticeable exception to the statement that in no case does Carleton record an event given by Temple and
not by Boyer. For Carleton is made to tell of an awful windstorm that
passed over Nivelles shortly after his arrival in 1674 at the camp of William's army. At the close of his account of the storm, he adds, "And, if I
am not mistaken, Sir William Temple, in his Memoirs, mentions somewhat
of it, which he felt at Lillo, on his return from the Prince of Orange's
camp, where he had been a day or two before." Boyer omits all mention
of this storm, which Temple describes very much as Carleton states.[61]
That fact, combined with the actual mention of Temple by name, would
seem to indicate that Temple's was the work before the author of the
Carleton story as he wrote. But would he not hesitate to mention Temple
if he were copying from him? To do so would give too good a clue to his
source and lead to a discovery of the fraudulent nature of the work which
he was fabricating. The event, moreover, was fully related in the "London
Gazette" which, as I shall show presently, was the real origin of the
account of it in the "Memoirs."

That this early part of the "Memoirs" was based upon Boyer rather
than Temple has more significance than at first glance appears. It means
that the borrowing extends beyond the year 1679 when Temple's "Memoirs" came to an end. Boyer's life of William III concludes with William's
death after the turn of the century, and the author of the Carleton narrative follows it for all the historical events prior to that time. This greatly
increases the portion of the work which is known to have been fabricated.
For, whereas Colonel Parnell supposed that twenty-three pages were
based upon Temple, it is now apparent that fifty-six pages have their
origin in Boyer.

An interesting bit of evidence for the use of Boyer for the period
subsequent to 1678 is afforded by the gaps in the Carleton narrative. With
the year 1679 Temple's "Memoirs" comes to a close, and Boyer, finding

---

[59] Boyer, *William III*, I, pp. 115-16.

[60] Carleton, p. 34. It may be noted that Kennett's *History*, III (1706), p. 363,
having plagiarized from Temple copiously, changes to Boyer shortly before the
account of this battle, and copies him slavishly. It seems needlessly to complicate
matters, however, to suppose that the author of the *Memoirs* consulted Kennett
in addition to Boyer and the *Gazette*.

[61] Carleton, p. 12; Temple, I, p. 385 ff.

himself out of materials, skips over the following five years. This leaves
Carleton without material, likewise, for his pretended memoirs; and so
he too skips over those same five years resuming activity again with Boyer's
account of the year 1684. But in the following year, 1685, Boyer wanders
from the history of William into a dull discussion, lacking in narrative,
of the reign of James II. Carleton, again out of material, has another
period of inactivity, and again resumes his memoirs with Boyer following
the accession of William and Mary in 1689.[62]

But the borrowings from Boyer have to do, in the main, with the
larger aspects of the narrative, such as the conduct of the various commanders, the general features of the battles, and the connecting thread of
events which leads on from year to year. For the particulars of the story,
however, the author of the "Memoirs" turned to the "London Gazette," and
occasionally to other periodicals, notably the "Post Boy." That some of
the accounts in the "Memoirs" may have been concocted from data in
the "Gazette" Colonel Parnell suspected, but farther in that direction
he did not go. It should not seem strange, however, that an author at
work inventing a pretended memoir should dig up information from old
periodicals. It is from them that he may secure those realistic details
which appear to show a more intimate acquaintance with events than can
be gleaned from histories.

With these two important sources in mind, namely, the "London
Gazette" and Boyer's "William III," we shall see that the "Memoirs"
relates for the period closing with the peace of Ryswick in 1697 little or
nothing, with the exception of the naked outline of Carleton's activity
and some anecdotes of a non-historical character, which was not in 1728
accessible in print, and which, moreover, was not based upon those
printed records.

The opening account of the battle of Solebay is, as I have intimated,
based upon the various dispatches in the "Gazette." Temple and Boyer
pay little attention to the engagement. The "Gazette," however, keeps up
a running fire on the subject from no. 674 (May 2-6,1672), which reports
the preparation of the English and French fleets to meet the Dutch, to
no. 684 (June 6-10), which gives the casualty list. The passages most
clearly indebted to the "Gazette" will now be compared with those from
which they were directly or indirectly taken.[63]

[62] Carleton, pp. 37, 39; Boyer, I, p. 120; pt. ii, p. 26.

[63] It is possible, of course, that instead of following the *Gazette* the author of
the Carleton account was using some history not yet considered which had incorporated a good deal of the *Gazette's* diction in its relation. But in view of the
fact that later parts of the *Memoirs* appear to be indebted directly to the *Gazette*
this presumption is unlikely to be true.

"Memoirs," pp. 1, 2.

"The fleet set sail . . . about the beginning of May, *in order to join* the French fleet, then at anchor in St. Hellens Road, under the command of the Count de Estree."

"The London Gazette," no. 674.

"Whitehal, May 5 . . . the Count d'Estrees, vice-admiral of France, was with the Squadron of French ships arrived at St. Helens . . . His Royal Highness . . . was passed . . . with his Majesties fleet . . . *in order to his conjunction* with the said squadron."

P. 2.

" . . . We sailed directly towards the Dutch coast, where we soon got sight of their fleet; . . . the *Galloper* lying between . . . it was resolv'd . . . to sail directly for Solebay . . . "

No. 680.

"Whitehal, May 23 . . . we weighed and stood to the southward; at five a clock we saw the Dutch fleet . . . at 12 we passed by the *Galloper* . . . At eight a clock we were before Sould Bay . . . "

P. 3.

"It was *about four in the* morning of the 28th of May . . . when we first made the discovery . . . *about eight* . . . the Blue Squadron . . . began to engage . . . the Amsterdam Squadron . . . The fight lasted till ten at night . . . "

No. 681.

"Southwold, May 28, past nine at night. *About five* . . . *this Morning* his Majesties fleet . . . discovered the Dutch . . . *about seven* the Dutch engaged with the Blew Squadron . . . they ceased from firing between eight and nine this night."

Attention should be called to the fact that, though the author of the "Memoirs" twice copies the "Gazette's" use of the qualifying word "about" with regard to the precise hours at which the events occurred, he persists in every case in differing by one hour as to what the time was.

Pp. 4, 5.

" . . . the Royal James . . . (after strenuous endeavours . . . to disengage her from two Dutch fire ships . . . one athwart her hawsers . . .) took fire, blew up and

perished; and *with her* a great *many brave gentlemen* . . . amongst them the Earl (of Sandwich) himself, concerning whom I shall . . . add, that in my passage from Harwich to the Brill . . . the master of the pacquet boat told me that . . . discovering a corpse . . . it proved to be that of the Earl of Sandwich . . . "

No. 681.

(Continuation of the preceding) " . . . the Royal James being overprest with men of war and fireships, a flagship laid himself thwart his hawse . . . three fireships attacked the Royal James two of which he sunk; the other took place and burnt him . . . "

(Note this sentence from Kennett's "Complete History," III, p. 288.
" . . . the Royal James . . . was at last burnt . . . and the noble Earl (of Sandwich) *perished in her with many brave* gentlemen . . . ").

"Harwich, June 10.
This day the body of the . . . Earl of Sandwich (was) discovered . . . by one of his Majesties ketches . . . "

Pp. 5.

' " . . . the Katherine was taken and . . . *Sir John Chicheley made* prisoner, her sailors soon after *finding* the opportunity . . . seiz'd all the Dutch sailors . . . and brought the ship back . . . together with all the Dutch men prisoners . . "

No. 681.

" . . . *the Catherine was taken, and Sir John Chichely* . . . put aboard of the Dutch ships, and all the men under the hatches . . .

the prisoners . . . *found* a way to break out upon the Dutch, and redeemed . . . their ship, and about 16 or 17 of the Dutch prisoners are brought ashore . . ."

On page 7, the "Memoirs" gives a long list of the names of "those English gentlemen who lost their lives, as I remember, *in this engagement,*" plainly compiled (with slight changes) from the list of those killed or injured *"in the late engagement"* given by no. 684 of the "Gazette." From the account of the English losses (that is to say, from the casualty lists), both the "Memoirs" and the "Gazette" pass to a consideration of the Dutch vessels sunk.

P. 8.

" . . . the Dutch had one man of war sunk though so near shore, that I saw some part of

her main mast remain above water."

No. 684.

" . . . a great Dutch man of war . . . was seen to sink . . . off of Orfordness . . . some days after, the wrack of this ship was seen by his Majesties fleet as they passed . . . as was also another . . . *her masts . . . standing out of the water* . . . "

It is now clear that whoever wrote the account of the Solebay episode was not present (as we have good reason to believe Carleton was) at that engagement, and that those details in that account which purport to reveal the personal recollections of Carleton are either untrue, as in the case of the master of the packet boat who pretended to have been the discoverer of the body of Sandwich, or are pillaged from the "Gazette" and other sources.

To continue chronologically, we recall that two years later Carleton went to Flanders to serve as a volunteer under the Prince of Orange. The "Memoirs" records that fact, but, as has been shown, contradicts itself by designating two several routes for the journey from England to the Lowlands, manifesting thereby both ignorance of, and indifference to, the matter. Carleton's first experience in Flanders, as the story correctly asserts, was at the battle of Seneffe. But further information of his conduct on that occasion the writer did not possess; for he borrows his narrative of the engagement completely from Boyer and the "Gazette."

From Boyer came the general facts:[64] the location of the army at

[64] Boyer, I, p. 49ff.: *Memoirs,* p. 13.

Nivelles; the decision to march to Bins or Binch; the disposition of the confederate army; the fact that Condé, the French commander, viewed the march from a vantage point; and the account of the battle as a whole. The one paragraph which the "Memoirs" uses so carelessly as to betray the fact is as follows:

"Memoirs," p. 14.	Boyer I, p. 51.
"Had the Prince of Condé contented himself with this share of good fortune, his victory had been uncontested: but being push'd forward . . . he resolv'd to force the whole confederate army to a battle."	"If the Prince of Condé had contented himself with this success . . . he had left no dispute of a victory; but lur'd on . . . He followed . . . and drawing out his whole army . . . brought it to a set battle."[65]

The more minute details, pertaining to Carleton himself, came from the "Gazette." The storm reported as happening upon Carleton's first day in camp is based upon paragraphs in the issue of that periodical for July 27-30, 1674 (no. 907), and not upon the account given by Temple, though the "Memoirs" mentions Temple in this connection. In addition to the reason advanced previously for regarding it as unlikely that the author would have cited Temple by name here had he been the source, namely, that he would have been inviting detection, is the fact that the Carleton report of the storm is unmistakably nearer in substance to the "Gazette" than to Temple. The latter stated that the storm lasted all night,[66] whereas both the other narratives describe it as lasting but a half hour; otherwise all three are pretty much in agreement. What actually happened is this. The author of the Carleton account, having taken the facts of the storm from the "Gazette," felt secure in citing Temple's "Memoirs" in corroboration of his assertions. This implies that the author was familiar with that portion of Temple's writings,— a fact which I shall later advance as an argument for that author being Defoe, who in his "Storm" (1704) quoted the whole of Temple's report of this tempest.

The details concerning Carleton's actions in the battle of Seneffe were fabricated from the reports in the "Gazette" of August 10-13, 1674, (no. 911) . In the "Memoirs" Carleton, who along with the other English volunteers had been placed in the Prince's guard, is made to tell of being stationed with Vaudemont's troops in the rear where he suffered the first fury of Condé's attack. Having saved his life by dextrously vaulting a

[65] Taken verbatim from Temple, I (1720), p. 388. See *English Historical Review*, VI, p. 131.

[66] Temple, I, p. 385; *Gazette*, No. 907; Carleton, pp. 11-12.

hedge before which his comrades were being slaughtered, he witnessed the remainder of the fight from a point of vantage.[67]

All this is agreeable to the "Gazette's" reports that in the first fury of the attack "those that conducted the Prince of Orange's baggage which was in the rear of the army, thought it was time to shift for themselves"; that the rear troops "on their left hand . . . . had a great hedge"; and that, being routed and put into confusion, "those that were not killed or taken prisoners were forced to retreat in great confusion" to a "hill beyond the Priory of St. Nicholas," from which they could see all that passed below.[68] Carleton's statement that the valor of the Prince of Orange "led him into the middle of the enemy" is, likewise, from the "Gazette."

So it goes. From one or the other of these two sources, Boyer and the "Gazette," was taken every material statement of the "Memoirs" concerning the battle. The succeeding account of the Prince of Orange's movements until he settled down to the investment of Oudenard is based upon Boyer, with a suggestion from the "Gazette" about the Mareschal de Humiers.[69] The report of the seige of Oudenard and the treachery of Souches of the Imperial army and the seige of Grave is closely fashioned after Boyer, as is likewise the statement that the Prince soon after fell ill of the small pox.[70] Some few stray details, such as the marching of Chamilly to Charleroy, the replacing of Souches by Sporke, and the thanksgiving for the recovery of Grave, are from the "Gazette."[71]

Passing on to the very brief mention of the campaign of 1675 (centering about the siege of Limburgh), we find it similar to the succinct account in Boyer.[72] The report of the siege of Mastricht, the only event recorded by the "Memoirs" for the year 1676, is, on the other hand, based almost wholly upon reports in the "Gazette."

Carleton was, as we know upon other evidence, present at this siege, where he was wounded. Further than that our information does not extend; nor does the "Memoirs" add to it. The narrative reports that he took part in both the principal assaults on the Dauphin bastion. The first assault succeeded, but, owing to the awkward handling of a grenade, the attacking party after holding the post a short time was thrown into confusion ending in retreat and the consequent loss of all that had been gained. One of the slain, the "Memoirs" goes on to say, was an ensign in

[67] Carleton, p. 14ff.

[68] *London Gazette,* No. 911, Amsterdam letter of August 17, and the Paris letter of August 18.

[69] Carleton, p. 18; Boyer, I, p. 53ff.; *Gazette,* No. 918.

[70] Carleton, pp. 19-21; Boyer, I, pp. 54-5, 67.

[71] Carleton, pp. 19-21; *London Gazette,* Nos. 934-5.

[72] Carleton, p. 22; Boyer, I, p. 67.

Fenwick's whose commission was bestowed upon Carleton in reward for his conduct. The second assault was led by Captain Barnwell of Fenwick's, who says Carleton, "was now my captain." Though Barnwell lost his life, the attack was successful, and, in spite of the springing of several mines by the enemy, the post was held secure.[73]

One false statement here I have already pointed out; Carleton was not commissioned as an ensign for four years at least after 1676, and he never at any time belonged to Fenwick's. Barnwell could not, therefore, have been his captain. Barnwell was, however, a real person, and the leader of the second assault,—a fact revealed in the "Gazette" (no. 1119).

Both assaults described in the "Memoirs" are set forth fully in the various issues of the "Gazette" from No. 1116 to No. 1119, which relate, exactly as does the Carleton story, the incident of the loss of the bastion after the first assault, owing to the falling short of a grenade. The plans for the assaults and the springing of the mines by the enemy are likewise taken by the author of the "Memoirs" from the same source.[74] The incident of the Prince of Orange waving his hat after an arm wound to show the slightness of the injury is from Boyer.[75] Such bits of information are introduced frequently by the phrase, "I remember," to give the air of originality to the narrative.

The next event related by the "Memoirs" after the siege of Mastricht is the attempt of the Prince to relieve St. Omers in the following year. The passage of time receives scant attention throughout the book; the author jumps from one important event to the next as it pleases him,— a fact which in part accounts for the interest of the story, as it does away with the tedious matters which obstruct the path of the conscientious historian. The account of the action around St. Omers is entirely from Boyer, who mentions all the circumstances given in the "Memoirs," namely, the fact that the Spaniards failed the Prince and that he had to depend upon troops in Dutch pay only; the incident of the Prince in the heat of the fight striking a cowardly officer across the face with his sabre in order to identify him later for hanging; and the details of the fighting.[76]

The next event, the battle of St. Denis, I have already shown to be described almost wholly after Boyer, with some details, such as the casualty list, from the "Gazette."[77] I have, furthermore, called attention to the fact that the "Memoirs" imitates Boyer in skipping over the years intervening between 1679 and 1684.

[73] Carleton, p. 24ff.
[74] Nos. 1118-1119.
[75] Carleton, p. 30; Boyer, I, p. 75. See also Temple, I, pp. 426-7.
[76] Carleton, pp. 30, 31; Boyer, I, p. 88-9. See also Temple, I, p. 444-5.
[77] No. 1,329.

For the year 1684 the "Memoirs" relates briefly the siege of Luxembourg, taking the few details from Boyer, and, in precise agreement with the latter's statement that in 1685 the English and Scotch regiments in Flanders were sent home by the Prince to aid in the suppression of Monmouth, records that Carleton returned to England in 1685.[78]

Passing rapidly over the next three or four years, the "Memoirs" borrows the account of the campaign in Scotland in 1689 and 1690 from both Boyer and the "Gazette." The statement that upon arriving in Scotland Carleton's regiment was quartered at Leith, and the mention of the surrender of Edinburgh Castle commanded by the Duke of Gordon are authorized by Boyer. The account of the fight at Strath Spey and of the taking of Lethindy Castle, though based upon Boyer, was supplemented by information from the "Gazette," which gives the fact that Cannon and Buchan (miscalled Balfour in the "Memoirs") were taken by surprise and compelled to flee in their night clothes.[79] Some of the stilted phraseology of the "Memoirs" in describing the Highlanders is not a little like Boyer. The latter refers to them as "a sort of savage that disdains to submit to any man that is not as wild as themselves." Similarly, Carleton speaks of "hunting for somewhat wilder than their wildest game, namely, the Highlanders."[80]

That the "Memoirs" errs in chronology by relating the building of the fort at Inverlochy as happening before the fight at Strath Spey and Lethindy Castle has been pointed out by Colonel Parnell. Concerning the taking of Lethindy Castle of which the "Memoirs" makes much, it should be said that few of the details given therein are to be found either in Boyer or the "Gazette." Carleton is made to tell of taking the stronghold singlehanded through his daring use of grenades, and of the general's complimentary report to court of his conduct which won for him a captaincy in Tiffin's. The official report, as we have already seen, makes no mention of Carleton, and his commission in Tiffin's, furthermore, did not follow until two years subsequently to that event; we have, therefore, the strongest reasons for suspecting the truth of the whole incident. These reasons are supported by the fact that, though a mine is mentioned as being placed under the castle, none of the authentic reports speaks of grenades.

The year 1691 the "Memoirs" passes over to tell of Carleton's arrival at Portsmouth where he took charge of his company in Tiffin's in time to hear the firing at sea between Russel and Tourville at the battle of La Hogue in 1692. The accounts of this engagement, of the Duke of

[78] Carleton, p. 37; Boyer, I, p. 120, pt. 2, p. 26.
[79] Carleton, pp. 39-45; Boyer, II, pp. 43, 55, 170; *Gazette*, No. 2,556.
[80] Carleton, p. 40; Boyer, II, p. 169.

Leinster's expedition, of the landing of Tiffin's at Ostend, of the battle of Steenkerke, and of the fortifying of Dixmude, are all taken from Boyer. I have already called attention to the fact that, though Carleton is made to relate the events of the battle of Steenkerke with the same pretention to first hand knowledge which is manifested in his reports of other engagements, he is positively known to have arrived in Flanders after the battle was over.[81]

The happenings of 1693 related in the "Memoirs" are few, consisting principally of the statement that Carleton's regiment was stationed on duty in the Tower of London, and that by the spring of 1694 it was again in Flanders. We know that Tiffin's actually was in England during 1693 until November when it returned to the wars on the continent.[82] But whether or not it was on duty in the tower, or, if it was, whether a powder explosion there was narrowly avoided, we can only conjecture.

For the year 1694 the "Memoirs" gives only an account of the long march, plainly borrowed in detail from Boyer.[83] The year following, however, the author makes the most of. Carleton, as we have seen, is made to tell at length of his exploits in connection with Vaudemont's famous retreat from Arseel, in the bombardment of Brussels, and in the siege of Namur, though he certainly was not at Namur, and probably was not with Vaudemont either at Arseel or in Brussels. The bitter attack on Kenoque in which he is known to have participated the "Memoirs" does not mention; it appears, in fact, that Tiffin's was stationed before Kenoque during most, if not all, of the summer.[84] These facts in themselves are sufficient proof that whoever was composing the "Memoirs" was paying little attention to the actual movements and performances of George Carleton. It is not surprising, therefore, to find that the narrative for the year was based upon published records, the accounts of Arseel and Brussels being taken from Boyer, and the report of the assaults upon the Namur citadel, in the main, from the "Gazette."[85]

The notorious conspiracy against William III occupies the "Memoirs" for the year 1696. Carleton is made to say that when the danger became known the troops in Flanders were hurried home, and that, being at Whitehall, he was notified that two only of the regiments were to land and that the others were to return to Holland. Meeting with Lord Cutts, whose attention he had attracted during the attacks on Namur, he was

[81] Carleton, pp. 45-49; Boyer, II, pp. 328, 330-331, 334-337, 339.

[82] Luttrell, Brief Relation, III, pp. 223, 230; Carleton, p. 50-51.

[83] Carleton, pp. 52, 3; Boyer, II, pp. 391, 2.

[84] English Historical Review, VI, p. 116; Luttrell, Brief Relation, III, p. 491; London Gazette, No. 3,088.

[85] Carleton, pp. 53-60; Boyer, III, pp. 67-96; London Gazette, No. 3,100.

employed by his lordship in the apprehending of some of the conspirators. Thus Carleton met the young Richard Steele, secretary to Cutts, and Porter, De la Rue, and Harris, former members of the plot who had turned witnesses. Hearing that Cassels, one of those sought, "was at Mr. Allens in the Savoy, under the name of Green," Carleton, with Porter and the other two, took him, and a little later Blackburn, who was discovered through the aid of a sputtering Dutchman.

Here is another interesting fabrication. Carleton, not having been at Namur, could not have known Cutts in connection with that event. His regiment, moreover, was not one of those ordered to land; he could not therefore, have been lounging about Whitehall leaving his company to take care of itself at Gravesend. As for the general facts of the conspiracy they lay open in Boyer. Though neither Boyer nor Blackmore, in his lengthy history of the conspiracy,[86] mentions such minor matters as the arrest of Cassels and Blackburn, the newspapers gave the author just the information he needed. The "Post Boy" reported by name all the English regiments returned from Flanders, stating that three only were to land and that the others were ordered back to the Lowlands.[87] The capture of Cassels is described, with all the details mentioned in the "Memoirs," in the "Flying Post" as follows: "Monsieur De la Rue . . . . having viewed the prisoners in Mr. Allen the messenger's custody, singled out one who went by the name of Green, but proves to be Cassels . . . . who was thereupon examined and committed." The "Gazette," likewise, gives both the proclamation for the arrest of the conspirators and the notice of the apprehending of Blackburn and Cassels, indicating that the latter was not mentioned in the proclamation.[88]

Here we have every material detail of the affair mentioned in the "Memoirs" except the instrumentality of the sputtering Dutchman in the capture of Blackburn. The circumstances of the plot were, moreover, well-known to many Londoners of 1728 who (among them Defoe) could have supplied such a point from memory, or even have invented it if need be.

The rest of the year 1696 and the year 1697 to the peace of Ryswick the "Memoirs" passes over lightly, there being little fighting to relate. Two incidents are told; one is concerning a stratagem by which Carleton outwitted a party from a neighboring French garrison, and the other is about the attempt of a spy to set fire to the ammunition wagons. The

[86] Sir Richard Blackmore, *History of the Conspiracy,* 1723.

[87] *Post Boy,* Nos. 129, 133, (March, 1696).

[88] *Flying Post,* No. 138 (31 March-2 April, 1696) ; *Gazette,* No. 3,171 (30 March-3 April, 1696).

former bears traces of being modelled after a similar trick by Sir Richard Hawkins in Purchas,[89] and the other is part of a series of anecdotes of powder explosions related in the "Memoirs," both of which facts will be mentioned later in connection with the evidence for ascribing the narrative to Defoe. Otherwise the passages offer little that can be tested. If, however, these incidents are the genuine experiences or recollections of Carleton they differ from any others discoverable in the story.

The relation of Carleton's activity between the peace of Ryswick and the expedition to Spain in 1705, having to do with Carleton's being placed on half-pay and with his pretended elevation to Peterborough's staff, has, as we have seen, a thin substratum of fact completely submerged beneath a mass of unmixed fiction. Passing on to the account of the war in Spain, we find a situation which differs little from that of the preceding narrative.

We may examine more hurriedly the sources of these later portions of the Carleton narrative, for a comparison of the story with its principal sources, already discovered, makes clear that it is no more trustworthy as a memoir than preceding parts, being fabricated almost in toto from previously published records. For the Spanish adventures Colonel Parnell found the principal sources to be Dr. Freind's "Account" and the letters of the Countess D'Aulnoy, with minor obligations to such works as Swift's "Conduct of the Allies," Mrs. Manley's "New Atalantis," Temple's "Miscellanea," and a few others. But though the author of the "Memoirs" certainly used Freind's book and the D'Aulnoy letters extensively, it is extremely uncertain that he used the others set forth by Parnell. The supposed borrowing from Temple's "Miscellanea" has to do only with an anecdote to the effect that "Don Quixote" had laughed away Spanish chivalry, an idea which I am ready to grant that the author (whom I believe to have been Defoe) may have taken from Temple. But the resemblances of the "Memoirs" to passages of Swift and Mrs. Manley are confined to a sentence or two, and are not very convincing except to one prejudiced, as Parnell was, in favor of attributing the story to Swift.[90]

But a hitherto unnoticed source, more important and more certain than these last (Temple, Swift, and Mrs. Manley)," is Abel Boyer's "Queen Anne."[91] We have already observed that Boyer's "William III" furnished the principal materials for the "Memoirs" between the years 1674 and 1697. It is not unlikely, then, that the continuation of the "Memoirs" should have been based upon Boyer's continuation of the history of

[89] Purchas, XVII, p. 95-6.

[90] *English Historical Review*, VI, pp. 127, 133-4, 134-7.

[91] Abel Boyer, *The Life of Queen Anne*, 2 vols., 1721. It is barely possible that the borrowing was actually done from Boyer's *Annals* upon which his *Queen Anne* was based.

English sovereigns. After following Boyer for awhile, however, the author of the Carleton story turned to Freind, whose narratives were more suitable to his purpose. Indeed he might have begun with Freind had the latter written a narrative of, instead of a series of reflections upon, the capture of Barcelona. Freind's main purpose being to clear Peterborough's reputation of specific charges against his conduct, he assumes a general knowledge of the siege, and devotes himself almost entirely to answering complaints. The "Memoirs" is, indeed, not entirely free from a disposition to do the same thing; and we have, therefore, a number of pages devoted to defending Peterborough.

Upon Boyer the author of the "Memoirs" based his account of the voyage to Barcelona. Both writers mention the sailing with Sir Cloudesley Shovel to Gibraltar, where the Prince of Hesse joined them; the sailing from thence to the bay of Altea; the bringing of provisions to Duke Charles by the people thereabouts who acknowledged him as their sovereign; the sending of ships which captured Denia; and the leaving of General Ramos as governor there.[92]

The account of the capture of Barcelona,—the basis of the Peterborough legend to which Lord Macaulay and others have given full credence,—is based upon Boyer, Freind, and newspaper accounts, probably those in the "Gazette."[93] All the reports of the councils of war and the petty jealousies and misunderstandings (for which we are told Peterborough was in no way to blame) are contributed by Freind, who devotes page after page to the detailed accounts of those councils, and to comments upon them.[94] The general narrative of the siege is as Boyer gives it, except that under the influence of Freind the credit for the attack on Montjuic, one of the principal strongholds of Barcelona, is given to Peterborough instead of the Prince of Hesse.

Wherever the Carleton narrative departs from Boyer or the contemporary accounts it can be shown to be fabricating. The account of the death of the Prince of Hesse, who fell in the attack on Montjuic, is a curious mixture of truth and fiction. The statement that the troops were deserting their posts in a panic when Peterborough appeared on the scene and by his example persuaded them to return to the attack, is substantially true, as the author may have learned from reading Boyer; but when he goes on to say that Carleton was the bearer of the news of the panic he is

[92] Carleton, p. 78ff; Boyer, *Queen Anne*, I, pp. 312-4, 318.

[93] The *London Gazette* for the period of the war in Spain I have not seen; but the echoes of the war which are to be found in the *Boston News-Letter* indicate that the author of the *Memoirs* was utilizing such materials.

[94] This is true especially of the first part of the work; later portions give uninterrupted scope to the narrative.

fabricating; for Colonel Rieutort is known to have met the Earl with the warning.[95]

A curious evidence of the dependence of the author of the "Memoirs" upon Boyer is reflected in the spelling of the name of the Count D'Asfelt. From the fact that the "Memoirs" in every case gives the name incorrectly as D'Alfelt, Mr. Doble argued that Defoe must have had a peculiar way of writing the letter "l" which led to an error in the printing. As one may observe, however, from facsimile reproductions of Defoe's writing, his letter "l" is normal and legible. The fact is that the error arises from a too literal dependence upon Boyer who likewise gives the Count's name as D'Alfelt.[96]

Immediately after relating the surrender of Barcelona, and of the nearby places, Lerida, Tortoza, Tarragona, and Gironne, the author of the Carleton story turned from Boyer's account to Freind's, incorporating in his narrative every usable scrap of information which Freind had to offer, and betraying the fact in nearly every paragraph, as Parnell has shown.[97] This carries the narrative forward to the siege of Alicante.

Just what work the author used after that point (when Freind's "Account" comes to an end) has not yet been determined. But that some history or histories and periodicals were relied upon is obvious from the fact that subsequently the "Memoirs" relates very few military actions in which it is even pretended that Carleton took part, devoting its attention mainly to the Spanish campaigns in general with little regard for the fact that Carleton did not witness them. Even the operations which took place after Carleton's capture in 1708 are described in full, as the battles of Saragossa, Villa Viciosa, and Breuhiga, and the springing of the Alicante mine,—for his information concerning which the author frankly confessed that he was indebted to the "best authorities."[98]

The most important of all the sources of the "Memoirs," from which came the pretended observations of Carleton upon Spanish customs and places, and upon which were based his adventures as a prisoner of war, is a work entitled, "The ingenious and diverting Letters of the Lady—— Travels into Spain. Describing the devotions, nunneries, humours, customs . . . . and recreations of that people. Intermixt with great variety of modern adventures, and surprising accidents. . . ." This interesting composition of the Countess D'Aulnoy, which went through at

[95] Boyer, I, p. 322; Parnell, *War in Spain*, pp. 131-3; Carleton, p. 105.

[96] Carleton, p. 235; Boyer, II, p. 7, and elsewhere.

[97] Carleton, p. 123; Boyer, I, p. 330. *English Historical Review*, VI, p. 134ff. The parts of the Carleton story which owe their origin to Freind are those included approximately between pages 123 and 179.

[98] Carleton, p. 237.

least eight editions in English previously to 1728, is the origin of approximately the last half of the "Memoirs."

The nature of the indebtedness of the author of the Carleton story to the Countess's letters was indicated briefly by Colonel Parnell, who cited by page and topic the more striking resemblance between the two works. Upon close examination the borrowings prove indisputable. Carleton's return to England through Spain to St. Jean de Luz follows with minor variations the precise route by which the Countess passed from thence into Spain; they go through the same cities and villages, describe them in the same manner, and have similar adventures by the way.[99]

From the letters of the Countess, moreover, came the more detailed description of famous historical places in Spain, such as the monastery of Montserrat, the city of Saragossa, the water works of Aranjuez, and Madrid and its environs.[100] The two descriptions of Madrid have in common nearly every point mentioned by the author of the "Memoirs." Among many others, they agree in such statements as that Madrid has no walls;[101] that therein ambassadors are exempt from the king's tax on wine;[102] that the large bridge across the Manzanares (which runs dry in summer) gave rise to a jest that the King would have done well to build a river first;[103] that the streets are full of filth, owing to the lack of proper sewage disposal;[104] and that the patron of St. Isadore's chapel rose from being a poor laboring man to sainthood.[105] Each comments, furthermore, upon the fact that the natives seldom drink to excess, owing to the fact that drunkenness incapacitates a man as a witness in court;[106] upon the inferiority of Spanish music and Spanish drama;[107] upon the seclusion of women, the intrigues which they carry on incognito, and the extreme jealousy of husbands, who murder their rivals upon the slightest provocation;[108] upon the Lent ceremonies, and upon the bull feasts, which both describe at great length;[109] upon the Inquisition;[110] upon the fact that no men sleep in the king's house; and upon the four orders of knighthood

---

[99] Carleton, p. 322ff.; D'Aulnoy (1708), p. 2ff.; *English Historical Review*, VI, p. 133ff.

[100] *English Historical Review*, VI, pp. 133-4.

[101] Carleton, p. 304; D'Aulnoy, p. 132.

[102] Carleton, pp. 304-5; D'Aulnoy, p. 134.

[103] Carleton, p. 305; D'Aulnoy, p. 170.

[104] Carleton, p. 318; D'Aulnoy, p. 232.

[105] Carleton, p. 308; D'Aulnoy, p. 151.

[106] Carleton, pp. 272, 3; D'Aulnoy, p. 213.

[107] Carleton, pp. 312-3, and elsewhere; D'Aulnoy, pp. 21, 151, 239, 253, 258.

[108] Carleton, pp. 276-7; D'Aulnoy, pp. 231-5, and elsewhere.

[109] Carleton, p. 263ff.; D'Aulnoy, pp. 178-188.

[110] Carleton, p. 253; D'Aulnoy, p. 242ff.

in Spain.[111] With the countess's acquaintance, Don Augustin Pacheco, compare Carleton's friend, Don Felix Pacheco, erroneously given as Pacheo in the nineteenth century editions of the "Memoirs," one of which Parnell used.[112]

Though this must suffice as an indication of the nature and extent of the borrowings of the author of the "Memoirs" from the Countess's relation, it does not take into account any considerable portion of them. A strict comparison of the pretended observations of Carleton with those of the Countess reveals that a negligible part remains to attribute to Carleton or to the real author.

This survey of the sources of the "Memoirs" has been wearisome, but necessary. The Carleton myth must be effectually laid. The book is not a genuine memoir of Captain George Carleton. Though containing a great deal of fact, it is, in its larger aspects, entirely a fiction, to which Carleton contributed only the title and the path of the action; that is to say, it records many events of history with a fair degree of accuracy, but the accounts of those events are not the genuine reminiscences of any one's experiences. The statements of the narrative are based upon materials gathered painstakingly from Boyer's "William III" and "Queen Anne," Freind's "Account," the D'Aulnoy letters, and the "London Gazette." The fictions are embroidered around facts mentioned in these sources.

It is unthinkable that Carleton could have written a work purporting to be about his own experiences covering a period of forty-one years without manifesting some unmistakable first hand acquaintance with the actions which he was describing. Not only does the "Memoirs" ignore and distort at will events in his life, and attribute to him many actions which prove to be fictitious, but it borrows its narrative from beginning to end. Only childish credulity could lead to continued belief that he had any hand in its concoction.

Just as the "Memoirs" ignores and distorts Carleton's activity, so does it pay no attention to his sentiments. Hardly to be expected from an old soldier is the sententious interest in religion and zeal for protestantism, especially the controversial spirit manifested toward such subtle points of doctrine as predestination and the Roman Catholic doctrine of purgatory. Homilies on drinking and duelling sound even more strange from the pen of a man who had been cashiered for duelling. Equally strong evidence against the supposition that Carleton wrote the book is the fact that Lord Galway, who mercifully befriended him at the time of his court martial and procured him his half-pay pension, and who gave him

[111] Carleton, p. 307; D'Aulnoy, p. 99.
[112] See Scott's edition, p. 319; Carleton, p. 243; D'Aulnoy, p. 195.

employment in Spain, is repeatedly maligned in the "Memoirs." This disposes of Carleton's claim to being the fabricator of a narrative which manifests no interest whatever in his actual conduct.

III. Did Swift Write the "Memoirs"?

The next claimant, Dean Swift, Mr. Doble disposed of long ago. The only forceful argument in favor of Swift is that of Colonel Parnell, who believed that the book was written with Peterborough's knowledge and consent for no other purpose than to rehabilitate the fallen reputation of that nobleman. The earlier account of Carleton's career in Flanders, and the concluding narrative of his sojourn as a prisoner in Spain, Parnell regarded as the prologue and epilogue, respectively, to the drama, or *raison d'être* of the book, the central portion relating to Peterborough's conduct in Spain. Here was the situation as Parnell describes it. In 1728 Peterborough joined with his intimate associates, Swift and Dr. Freind, in a scheme for fabricating this narrative on the basis of some notes or jottings procured by Swift from Carleton, who, a needy old soldier of seventy-six, had been living for many years in Dublin. With information secured from Peterborough and other sources, Swift retired into the country late in the summer of 1728 to frame the narrative which should again make Peterborough a popular hero.[113]

Mr. Doble, however, has pointed out that, though Swift did actually retire into the country during the summer of 1728 conceivably to write, the "Memoirs" was already in print[114] and on sale at the time. During the two years preceding the publication of the book, moreover, Swift was not likely to have lent a hand to such an undertaking. His visit to London in the summer of 1727 was marred by political disappointment, physical weakness, and the certainty that Stella could not long survive.[115] His gloom was deepened in August by reports that she was sinking. In September he said to Sheridan, "I am able to hold up my sorry head no longer." After contemplating turning his back on his misery by going to France, he changed his mind and, in October, returned to Dublin. Stella died at the very end of January, and the "Memoirs" came out in London on the 16th of May.

Colonel Parnell's clever assumption that the "Memoirs" was a bit of propaganda issued by Peterborough and his friends, likewise, proves to be erroneous. For neither Peterborough himself nor any of his associates

---

[113] *English Historical Review,* VI, pp. 149-150.

[114] *Academy,* XLIII, p. 394.

[115] The facts of Swift's life have been taken from Leslie Stephen's account in the *Dictionary of National Biography.* See also, the *Academy,* XLIII, p. 394.

ever betrayed any knowledge of the scheme. Pope, who could not have been left out of such a secret, shows clearly that he knew nothing of the matter. For his letter to Aaron Hill, written three years later, expressed regret that Peterborough had *not* had his papers put together and published in order to create a more favorable opinion of his activity in Spain, and the hope that Hill himself, than whom (Pope says) no one was better qualified for the task, was contemplating the carrying out of that scheme.[116] Obviously, then, Swift had not previously to 1731 taken part in a plan for retrieving Peterborough's lost reputation by editing a narrative founded upon his papers. That the "Memoirs" praises Peterborough highly, I grant; but that praise came from another admirer than Swift.

Further evidence that Swift had no part in the composition of the work may be found in its style and its tone. There is, as Mr. Doble has remarked, a triteness about many of its passages which Swift could not have endured.[117] This is well illustrated in such phrases as "what Sir Walter Raleigh finely calls," "the immortal Shakespeare," and "the excellent Hudibras," and in such circumlocutions as these: "But my good fortunes not allowing me to participate in those glorious append-ages of the English arms" (meaning Marlborough's victories in Flanders), and "under this sort of uncertain settlement I remain'd with the patience of a Jew, though not with Judaical absurdity, a faithful adherer to my ex-pectation."[118] Such affected and awkward sentences cannot, I think, be paralleled in any of Swift's known writings. Professor Saintsbury's opinion that as concerns matters of style the "Memoirs" should be at-tributed to Swift rather than to Defoe is complimentary neither to his own judgment, nor to Swift's prose style.

A final reason for denying to Swift the doubtful honor of having been the fabricator of the Carleton story is the fact that the opinions and senti-ments therein expressed towards various historical characters are violently opposed to the known and frequently spoken opinion of Swift towards these men. Were there no other evidence, this alone would suffice to eliminate him from consideration. Lord Cutts, whom Swift had vilified repeatedly and upon whom he had poured the biting venom of his hatred in the "Salamander," is made to play an honorable part in the story and given high praise.[119] Steele, of whom Swift wrote in the following year,

> Thus Steele who own'd what others writ,
> And flourished by imputed wit,
> From perils of a hundred jayles,
> Withdrew to starve and dye in Wales,

[116] *Academy*, XLIII, p. 394.
[117] *Academy*, XLIII, p. 439.
[118] Carleton, pp. 72, 74.
[119] *Ibid.*, pp. 74-5.

is referred to courteously in the "Memoirs" as "Mr. Steel, now Sir Richard." Equally unexplainable, were Swift the author, would be the praise of Stanhope, a staunch Whig, a manager of Sacheverell's trial, and a poor general, and the dedication to Lord Wilmington. The latter, from whom Swift could have had no hope of preferment, having written shortly before the "Memoirs" was published, "As to Richmond Lodge and Market Hill, they are abandoned as much as Sir Spencer Compton," is praised for his services to the cause of liberty,—an obvious reference to his part in the trial of Sacheverell. Though Swift must have despised Sacheverell, he could not have, as Mr. Doble has remarked, considered his Whig prosecutors as acting in the cause of liberty.[120]

There is, then, not only insurmountable external evidence against attributing the "Memoirs" to Swift, but, also, equally strong internal indication that he had no part in its fabrication. He may, therefore, be dismissed from further consideration.

IV. *Did Defoe Write the "Memoirs"?*

But what is true of Carleton and Swift, namely, that every indication is against their having participated in the composition of the book, is distinctly untrue of Defoe, the only other writer seriously suggested as the author. The more closely the book is examined the more convincing is the proof that it came from his pen. Everything that we know of his style, method of composition, interests in history and books of travel, his frequent phrases in foreign languages, especially French and Latin, his use of sources, his favorite sentiments and ideas and anecdotes, his moral seriousness and interest in religious controversy, and the impudence with which he put forth fiction as fact,—all these we find abundantly manifested in the "Memoirs."

Colonel Parnell, who argued strenuously that Swift was the writer of the story, excluded Defoe upon such grounds as his sturdy manly honesty and his illiteracy; that is to say, his lack of acquaintance with the classical languages quotations from which abound in the book. He is of course thinking of the Defoe of Chalmers and the earlier nineteenth century biographers, rather than of the Defoe revealed to us through the researches of Mr. Lee, Mr. Aitken, and Professor Trent. Parnell, moreover, shows no familiarity with the works of Defoe, in which occur frequently classical quotations of a sort precisely like those in the "Memoirs."

Whereas, as we have seen, there are serious external reasons why in the year or two previously to the publication of the Carleton story Swift would not have been likely to attempt such a work, no such obstacles are

[120] *Academy*, XLIII, pp. 394, 462.

known to exist in the case of Defoe. In 1728 he was in London, actively engaged in writing under pseudonyms works of various sorts.[121] Though it is true that after 1724, when the "New Voyage" appeared, he is not known to have produced an original fictitious narrative of any considerable length, he was, as we have good reason to believe, writing accounts with a basis in the experiences of actual adventurers. Works of a nature similar to that of the Carleton story which have long passed for authentic but which recent investigators think were at least in part reworked by Defoe are the "Voyages of Captain George Roberts" (1726) and "Madagascar: or Robert Drury's Journal" (1729).[122]

But as Carleton and Swift lived in Dublin, whereas Defoe was a Londoner, Parnell thinks it more likely that Swife rather than Defoe should have come in contact with the old soldier. We know, however, from records in the Treasury Office[123] that so late as 1722 Carleton was still petitioning for pay for his services during the war in Spain which had closed a decade earlier; there is more than a suggestion of this very thing in the "Memoirs," where mention is made of his attending some years after (that is, after 1706) the meetings "at their house in Darby Court in Channel Row" of "the commissioners for stating the debts due to the army."[124] At such a time he must have been, as the narrative suggests, present in London with memoranda drawn showing not only the nature and extent of his services in Spain, but those also of his earlier career. That Defoe, who was in the employ of Stanhope and other government officials as late as 1718 and possibly even later, after Carleton is known to have begun his petitioning for back pay,[125] may have come in contact with Carleton at this time and procured from him an oral or a brief written sketch of his service is not improbable. 1722 is the year of the publication of the "Memoirs of a Cavalier," and conceivably Defoe at the time may have been gathering more materials for similar works. There is evidence, moreover, of Carleton's having been in London even later than 1722. For upon his death prior to December 4, 1730, the execution of his will was left to his principal creditor, a Mary Toms, of St. Margaret's Parish, Westminster. Is it not of significance that at his death he should have been indebted to some one in or near London? And, though the matter is of little importance, since we know almost nothing of the movements of either Carleton or Defoe during the years preceding 1728, Defoe was

[121] Trent, *Defoe*, p. 257ff.

[122] Trent, *Defoe*, p. 262; Pasfield Oliver, Introduction to *Madagascar* (1890).

[123] Calendar of Treasury Papers, 1720-1728, CCXLI, 1722, pt. i, p. 177, "Report of the Commissioners for examining debts due to the army . . . "

[124] P. 170. See also a similar statement on p. 108.

[125] *English Historical Review*, VI, p. 109.

not completely out of touch with Dubin. Late in 1725 the first volume of his "Complete English Tradesman" was issued there by subscription.[126] Slight as all this is, it indicates that Carleton was not out of communication with London and that Defoe had interests in Dublin. Further than this we are not likely to get.

But whether or not Defoe and Carleton ever met or were ever in direct communication, there can be no reasonable doubt that Defoe wrote the "Memoirs" using the pretended author's career as a nucleus about which to gather a cluster of incidents, some true and some false, but practically all taken, not from Carleton's memory or diary, but from previously published histories and newspapers.

The "Memoirs" are obviously like all of Defoe's other long narratives, being fiction with a slight basis in fact, but parading as entirely genuine. "Robinson Crusoe," "Captain Singleton," "Journal of the Plague Year," "Moll Flanders," "Memoirs of a Cavalier," "Colonel Jacque," "Roxana," and the "New Voyage," all pretend to be historical accounts. The story of Colonel Jacque was in 1734 included in a collection of lives of actual rogues.[127] The frequency with which his "Journal of the Plague Year" and his "Memoirs of a Cavalier" have imposed even upon discriminating readers is well known. The latter work, especially, had to undergo a long period of uncertainty before being admitted to the list of Defoe's writings. So late as 1895, on the eve of the publication of Mr. Aitken's edition of the Defoe narratives, the "Athenæum" expressed grave doubts as to the propriety of incuding the Cavalier's story. The weight of Mr. Aitken's authority, however, and that of Professor Trent's, seem to have silenced all opposition.[128]

The resemblance of the Carleton narrative to that of the Cavalier is indisputable. Both are strictly military in their scope, telling nothing of the inner lives of their heroes. The Cavalier, if he was an actual person such as Carleton was, may or may not have been married; the story gives no hint of it. Carleton we know had a wife and three children at least,[129] but such matters do not find a place in his story. There are related, to be sure, some adventures of gallantry in Spain. But, though almost wholly invented from anecdotes in the Countess D'Aulnoy letters, these adventures are very similar to experiences in the continental military

---

[126] Curiously enough, one of the subscribers was a "Josh. Carleton," who obligated himself for a half-dozen copies.

[127] Captain Charles Johnson, *Lives and Adventures of the Highwaymen.*

[128] *Athenæum*, 30 March, 1895, p. 408.

[129] *English Historical Review*, VI, p. 109. Colonel Parnell thinks there is a possibility that Carleton was not actually married, Galway's phrase, "une femme," being capable of two interpretations.

careers of both the Cavalier and Colonel Jacque, and suggestive of the creator of Moll Flanders and Roxana.

The similarity of the situation in the three narratives, namely, those of the Cavalier, Colonel Jacque, and Carleton, is significant. The Cavalier, having journeyed through France into Italy where, as an onlooker, he accompanied for a time the Duke of Montmorency's army, leisurely travelled about previously to joining the forces of Gustavus Adolphus in Germany. He is made to comment upon the character of the Italians (as Carleton does upon that of the Spaniards), and to tell particularly of his adventures with a woman of splendid equipage who nevertheless turned out to be a courtesan.[130] Similarly Carleton is lured into an acquaintance with an agreeable Spanish woman whose inquiries were "not often improper" and from whose designs he is finally saved through the warning of the daughter of the woman with whom he had his lodgings.[131]

Like the Cavalier and Carleton, Colonel Jacque at one time became engaged in the continental wars, serving in the French army in 1701 and 1702. At this point his story takes on a tone identical with that of the other two more strictly military narratives. Precisely as Carleton is made to tell of his great exploit at the capture of Lethindy Castle, so Colonel Jacque relates that his intrepid action saved Cremona from the attack of the enemy; as a result, the conduct of each is mentioned "with some particularities" in an "account to the court" and each is rewarded with a promotion: Lieutenant Carleton becoming a captain, and Captain Jacque becoming a lieutenant colonel.[132] Like Carleton, furthermore, Colonel Jacque later was made prisoner and sent on parole to Trent among the Milanese, and like him was in the good graces of the daughter of the family with whom he lodged.[133]

I have already stated that the Carleton story deals largely with the general features of campaigns, and with the policies of statesmen and generals behind the action, and that it gives the impression of having been written either by an historian or by some general or statesman who had no local or particular viewpoint. Precisely this may be said of both the "Memoirs of a Cavalier" and the military portions of "Colonel Jacque." All three are continually pointing out the reasons why Richelieu, or the Prince of Orange, or Prince Eugene did thus and thus. The old Queen Mother of France, the Cavalier thought, understood better than Charles I how to handle popular outbursts.[134]

---

[130] *Memoirs of a Cavalier* (Everyman), p. 30.
[131] Carleton, p. 276ff.
[132] Carleton, p. 45; *Colonel Jacque,* II (Aitken edition), p. 42.
[133] *Colonel Jacque,* II, p. 58.
[134] *Memoirs of a Cavalier,* p. 17.

That in the account of Carleton's action in the battle of Seneffe the author is satirizing the military profession has been argued by Colonel Parnell, who believed that Carleton is made to proclaim his conduct as unsoldierly in a memoir which is ostensibly written to set forth his valor. This he used as evidence for assuming Swift to have been the author. But Colonel Parnell is evidently unfamiliar with these earlier adventures of the Cavalier, in which he too shows a wholesome regard for his flesh by twice fleeting at the first assault. "I was," he says concerning the first occasion, "but a raw soldier, and did not like the sport at all . . . . I ran away very fairly, and my companion with me . . . . and being not much known in the army, we came into the camp in an hour or two after, as if we had been only riding abroad for the air." The second time he took refuge in a wood.[135] This tallies exactly with Carleton's account, which I have shown to be a fabrication, of how he fled at the Prince of Condé's first attack, and climbing over a hedge by jumping upon the backs of his scrambling comrades, escaped to a place of safety.

The whole action of the battle of Seneffe gives every indication of having been written by the pen which recounted the engagement just cited from the Cavalier's story. It is a strange coincidence that a long sentence forming a whole paragraph in the latter narrative should reappear with slight changes in the other, a sentence, moreover, which Parnell believed to have been plagiarized from Temple and which does actually owe something to Boyer.

Boyer, "William III," I, p. 51.

"If the Prince of Condé had contented himself with his success . . . he had left no dispute of a victory; but lured on by the hope of one more entire . . . He followed . . . and drawing out his whole army . . . brought it to a set battle."

Carleton, p. 14.

"Had the Prince of Condé contented himself with his share of good fortune, his victory had been uncontested: but being push'd by a vehement heat . . . he resolv'd to force the whole confederate army to a battle."

"Memoirs of a Cavalier," p. 22.

"Had the Duke of Savoy contented himself with the defeat of five regiments . . . he had come off with honor; but endeavouring to break the whole party . . . the obstinate resistance . . . lost him his advantages . . . and had not night parted them he had been entirely defeated."

This type of sentence is common with Defoe, as is illustrated by an example in "Robinson Crusoe,"

[135] *Ibid.*, pp. 20-23.

"Had William Atkins and his men retired immediately as soon as they had fired . . . the savages had been effectually routed. . . . But . . . ,"

and a similar one in "Colonel Jacque."[136] Consequently when he ran across Boyer's "if" clause, he instinctively substituted for it the "had . . . . had" construction which was more in keeping with his own practice.

It is my opinion that not a great deal of search would be required to show that the continental adventures of the Cavalier and of Colonel Jacque are based upon published histories and newspapers just as the Carleton story is. In fact, there is already partial proof of the assertion; Mr. Aitken pointed out that the Cavalier's adventures under Gustavus Adolphus were indebted to the "Swedish Intelligencer," and that his later career in the English civil wars occasionally shows traces of the influence of the memoirs of Ludlow and Whitelock.[137] The three narratives, those of the Cavalier, Colonel Jacque, and Carleton, are alike in substance, giving attention chiefly to the larger features of the campaigns which could be found in printed records, and setting forth their hero's adventures in the same style and with similar details.

Defoe's knowledge of history is amazingly wide, if not always accurate. A glance at his numerous works of an historical character, including of course the stories of the Cavalier and of Colonel Jacque, well illustrate that fact. His earlier poems, such as the "True-Born Englishman," and the others contained in the collected editions of 1703 and 1705, allude to many of the events described in the three fictions which I have been comparing. Among others he speaks of Seneffe and relates the incident of the holding Mareschal Boufflers at the surrender of Namur, an incident related also in the Carleton story.[138] The engagement of Solebay with which that story opens Defoe had described four years earlier in the "Tour."

He is, moreover, constantly commenting upon the policies of commanders and statesmen, showing, in fact, all the interests and information which we should expect on the part of the author of the "Memoirs." As early as 1697, in the "Essay on Projects," he showed his interest in broad schemes for national development; the "Shortest Way," "Hannibal at the Gates," "What if the Pretender should come?" "Secret History of the White Staff," and "Plan of the English Commerce," are a few of the many of his writings which illustrate this trait of his thinking.

The method of securing the materials for the Carleton narrative agrees with what we know of his procedure in his other novels. In "Robinson

---

[136] *Robinson Crusoe*, II, p. 94; *Colonel Jacque*, II, p. 60.
[137] Introduction to *Memoirs of a Cavalier*, pp. xv, xvi, xvii.
[138] *Works*, I (1703), p. 26; II (1705), p. 128ff.; *Tour*, I, i, p. 83.

Crusoe" and "Captain Singleton," we have seen, he turns to the records of previous writers for the background of his story. Crusoe's voyage from Bengal to the coast of China is based upon Dampier's account of a voyage over precisely the same route; his journey from Peking to Archangel traverses the path which Ides had marked out. Defoe's use of Ides's narrative is precisely the use made in the Carleton story of the D'Aulnoy letters. Just as Crusoe travels from *China* to *Russia* over the course by which Ides had gone from *Russia to China,* so Carleton travels through *Spain into France* by the route marked out for him by the Countess D'Aulnoy in going from *France into Spain.* In each case the hero is reversing the direction of the original journey.

All this is typical of Defoe's interest in works of travel and in topography. Practically all his novels reveal such interests, and nearly all have land journeys. Crusoe, at the end of Part I, returns to England from Lisbon overland through Spain and France; at the end of Part II he sets out homeward from China by way of Tartary and Muscovy. Singleton and Avery (Defoe's), upon quitting the pirate trade, return overland from Asia to Europe. Singleton's hazardous venture across Africa, and that of the unnamed hero of the "New Voyage" across the Andes of South America are other illustrations of this fact. More like the leisurely journey of Carleton through Spain, is the Cavalier's wandering through France, Italy, and Germany, and his indulgence in various diversions by the way.

Shortly before 1728, moreover, Defoe had written the "Tour," a three volume work purporting to recount a series of journeys about in England.[139] In it he follows the narrative method, telling as he passes from point to point what he saw and heard that was of interest, including the physiographical features of the country, the occupations of the people, and various incidents and anecdotes. The later portions of the Carleton narrative, especially, betrays this same interest in topography. Though detailed to act as engineer to a besieged city, Carleton loiters several days on the way in order to visit the famous monastery at Montserrat, which he describes at length. The bull feast, similarly, is one of many such customs which he describes in detail. The relation of the journey home at the end of the war is, as we have seen, precisely in the manner of Defoe's stories of travel, and like them is fabricated from the account of an actual traveller.

There are a number of other such manifestations in the "Memoirs" of interest in books of travel. Carleton's description of the locusts which

---

[139] *A Tour thro' the Whole Island of Great Britain,* I (1724), II (1725), III (1727).

swept across the Mediterranean from the Barbary coast to Spain gives strong indication of being borrowed from Purchas. The latter's condensation of John Leo's history of Africa tells of a swarm of locusts in Morocco which covered the surface of the earth and devoured the crops. A more significant instance, resembling in detail the Carleton account, Purchas gives in his report of Sir Francis Alvarez's journey to the court of Prester John in Ethiopia. Both Carleton and Alvarez speak of the number of insects as sufficient to hide the sun; both speak next of their devastations: they consume the leaves from the trees and every thing green; both relate that the insects finally perish in the streams and lakes, after which their bodies are left in heaps (mountains, says Alvarez; hills, says Carleton); and finally both mention the intercession of priests in behalf of the plague stricken people.[140] Who is more likely than Defoe to have recalled from his reading in Purchas this account of African locusts? That he speaks of Barbary locusts in the "Complete English Tradesman" is the assertion of Mr. Doble.[141]

Incidents similarly indicative of Defoe's interests in such matters are the storm which swept over the camp in Flanders the evening of Carleton's arrival there in 1674, and the earthquake related as occurring soon after. The storm was an actual event, the account of which we have traced to its source in the "Gazette," though a report of it in the "Memoirs" of Temple is alluded to therein. Defoe's interests in storms is well known. He seized the opportunity of issuing with copious details from all parts of England a description of the great November storm of 1703. And in that work, as I have intimated, he quotes in full the very passage from the Temple memoirs to which the Carleton account alludes. Two important storms figure in "Robinson Crusoe," and in both the "Storm" and "Robinson Crusoe," moreover, earthquakes are described.[142]

Carleton's comparison of the opening at the top of a hill to the "mouth of one of our coal pits," and of the habitations of the Highlanders to the huts of the Arabs and Tartars, and his reference to the Potosi mines, likewise, point to the Defoe of the "Tour" and of the books of travel.[143] Not only had he described the coal mines of northern England in the "Tour," but in "Robinson Crusoe" he had described the dwellings of the Tartars,[144] and in half a dozen places, according to Mr. Doble, he had

---

[140] Purchas, V, p. 364; VII, p. 29ff.; Carleton, pp. 234-5.

[141] *Academy*, XLIII, p. 462. The phrase "thick as the locusts which in Egypt swarmed," in the *True-Born Englishman*, is an obvious allusion to the Mosaic account of the plagues in Egypt.

[142] *Robinson Crusoe*, I, p. 88; *Storm*, p. 225.

[143] Carleton, pp. 40, 172, 308.

[144] *Robinson Crusoe*, II, p. 295.

mentioned the famous Potosi mines of South America, which figure so prominently in seventeenth century voyages.[145]   Another incident which points significantly to Purchas as its origin is that of the stratagem by which Carleton in 1696 outwitted a party from a nearby French garrison.[146]

Pointing likewise to Defoe are a number of devices manifested in the "Memoirs" and in the management of its publication.   The significance of the change of title has been pointed out by Mr. Doble.[147]   The book, first issued as "The Memoirs of an English Officer. . . . By Capt. George Carleton," was about ten days later reissued as "The Military Memoirs of Capt. George Carleton. . . . "   Obviously the work was not selling rapidly,—a condition which the new title page was intended to remedy. Similar substitutions of new title pages in the known works of Defoe were made in the case of "The Storm," "Conjugal Lewdness," and the "Essay on Apparitions."

Like Singleton and the Cavalier, not to mention a number of Defoe's minor characters, Carleton is credited with a knowledge of Latin.   His restless disposition which induced him to engage in the wars in Flanders and later forced him into the conflict in Spain, links him more closely to Crusoe and to nearly all of Defoe's heroes.[148]

Other instances of Defoe's literary mannerisms abound in the "Memoirs."   There are two formulas with which incidents are, in general, introduced in the "Memoirs"; one of these is the phrase, "I cannot (or must not) omit here"; the other is, "I remember."   The first, apparently, is used when the author is inserting an anecdote of his own in what he considers a fitting place; the second, when he is trying to give an air of genuineness to incidents which he is borrowing from the histories before him.   The former, occurring no less than six times in the "Memoirs," Defoe had employed frequently in the first volume of the "Tour," in one case using it both at the beginning and at the end.   Four instances of the use of the phrase may be found in the "Storm," and numberless variations of it in "Duncan Campbell."[149]   The other phrase, "I remember," used in the Carleton narrative seven times, is sufficiently prevalent in the acknowledged writings of Defoe, occurring a half dozen times in "Duncan Camp-

[145] For Defoe's mention of the Potosi mines, Mr. Doble (*Academy*, XLIII, p. 483) cites: *Complete English Tradesman* (1841), p. 256; *Review*, III, 16; *New Voyage* (1724), p. 363ff.; and *Complete English Gentleman*, p. 105.

[146] Carleton, p. 65ff.; Purchas, XVII, pp. 95-6.

[147] *Academy*, XLIII, p. 394.

[148] *Captain Singleton*, p. 5; *Memoirs of a Cavalier*, p. 7; Carleton, p. 78.

[149] Carleton, pp. 5, 9, 109, 121, 122, 311; *Tour*, I, i, p. 87; iii, pp. 62, 77, 78, 93; *Storm*, pp. 77, 199, 271; *Duncan Campbell* (1720), pp. 124, 140, and elsewhere.

bell," and elsewhere.[150] The trite manner employed in the "Memoirs" to introduce quotations has already been pointed out as evidence that Swift did not compose the work. Precisely similar to Carleton's "the immortal Shakespeare" and "the excellent Hudibras," are Defoe's "the immortal Virgil," "the famous Torquatus Tasso," and "the learned Camerarius,"—all from "Duncan Campbell."[151] The sentence with which Carleton closes the anecdote of Spragge's pigeons, "What sort of instinct this could proceed from, I leave to the curious," is almost precisely that with which Defoe, in the "Tour," concludes a similar anecdote about swallows: "How these creatures know . . . . this . . . . we must leave to the naturalists." Other uses of this phraseology appear in the "Memoirs" as well as in the "Tour" and "Duncan Campbell."[152] Carleton's "true Englishmen" and "true-born Spaniard" suggest Defoe's best-known poem, the "True-Born Englishman."[153] That Defoe liked in this way to call attention to his previous writings is evident from the manner in which he plays upon the phrase, "the shortest way," in his tracts.

The use of the qualifying adverb with adjectives is common to the "Memoirs" and the known works of Defoe. Such combinations as "transcendently odoriferous," frequent in the Carleton story, are in strict accord with Defoe's "inimitably resolute," "eminently wicked," and "agreeably pleasant."[154]

Carleton's "bigots of bigotry" is suggestive of Crusoe's "bubbles of all bubbles."[155] Compare, likewise, the former's "Quixotism" and "incendiarism" with Defoe's Jacobitism, devilism, wizardism, epicurism, idolism, beauism, and blockheadism.[156] Carleton coins "impocketed,' and Defoe coins "implunged," "enregistered," and "enarched." The exclamation, "No!" occurs three times in the "Memoirs" and frequently in the known writings of Defoe. Carleton's use of "our naturalists" is common with Defoe; it occurs also in works of travel, of which he was a wide reader.[157]

Suggestive of Defoe, furthermore, is Carleton's phrase, "a rape upon nature." For in the "Complete English Tradesman" he had written: " . . . . raising plants by mere violence, and . . . . a rape upon the earth

---

[150] Carleton, pp. 7, 30, 31, 193, 221, 225, 314; *Duncan Campbell*, pp. 69, 106, 211, 226, 240, 282; *Tour*, I, i, p. 131.

[151] Carleton, pp. 42, 71; *Duncan Campbell*, pp. 112, 193, 198, 240, 278.

[152] Carleton, pp. 9, 235; *Tour*, I, i, p. 119; *Duncan Campbell*, pp. 78, 242.

[153] Carleton, pp. 48, 279.

[154] For fuller consideration, see Mr. Doble's discussion in the *Academy*, XLIII, p. 438.

[155] Carleton, p. 184; *Robinson Crusoe*, III (1720), p. 263.

[156] *Academy*, XLIII, p. 438.

[157] Carleton, p. 9; *Storm*, p. 12; *History of the Devil*, p. 328, and elsewhere; *Academy*, XLIII, p. 438.

. . . . what rapes are committed upon nature . . . "; and in "Robinson Crusoe" he referred to the solitude of a hermit as causing "his soul to commit a rape upon his body" and as being "a rape upon nature."[158] Both Carleton and Defoe, as Mr. Doble has observed, appear to have forgotten their Euclid. The former refers to the difference between Whigs and Tories as being as unreconcilable as "direct angles," and the latter speaks of "all sorts of indirect angles."[159]

The few French phrases in the Carleton narrative, such as "en passant," and "minister petite," are of a kind with those frequently employed by Defoe. "En passant" occurs in the Cavalier story and in the "Tour." The introduction to the first part of the "Complete English Tradesman" has the phrase, "so 'opinionatre,' as the French well express it"; and the "Tour" has a similar remark.[160] Most of the Spanish words used in the "Memoirs" appear also in the acknowledged works of Defoe. Carleton's one venture into Italian is not without significance. He speaks of the donkey of Montserrat as "the poor Borigo," and Defoe, in the "Essay on Apparitions," refers to one as "a poor Boricco, as the Italians call him."[161]

Turning next to the ideas and sentiments expressed in the "Memoirs," we shall see that all of those circumstances which conflicted with our assuming either Carleton or Swift to have been the author, fall into harmony if, instead, we suppose Defoe to have composed it. The inconsistency of asserting that Swift wrote the numerous passages warmly praising his known enemies was fully realized by Colonel Parnell; he was, therefore, compelled to torture those passages into giving a satiric meaning. No such straining after consistency, however, is necessary if we accept Defoe as the writer.

The attitude of the "Memoirs" towards the various characters mentioned therein is that of Defoe. The dedication praises Wilmington for his services in the cause of liberty,—an allusion, as has already been pointed out, to his part in the prosecution of Sacheverell, who was for years one of Defoe's favorite bugbears.[162] The frequent but judicious praise of William III is to be expected from the author of "The True-Born Englishman," who had been favored by the attention of that mon-

---

[158] Carleton, p. 233ff.; *Complete English Tradesman*, I (1841), p. 288; *Robinson Crusoe*, III, p. 6.

[159] Carleton, p. 350; *Review*, II, p. 476. For additional examples of the similarity of Carleton's and Defoe's vocabulary see Mr. Doble's article, *Academy*, XLIII, p. 438.

[160] *Memoirs of a Cavalier*, p. 122; *Tour*, I, ii, p. 124.

[161] Carleton, p. 219; *Apparitions,* p. 373. The last reference is from Mr. Doble, *Academy*, XLIII, p. 438.

[162] *Academy*, XLIII, p. 394.

arch, but who was aware of his faults. The courteous reference to Sir Richard Steele, of whom Swift spoke in the most biting terms, points likewise to Defoe who admired him.[163] Likewise admired by Defoe was Lord Cutts, the hero of many campaigns, and Peterborough, whose "fire and fury" he praised in the "Review." Upon Stanhope the "Memoirs" goes out of its way to lavish praise; he was not a good general, he meant nothing to Carleton, and he was probably unacquainted with Swift, differing from him in both politics and religion. Defoe, however, had been in Stanhope's pay in 1718, and had, therefore, a particular reason to be grateful to him. Mr. Doble thinks, moreover, that, though in 1728 Stanhope was dead, Defoe by thus praising him was trying to curry favor with his kinsman, the Earl of Chesterfield. The competence of Galway, to whom Carleton was under deep obligation, but whom the "Memoirs" maligns fulsomely, Defoe had discussed in the "Review."[164]

It has hitherto passed unobserved that likewise reconcilable with previous utterances of Defoe is the defense of James II, against whom he took up arms in 1688, and perhaps in 1685 also. Tolerance is one of his characteristics. We find him in "Robinson Crusoe" speaking of the Catholic missionaries not without praise and even allowing one to direct the spiritual welfare of the colony on Crusoe's island. In the "Memoirs of a Cavalier" and elsewhere, this staunch Whig and dissenter extenuates the conduct of Charles I. So in the "Tour" he wrote with identically the same attitude towards James II which the author of the Carleton story manifests.

"I am very sensible," remarks the author of the "Memoirs," "later times have not been over favourable in their sentiments of *that unfortunate Prince's* valour, yet *I cannot omit* the doing a piece of justice to his memory." In like manner Defoe, speaking in the "Tour" of the little place where James II was made prisoner in his flight of 1688, says: "*I must mention it* to the reproach of the people of Feversham, let the conduct of *that unfortunate Prince* be what it will, that the . . . . rabble can never be excus'd, who treated the King . . . . with the utmost indecency . . . . till some neighboring gentlemen . . . . who understood their duty better . . . . preserv'd (him) from farther violence. . . ."[165]

The failure to mention the Glencoe massacre in connection with the fort at Inverlochy, and the remarks at the end of the "Memoirs" concerning the peace of Utrecht are other manifestations of Defoe's political sympathies. The massacre, which occurred just a month before Carleton's

---

[163] *Ibid.*, p. 394.

[164] *Academy*, XLIII, p. 394; *Review*, III, pp. 219, 386; Carleton, p. 238.

[165] Carleton, p. 4; *Tour*, I, ii, p. 31.

actual departure from Scotland to join Tiffin's at Portsmouth, Swift could not possibly have overlooked. The fort at Inverlochy Defoe had described in the "Tour." Concerning the peace of Utrecht, Carleton remarks that upon his arrival in London at the end of the war he found "some arraigning, and some extolling of a peace; in which time has shown both were wrong." Swift, as Mr. Doble points out, had taken too partisan a share in the negotiations to allude to it so; whereas Defoe, though he argued for it at the time as the best thing to be done under the circumstances, later expressed no sympathy with it.[166]

Adding to the weight of the similarities already presented as existing between the author of the "Memoirs" and Defoe is the great number of favorite ideas which they have in common. One of these is the subject of birds. In addition to the anecdote of Spragge's pigeons, Carleton mentions them upon a number of occasions and in a manner suggestive of Defoe. The body of Sandwich, Carleton relates, was discovered through the presence of gulls hovering over it as it floated at sea,—a detail clearly added by the author, since it was not present in his source. The soldiers' hats flying about during a windstorm he can "resemble . . . . to nothing better than those flights of rooks, which at dusk . . . . seek their roosting places." The single file march of the Highlanders reminds him of "geeze in a string." His gazing at a flock of ducks in the water before him gives him timely notice of the beginning of an earthquake. And while a prisoner in Spain he sees a "most surprising flock of eagles." In the first volume only of the "Tour" Defoe had four years earlier written of eagles, swallows, swans on a lake, and the crows or Cornish Choughs of Scilly.[167]

But of especial significance, it seems to me, is an anecdote concerning swallows which Defoe relates immediately following his summary in the "Tour" of the Solebay fight; for the author of the Carleton story, likewise, concludes his account of Solebay with an anecdote of birds, that of Spragge's pigeons. The two stories are as follows.

"Memoirs," pp. 9, 10.

"I cannot here omit one thing, which to some *may seem trifling;* though I am apt to think our *naturalists* may have a different opinion of it, and find it afford their fansies no *undiverting* employment . . . We had on board the London . . . *a great number of pidgeons,* of which our commander was very fond. These, on the first firing of our cannon, dispers'd . . . and were seen no where near us during the fight. The next day . . . a brisk gale . . . drove our fleet some leagues to the southward . . . yet the day after they all returned safe aboard; . . . some persons admiring at the manner of their return . . . Sir Edward Sprage told them, that

---

[166] *Academy,* XLIII, pp. 462, 483.
[167] Carleton, pp. 4, 9, 12, 40, 50, 250; *Tour,* I, iii, pp. 62, 70, 126.

. . . when he left the Revenge . . . to go aboard the London, all those pidgeons, of their own accord . . . left the Revenge likewise, and removed on board the London, where I saw them. . . What sort of instinct this could proceed from, *I leave to the curious."*

"Tour," I, i, p. 83ff.

" . . . I think the following remark, tho' of so *trifling* a circumstance, may be both instructing, as well as *diverting.* . . I was some years before at this place . . . and observ'd in the evening *an unusual multitude* of birds sitting on . . . the church; curiosity led me to go nearer to see what they were, and I found they were all swallows . . . this led me to enquire of a grave gentleman . . . what the meaning was . . . I perceive, Sir, says he, you are a stranger to it; you must then understand . . . that this is the season . . . when the swallows . . . return to the country . . . from whence . . . they came; and this being the nearest to the coast of Holland, they come here to embark . . . and now, Sir, says he, the weather being too calm, or the wind contrary, they are waiting for a gale. . .

"This was more evident . . . when in the morning I found the wind had come about to the northwest in the night, and there was not one swallow to be seen, of near a million, which I believe was there the night before.

"How these creatures know that this . . . is the way to their home . . . *we must leave to the naturalists. . . "*

Is it not strange that two different authors should tell two stories of such similarity and connect them, not only with the same region, but also with the same event? Both Defoe and the author of the "Memoirs" associate birds with the idea of Solebay and the battle there. Attention further should be called to the fact that the similarity of the two anecdotes extends even to the phraseology employed. In each case the author has emphasized the large number of the birds, and has the point of interest lie in the question of instinct which guides their movements. Both, furthermore, begin with the apology that though the circumstance may be trifling it is diverting, and end with statements that are almost word for word the same. The inference that Defoe, having fabricated the Carleton account of the Solebay fight and desiring to give the atmosphere of genuine memoir to what is otherwise a common-place history, had recourse to the ideas which he connected with Southwold in the "Tour," written four years earlier, can hardly be evaded. Obviously the story of the swallows could not be repeated; so a similar one was substituted.

A second favorite topic common to the Carleton memoirs and to Defoe's "Tour" is that of powder explosions. Excluding the incident of the powder ship on the Maes, and the springing of the famous mine at the siege of Alicante (which Defoe describes in Applebee's "Original Weekly Journal"), Carleton tells of one considerable explosion and of two that were narrowly averted. One of the latter was in the Tower of London; some flooring gave way allowing 20,000 barrels of powder to drop upon other barrels of powder on the floor beneath. That "not one nail . . . .

in that large fabrick, should afford one little spark to enflame that mass of sulphurous matter" to the destruction of the entire city, perhaps, was a "providence strangely neglected at that time," he remarks. Upon another occasion in Flanders, a spy attempted to ignite the whole train of ammunition wagons.

The last powder incident related by the author is said to have occurred in Spain. Carleton was in charge of forty-five barrels of powder, which, through the carelessness of a Spanish civilian, was exploded. The concussion "threw down tiles, windows, chimney and all." Carleton's lieutenant, asleep nearby, was blown "all to pieces, several of his limbs being found separate . . . . all the soldiers who were standing . . . . were struck dead. . . ."[168]

To Defoe's interest in such explosions I have called attention in my consideration of "Captain Singleton." There, in the story of the siege of the hollow tree, he had related how Quaker William placed a mine in the mouth of the cave beneath the tree and therewith blew the native garrison out another opening. Like the victims of Carleton's explosion, they were pitifully torn and mangled, some of whom had "no arms, some no legs, some no head." Attention likewise has been called to a coal mine explosion related in the "Tour," with results similar to those just referred to in the Singleton and the Carleton narratives. Even Crusoe, it will be remembered, was so afraid of a sudden shock that would set off all his powder at one blast that he divided it into small parcels and placed them far apart.

Two other explosions, described in the "Tour," are significantly like the one experienced by Carleton in Spain. One occurred at the Woolwich ammunition works "in the time of a Dutch war." By accident a shell was ignited, blowing up "all the works with such a terrible blast and noise, as shook and shattered the whole town of Woolwich almost in pieces," and killing a number of men who were near. The second was the blowing up of a powdermill at another place. The frightful blast "shattered the whole town, broke the windows, blew down chimneys, and gable-ends not a few."[169]

The reference to providence in the Carleton account of the accident in the Tower, suggests another of Defoe's favorite ideas. The only way to explain the amazing fact that the powder was not ignited by the force of the fall, the author says in effect, is to accede to a belief in Providence. Allusions to Providence are one of the commonest features of Defoe's writings. The way in which Crusoe found himself cared for by Providence

[168] Carleton, pp. 28, 51, 69, 161-2, 239ff.; Lee, II, p. 470.
[169] *Tour*, I, ii, pp. 9, 20, 31.

needs no citation. The long essay in the "Serious Reflections" entitled "On Listening to the Voice of Providence," abounds in such discussions, relating particularly of the traveller who ascribed his good fortune to luck, without "the least sense of the government of Providence" in his affairs.[170]

The fly which, the "Memoirs" asserts, persisted in buzzing about General Richards just before his death at the springing of the Alicante mine has parallels in the "Essay on Apparitions" and elsewhere in Defoe's writings. Compare with it Crusoe's insistence upon the importance of obeying secret hints and mental impressions. Carleton's ideas on predestination, furthermore, agree with Defoe's as expressed in the "Essay on Projects," in the "Consolidator," and elsewhere.[171]

The censure of drinking and duelling in the "Memoirs" is such as Defoe frequently uttered. Carleton's remarks upon the unusual self restraint of the Spaniards in the matter of drinking were, as we have seen, based upon similar statements in the Countess D'Aulnoy letters. But the incident which he is made to relate of an English soldier who disgraced his country by his drunken antics in a public place before a great throng of Spaniards, is unmistakably suggestive of these lines which Defoe had long before written in the "Reformation of Manners."

> Brave T——n, who revell'd day and night,
> And always kept himself too drunk to fight;
> And O——d . . . . strove
> To let the Spaniards see the vice we love.[172]

The discussion of true courage, accompanying the anecdote of the cowardly duellist, has numerous close parallels in Defoe's known works. Commenting on this duellist, the author of the "Memoirs" says: "There is a bravery of the mind which I fansy few of those gentlemen duellists are possess'd of. *True courage* cannot proceed from what Sir Walter Raleigh finely calls the art or philosophy of quarrel. No! It must be the issue of *principle,* and can have no other basis than a steady tenet of *religion.*" In "Duncan Campbell" Defoe speaks of an ambush arranged with much *false courage,* and of the courage of younger brothers being turned into brutish rage, and of their being run through in quarrels. In the "Journal of the Plague Year" he writes of "a sort of *brutal courage* . . . . founded neither on *religion* or prudence," and in the "Review" of there being no "difference between bravery and coward-

---

[170] *Robinson Crusoe,* III, p. 202ff.

[171] Carleton, pp. 240-2; *Academy,* XLIII, p. 46; *Robinson Crusoe* (Dobson's reprint), p. 207; *Consolidator* (Morley), p. 307.

[172] *Collected Writings* (1703), p. 81.

ice, but what is founded in the *principle* they are engaged for." Finally, Mr. Doble calls attention to the verses from "Robinson Crusoe,"

> Among the worst of cowards let him be nam'd
> Who having sinn'd 's afraid to be asham'd;
> And to *mistaken courage* he's betrayed,
> Who having sinn'd 's ashamed to be afraid.[173]

Carleton's account of seamen praying in a storm recalls a frequent circumstance in Defoe's writings. In the "Pacificator" he remarks simply that seamen pray in time of storms. Crusoe mentions seeing some members of the crew at prayer during the Yarmouth storm; concerning the later storm which threw him upon his island he says, there was only time to say "O God." Roxana and her maid Amy, during a storm at sea, have recourse to prayer, as does likewise a member of the ship's crew. There is also one account at least of praying sailors in Defoe's "Storm" (1704).[174]

In his description of the Carleton storm, the author manifests another idea which Defoe held, namely, that the men of earlier times who lived about the Mediterranean shores, being less proficient seamen and having weaker vessels than the modern inhabitants of the west shores of Europe, were alarmed at storms which an English sailor, for example, would not regard as serious. "If Ovid, in the little Archipelagian sea, could whine out his *jam jam jacturus* (*tacturos?*)," says the "Memoirs," ". . . . what words . . . . could serve to paint our passions, or our expectations?" In the second chapter of the "Storm" Defoe treats "of the opinions of the ancients that this island was more subject to storms than other parts of the world," quoting from Horace, Juvenal, and others, and giving expression to their tendency to describe as severe storms which in England create little attention.[175]

Defoe's attitude toward the Boors of Holland, as illustrated by the incident related in "Robinson Crusoe" of their barbarous practice of putting in ovens to roast alive stragglers from the army, reappears in the same anecdote told in almost identical form in the Carleton story,—a circumstance of which both Mr. Doble and Professor Trent have made much. The time of the incident is given differently in the two narrations, but otherwise the accounts are alike. According to the "Memoirs" Carleton, "strolling" from his quarters, ventured to enter one of the

[173] Carleton, p. 6; *Duncan Campbell* (1720), pp. 162, 213-4; *Academy*, XLIII, p. 439. Mr. Doble there cites a number of other references for similar expressions from Defoe.

[174] Carleton, p. 347; *Works* II (1705), p. 158; *Robinson Crusoe*, I, pp. 11, 48; *Roxana*, I (1903), p. 187; *Storm*, p. 194.

[175] Carleton, p. 346; *Storm*, p. 13ff.

peasants' houses which he found unoccupied, but upon advancing a short way he observed at the mouth of the oven "the corpse of a man so bloated . . . . as left" him little room "to doubt that the oven had been the scene of his destiny." Withdrawing in haste, he hurried to the security of the camp. In "Robinson Crusoe" the story is of several English soldiers who, straying from camp and diverting themselves in a peasant dwelling, were set upon by the Boors. Two were killed, and a third was thrust alive into an oven where he smothered, the oven not being hot enough to burn him. The survivors escaped to the camp.[176] Another of Defoe's anecdotes reappearing with little change in the "Memoirs" is that from the "Tour" of a man fallen overboard from a ship; in the "Memoirs" the unfortunate man is Carleton himself. In each case the victim is able by the aid of the ship's ropes to sustain his position until rescue comes.[177]

The Carleton reference to the danger of "pestilential infection," an allusion probably to Dr. Mead's "Short Discourse concerning Pestilential Contagion," is indicative of the author of the "Journal of the Plague Year."[178] Carleton says that "our English sailors" have given to the guitar "the title of strum strums," and Defoe speaks of "our sailors who nickname everything."[179] The Carleton statement that Madrid is only a village Defoe had made shortly before in the "Complete English Trades-man."[180] Suggestive of the "good old Cavalier" of "Robinson Crusoe" and of the "Memoirs of a Cavalier" is the "old Cavalier" mentioned in the Carleton story.[181]

Ravished nuns of Port St. Mary figure both in the "Memoirs" and in the known works of Defoe.[182] The Carleton argument against purgatory, namely, the promise made to the thief on the cross, Mr. Doble thinks smacks of Defoe, who mentions the thief on the cross in the "Family Instructor."[183]

Indications of Defoe's hand in the fabrication of the "Memoirs" is clear from a consideration of the authors and works alluded to, as Mr. Doble has remarked. The principal ones are these: Raleigh, Temple, Shakespeare, "Hudibras," Erasmus, "Don Quixote," and Ovid.[184] Raleigh,

---

[176] Carleton, p. 32; *Robinson Crusoe*, III, pp. 192-3; Doble, *Academy*, XLIII, p. 439; Trent, *Defoe*, p. 210, Note 10.

[177] Carleton, p. 338; *Tour*, I, ii, p. 23.

[178] Carleton, p. 235.

[179] Carleton, p. 279; *Tour*, III, iii, p. 9.

[180] *Academy*, XLIII, p. 483; Carleton, p. 309.

[181] Carleton, p. 118; *Robinson Crusoe*, III, p. 143.

[182] Carleton, p. 248; *Works*, II, p. 106.

[183] *Academy*, XLIII, p. 483.

[184] Carleton, pp. 7, 12, 42, 71, 181, 244, 275, 291, 299, 341.

to whose family he claimed relationship, was a favorite hero of Defoe. His "History of the World,"[185] containing the statement to which the "Memoirs" alludes, was among the books in Defoe's library.[186]   That Defoe mentions Raleigh in at least eight of his other works, and always with the highest praise, is the assertion of Mr. Doble.[187]

Temple, as Mr. Doble observes, was too familiar for Swift to use, whereas Defoe frequently quoted from him, as in the case of the storm previously mentioned. "Hudibras" Swift is said to have known by heart; but Defoe twice uses the phrase "honor's trucklebed," from the couplet given in the "Memoirs."[188]   Erasmus he mentions occasionally, and "Don Quixote" very frequently.[189]   Of especial significance is the description in the Carleton memoirs of a Spaniard mounted on a mule and armed in such a ridiculous manner that he outdid "the ever renown'd Don Quixote" himself.   Crusoe, it will be recalled, met while in China a greasy don travelling in a state of perfect quixotism.[190]   In the preface to the "Serious Reflections," Defoe transforms an envious critic's comparison of "Robinson Crusoe" to "Don Quixote" into the highest praise, by showing that the latter was intended as a satire on a well-known Spanish character of the day.   The author of the "Memoirs" calls it a "facetious but satyrical romance."[191]

The very errors in the Carleton narrative are indicative of Defoe, who was a hasty writer and who wasted few tears over careless statements.   The contradictions of fact in "Robinson Crusoe," "Captain Singleton," and "Roxana" have already been commented upon; all of his longer works abound in them.   The "Memoirs of a Cavalier," though purporting to have been written previously to the battle of Worcester in 1651, and to have been preserved in manuscript until the time of publication, contains references to many events subsequent to 1651, and actually carries the story beyond that point; there are in it, moreover, allusions to works of Defoe's own composition.[192]

---

[185] VI (Oxford ed.), p. 459.

[186] *Athenæum,* 1 June, 1895, p. 706ff.

[187] *Tour,* I, iii, p. 85; III, p. 263; *System of Magic* (1840), pp. 18, 31; *History of the Devil* (Bohn ed.), p. 533; *Works,* II, pp. 61, 284; *Storm,* p. 4; *Plan of the English Commerce,* xiii, 148; *Robinson Crusoe,* III (1720), p. 244; *Review,* I, p. 145.

[188] Carleton, p. 71; *Academy,* XLIII, p. 438.

[189] *Academy,* XLIII, p. 395.

[190] Carleton, p. 299; *Robinson Crusoe,* II, p 258.   Mr. Doble has pointed out this parallel.   See, also, Carleton, pp. 213-5; 291.

[191] Carleton, p. 242.

[192] Aitken, Introduction to *Memoirs of a Cavalier,* p. xiii.

An error in the "King of Pirates" has striking similarity to one already pointed out in the Carleton story. We have seen that looking ahead in anticipation of Carleton's future voyage to the Lowlands, the author gives his route as being from Harwich to Rotterdam; but that when several pages later he arrives at the point when Carleton actually sets out, he sends him not from Harwich to Rotterdam, but from Calais to Dover. Obviously he had either forgotten the earlier statement or else suspected, what has proved actually to be true, that the reader would not detect the contradiction. The similar inconsistency in the "King of Pirates" has to do with Avery's journey (probably fictitious) across the isthmus of Darien, for which at two several times Defoe assigns two entirely different routes. In the first place Avery is made to state that having participated in the South Sea piracies under Sharp and Hawkins (Sawkins?) he was one of those who fought their way back sword in hand across the isthmus of Darien. A little farther on, however, when he wishes to give some sage counsel in regard to the dangers of the strait of Magellan, he cites his experiences thereabouts with Sharp and the buccaneers with whom he asserts he returned around Cape Horn from the South Seas.[193] This, of course, contradicts point blank the previous statement that he had fought his way back across Darien. The inconsistency is identical with the one concerning Carleton's journey to Holland, and proceeds from the same cause, either forgetfulness or indifference. That in neither case did the author possess information as to the route taken by his hero is probable. Defoe's characters frequently pass between Harwich and the Brill (Rotterdam) and between Calais and Dover; so that off hand he might send Carleton by either of these two routes, or by both, as he actually did.[194]

Even the classical tone of the "Memoirs," which Parnell thought far above Defoe, proves to be in strict accord with his other writings. As Mr. Doble has observed, Swift's knowledge of the classics was far above Defoe's whose frequent quotations from the Latin, especially, are often according to zeal rather than knowledge. In harmony with this Professor Trent remarks that Defoe had a wide command of foreign languages, but was often slipshod in the use of them.[195]

When we come to inquire into the character of the classical quotations of the Carleton narrative we discover them to be full of error.

[193] *King of Pirates* (Aitken), pp. 9, 19.

[194] *Tour*, I, i, p. 49; *Moll Flanders*, II (1903), p. 104; *Roxana*, I (1903), p. 192ff.; *Robinson Crusoe*, I, p. 338; *Memoirs of a Cavalier*, p. 6. Similar carelessness appears in the dedication of the memoirs of Carleton to "Spencer Lord Compton." Here was an error which could not pass unnoticed, and the reissue of several days later corrected it to "Spencer Lord Wilmington."

[195] Trent, *Defoe*, p. 5.

"Maecenas" is misspelt in the dedication; "Nihil obstabit eunte" is the blundering Latin given as the inscription on a French shield; "Dulci est pro patria mori" Defoe had satirically quoted and mistranslated elsewhere; Ovid's "jam jam tacturos" is misquoted as "jam jam jacturus." These facts have been shown earlier by Mr. Doble, who adds that the Latin epilogue was not written by a trained scholar.[196]

The allusions in the "Memoirs" to Hannibal and Scipio are such as we have a right to expect from Defoe, who in 1712 had written "Hannibal at the Gates," and who mentions Scipio in the "Tour," and both Hannibal and Scipio in the "Review," calling William III "the Scipio of his native country." The phrase from Vergil, "Hoc opus, hic labor," occurs dozens of times in the writings of Defoe, who upon one occasion inverts as Carleton does the order of the two members. The Carleton phrase "in terrorem" also was employed elsewhere by Defoe.[197]

Passing on to a consideration of the statements by which the author of the "Memoirs" supplements the facts given him in his sources, we find additional evidence for believing that Defoe was the author for whom we are seeking. Though the great body of the narrative was taken from published sources and, therefore, affords no indications as far as concerns substance of who compiled it, there are throughout the book traces of amplifying information contributed by the writer. Nearly always these point to a well-informed Englishman, particularly to a Londoner, and not infrequently to Defoe himself.

This is true of the paragraph in the "Memoirs" devoted to the *Catherine*. The facts of the capture and recovery of that vessel at the battle of Sole-bay were taken almost verbatim from the "Gazette," but the supplemental information that in a later fight she was commanded by the Earl of Mulgrave ("afterwards Duke of Buckingham"), who had a picture of her painted in his house in St. James Park, is a contribution of the author. The *Catherine,* as Mr. Doble shows, was no new subject with Defoe. He mentions her in the "Tour," where he speaks also of the fine pictures in the Duke of Buckingham's house; this house he had described earlier in the "Dyet of Poland."[198]

To the "Gazette's" bare mention of the Galloper, the "Memoirs" adds (erroneously) that it is a sand upon which the *Charles* was lost in the previous war. In the "Storm" Defoe called the Galloper a very dangerous sand, and in the "Essay on Projects" mentioned the *Charles* as "a first-rate ship, being of a reddish colour."[199]

---

[196] *Academy*, XLIII, p. 394; Carleton, pp. 36, 344, 352.
[197] *Academy*, XLIII, p. 394.
[198] *Academy*, XLIII, p. 439.
[199] Carleton, p. 2; *Storm*, p. 218; *Academy*, XLIII, p. 439.

That London was the standard of comparison both for Defoe and for the author of the "Memoirs" Mr. Doble has remarked. The latter likens a Spanish carnival to Bartholomew Fair, mentions "Major Harding, now a justice in Westminster," and speaks of "our oars on the Thames." The Carleton reference to the dexterity of London firemen particularly points to Defoe who in the "Tour" tells of the care taken in quenching London fires.[200] Defoe's knowledge of London was, of course, as intimate as that of Dickens with whom he has more in common than is often suspected.

Defoe's wide reading of history, manifested especially in his poems and tracts, which are studded with allusions to military achievements from the time of Richelieu and before to those of his own day, has already been commented upon. That he furthermore had the Spanish war at his fingers' ends is the assertion of Mr. Doble, who points out that at the time Defoe was conducting the "Review" and, therefore, was compelled to keep closely informed of all that passed. His contemporary allusions to the conduct of Peterborough and Galway have already been mentioned. Among other matters which he discussed and which are treated in the "Memoirs" are, the bloodthirsty character of the Miquelets; the taking of Barcelona; the French siege of Barcelona (including the raising of the siege and the eclipse accompanying it); the battles of Almanza and Villa Viciosa, and the springing of the Alicante mine.[201]

The author of the "Memoirs," furthermore, writes from an intimate acquaintance with the physical features of Gibraltar and of its value as a military stronghold. Such an acquaintance Defoe possessed, having the year previously to the publication of the "Memoirs" issued a work entitled "Evident Approach of a War . . . . (with) an exact plan and description of the Bay and City of Gibraltar." His "Complete English Gentleman" gives further indication of familiarity with Gibraltar and military operations before it.[202]

Though the major portion of the comments of the "Memoirs" upon Spain and its people were based upon suggestions taken from the D'Aulnoy letters, much of the same information Defoe possessed prior to the composition of the work. We know that he had visited Spain, and suspect that he may have lived there for a while. It is more than probable, too, that he had read the D'Aulnoy letters long before, and returned to them when composing the Carleton narrative. The Manzanares bridge, for instance, he mentions in the "Tour," and the Guadiana River twice in the "Tour"

[200] Carleton, pp. 184, 241, 331; *Tour*, II, ii, p. 148ff.; *Academy*, XLIII, p. 439.

[201] Carleton, pp. 98ff., 140ff., 208ff., 261; *Review*, III, pp. 310, 465, 221, 233, 314; VII, pp. 279, 509, 530; Lee, II, p. 470. Cited from Mr. Doble's article, *Academy*, XLIII, p. 482.

[202] *Complete English Gentleman*, p. 227; *Academy*, XLIII, p. 482.

and once in the "Review." Elsewhere he speaks of the Spanish bull feasts and Spanish wine.[203]

Stronger or more varied evidence that Defoe actually wrote the Carleton story can hardly be expected in the absence of direct contemporary testimony to the fact. The book from beginning to end is a fabrication; it could have been written by neither Carleton nor Swift; and it bears traces of Defoe's pen throughout. In substance and method of composition it closely resembles his other narratives, and it manifests in abundance his favorite ideas and sentiments, anecdotes, literary mannerisms, and power of securing credence. To the frank acceptance of the conclusion to which every indication unmistakably points, namely, that Defoe fabricated the "Memoirs," there is but one alternative: the taking refuge in the fantastic theory once advanced in certain quarters that Defoe had a literary double, or man Friday, who could exactly duplicate his style and manner of composition.

V. *The Composition of the "Memoirs of Captain Carleton"*

Having thus fully determined that the "Memoirs" came from his pen, we may proceed with the consideration of the way in which it was composed, a consideration greatly simplified by the facts already discovered as to the nature of the materials which entered into it. Carleton's contributions to the story are, as we have seen, very meagre. And we are now ready to cast aside as mistaken the idea, held by Lockhart, Doble, Stebbing, and others, that Defoe, "after his manner, worked up Carleton's anecdotes and reminiscences into literary shape"; for there are no traces of his anecdotes and recollections discoverable in the book. The great body of historic facts and semi-facts, being taken from previously published records, he had no reason to compile. The numerous anecdotes, such as those of birds, of powder explosions, of swarms of locusts, and of men baked in ovens, may likewise be ruled out, as they point directly to Defoe. We may, furthermore, modify Professor Trent's statement that we shall never know whether Defoe revamped a manuscript written by Carleton or an agent for him; whether he utilized Carleton's memoranda and conversation merely; or whether he made up the entire book on his knowledge of the events of the period and a few hints with regard to Carleton's personality and career derived from an unknown source. The first of these possibilities is now clearly untenable.[204]

[203] Carleton, pp. 305, 256; *Tour*, I, ii, p. 92; III, i, p. 126; iv, p. 83; *Review*, III, p. 27ff.; Lee, III, p. 460; *Works*, I (1703), p. 102; *Academy*, XLIII, p. 483.

[204] J. G. Lockhart, *Life of Scott*, III (1902), p. 74; Parnell, *English Historical Review*, VI, pp. 114, 149; Doble, *Academy*, XLIII, p. 483; W. Stebbing, *Peterborough* (1890), p. 55; W. P. Trent, *Defoe*, p. 264.

For our purposes as students of Defoe's literary method the very imperfections of the book have their merit. They enable us to analyze the composition more completely than is possible in the case of "Robinson Crusoe" and "Captain Singleton." Whether or not it is a work of great importance may be open to question, though men of literary judgment, such as Dr. Johnson, who sat up most of the night reading it, and Sir Walter Scott, have mentioned it with praise. That it was written with the care which was expended upon the narratives of Crusoe and Singleton few will contend. Its elements are to a less degree blended, and its style is inferior.

Our knowledge of the sources allows us to point out the tangible materials of which the story is composed. The discernible elements, four in number, are (1) the slender thread of Carleton's actual career; (2) the general historical facts from Boyer and Freind; (3) the more specific details from the "Gazette" and other periodicals; and (4) the non-historical anecdotes and topographical descriptions. Upon these materials Defoe expended no great degree of artistry. Though his powers were undoubtedly declining, he retained the gift of writing plausible, smoothly flowing narrative. In spite of the fact that many passages taken from other works are changed so slightly as to betray their origin, the story must be convincing, or else so many men would not have rushed in to defend its genuineness. In addition to Dr. Johnson and Sir Walter Scott, there have been William Lee, Sir Leslie Stephen, and many others, especially military men, who have believed it implicitly.

What Defoe did was this. The thread of Carleton's military activity he used as a general guide in searching for source materials in the histories, newspapers, and books of travel. Upon the basis of Carleton's career he erected a superstructure of the larger historical events which Carleton, though a minor participant in them, is made to recall; those are chiefly from Boyer and Freind. This structure he finished with fictitious accounts of Carleton's own performances fabricated from the newspaper reports of the more detailed happenings. These are to lend the air of close personal acquaintance with the events, an air which is only superficially present in the "Memoirs." Finally, complementing and adorning the work, are the entertaining observations and anecdotes which the leisurely and imperturbed narrative allows room for.

CHAPTER V

Defoe's Method of Composition

In the opening chapter of this study were set forth four explanations commonly given by writers on Defoe to account for his fundamental methods of narration. The first of these, that Defoe's fictions issued from the picaresque tradition of "Lazarillo de Tormes" and of the "English Rogue," was there shown to be in general unfounded. Our investigation of the materials of "Robinson Crusoe" now enables us, furthermore, to discard the assertions of Professor Cross and Dr. Wackwitz of specific instances of Defoe's use of ideas and details from the "English Rogue." "Robinson Crusoe," we may be sure, owes nothing discoverable to that, or to any other, picaresque narrative.

The other three explanations, emphasizing the place of mendacious journalism, the writing of biography (chiefly of criminals), and the writing of moral treatises, have to do more with his own earlier compositions than with the literary current to which he turned for materials and inspiration when he began his fictions. The value of all these to his training is obvious, though, as has been pointed out, the mendacious element in his journalism has been overstated, and though he wrote little biography until after "Robinson Crusoe" and "Captain Singleton" were published. The fourth explanation, accounting for his method as influenced by the writing of moral treatises, is most satisfactory of all, taking into account his long career as a miscellaneous writer, and especially his semi-fictitious works, such as the "Family Instructor" and the "Continuation of the Letters of the Turkish Spy."

These last three explanations define sufficiently, I think, the training which fitted him for the rôle of novelist, but not the source of the inspiration and of the materials of those novels. For that, as our study of his sources has shown, we must turn to the literature of voyages and travels and of authentic (or what passed for authentic) adventure.

Upon "Robinson Crusoe" we have detected the general influence of Hakluyt and Purchas, and the specific influence of a number of other works of similar character. Among them are: the published accounts of Selkirk's experience on Juan Fernandez, Knox's "Ceylon," Dampier's "Voyages," Misson's "Voyage of Leguat," Pitman's "Relation," Le Comte's "China," and Ides's "Travels." This, of course, includes only those works which we know were used by Defoe. In "Captain Singleton" there is, in addition to the general obligation to Hakluyt and Purchas, the detailed borrowing from Mandelslo's "Travels," "Leguat," the accounts of Avery, Dampier, Knox, and the "Bucaniers of America." Even in the "Memoirs of Captain Carleton" (an historical narrative) the influence of the Countess D'Aulnoy's "Letters" telling of her journey into Spain is marked, and slight traces of Purchas and of similar works of travel are apparent. Other parts of the Carleton story and the whole of the "Journal of the Plague Year" are deeply rooted in genuine records of histories and periodicals.

These facts have been demonstrated for "Robinson Crusoe," "Captain Singleton," and the "Memoirs of Captain Carleton" in this study. The sources of the "Journal of the Plague Year," the chief of which were pointed out by Mr. Aitken a quarter century ago,[1] have recently been considered in detail by Dr. Watson Nicholson, who, unfortunately, has misunderstood his problem.[2] For instead of studying the sources of the "Journal" for the light they may throw upon Defoe's methods, Dr. Nicholson has launched into an unwarranted and amateurish attempt to establish "the complete authenticity" of the "Journal," which, he argues, "is a faithful record of historical facts" and should be removed from the shelves of fiction to those of history. The "Journal" is not history. It consists of a mass of the actual facts of history borrowed from truthful records and mixed with considerable illustrative matter (fictitious and semi-fictitious) invented from suggestions in those records; and the whole is related as the actual experiences and recollections of a man who, unlike Carleton, appears to be entirely imaginary. The narrative is history only in the same sense as the Cavalier and the Carleton memoirs might be called history, and has long ago been so judged by Mr. Aitken and others.

That the "Journal" is not actually history in any true sense Dr. Nicholson himself knows and incautiously admits in numerous instances throughout his book. He concedes, for example, that much of the illustrative material is true only in that it is in keeping with the spirit of the time,[3]— a conception which would logically lead to classifying "Woodstock" and "Henry Esmond" as history. He confesses, furthermore, that Defoe's memory was a "fruitful source" drawn upon for the "Journal"; that he

---

[1] Introduction to *Journal of the Plague Year* (Everyman), pp. ix, xii, xiii.

[2] Watson Nicholson, *The Historical Sources of Defoe's Journal of the Plague Year*, 1919.

[3] Nicholson, p. 14ff. There he discusses parallels for the Solomon Eagle episode. The whole first chapter is an attempt to disguise the fact that the writer cannot substantiate many such accounts in the *Journal*.

possessed a "natural predilection for invention"; and that seeing he must soon exhaust his fund of information he was forced "to repeat his stories" and "to embroider upon his facts by circling round and round them."[4] Further evidence that the "Journal" is not reliable history is unnecessary, and Dr. Nicholson's contention may be dismissed as valueless.

An unfortunate result of Dr. Nicholson's procedure is that the useful information which he possesses of the detailed dependence of Defoe upon his sources is obscured and partially crowded out of his discussion to make room for his misguided effort to prove the narrative authentic. It is evident, however, that Hodges's "Loimologia," Vincent's "God's Terrible Voice in the City," and the weekly bills of mortality were, as Mr. Aitken asserted, drawn upon extensively in the fabrication of the "Journal," and that a number of other treatises on, and historical accounts of, the great plague of 1665 were used to a lesser extent.

Due in part no doubt to Defoe's dependence upon authentic narratives, whether of history or of travel, are the structural defects of his plots; that is to say, those features which appear to be defects in the light of more recent development of plot construction. He writes in imitation of true records. If the narratives of the military careers of the Cavalier and of Carleton are to pass as authentic, they must resemble history; if "Robinson Crusoe" and "Captain Singleton" are to receive credence they must resemble the genuine accounts of travellers and adventurers. Obviously these genuine records, whether of military activity or of travel, have little to offer as models of well designed plot.

"Robinson Crusoe," as others have remarked, imitates life in its very shapelessness. Crusoe endures two years of slavery at Salee, follows the life of a Brazil planter for four more, spends twenty-eight years on his island, trades back and forth in the East Indies for a half dozen years, wanders into China, and, finally, returns to England through Russia and Germany. Singleton starts out as a young sailor, drifts into piracy, acquires wealth, and likewise returns to England. The plot of the Carleton story does not differ in character from these two, though that of the "Journal of the Plague Year" is in some respects an exception.

The fact that Defoe is attempting to have his stories pass as authentic relations means that he must give the larger features of history and of geography with fidelity,—a truth which Dr. Nicholson apparently fails to understand. When he fabricates the journal of an imaginary saddler who endured the rigors of the great plague, or describes fictitious exploits of Carleton in the wars of Flanders, Defoe incorporates in the narrative a large proportion of authentic happenings; not to do so would lay him

[4] *Ibid.*, pp. 3, 89, 94, 98.

open to immediate detection as a writer of fiction. Where does he get those facts? He borrows them from histories and newspapers. In the invention of action the writer of historical fiction is always limited more or less to matters in which he will not seriously conflict with the statements of history.

It is evident that Defoe had no conscious intention of constructing what we now mean by plot. For the account of Crusoe's journey through Tartary and Muscovy, he consulted but one source, taking therefrom fact after fact without any great effort to transform them; the narrative, consequently, suffers a distinct loss of interest. Other portions of "Robinson Crusoe," such as the island story, and the African journey of "Captain Singleton" show clearly a desire upon the part of the author to concentrate upon a single problem, in the solution of which he subdues the vast collection of details from different sources to one unifying plan. The "Journal of the Plague Year," as is often remarked, has a unity arising from the nature of the subject. But even in the Carleton story there are traces of an effort to manipulate the incidents for the artistic purposes of fiction. The account of Carleton's activity at Fort Kenocque is omitted to make room for the invented exploits at Namur, which were to introduce him to Lord Cutts and the Earl of Peterborough. It is clear, therefore, that had Defoe attempted the construction of a unified plot he would have been successful.

That Defoe foresaw the value of the island situation in "Robinson Crusoe" and of the African journey in "Captain Singleton" is, as I have remarked earlier, unlikely. The island story is but a single episode, preceded and followed by other episodes. Apparently Defoe started out to send Crusoe upon a series of adventures, one of which was to be upon a desert island, but this last grew on his hands until it filled the rest of the volume, leaving the subsequent adventures to wait for a second part. In "Captain Singleton," similarly, his purpose appears to have been to write a tale of piracy; the African journey, however, absorbed his interest, and delayed the account of piracy.

These instances from "Robinson Crusoe" and "Captain Singleton" are sufficient indication that in the subdivisions the plot structure is firmer than in the novels as a whole. The narratives of Crusoe's Asiatic adventures and of Singleton's piracies, also, possess a degree of unity. All of his narratives studied have unity in the person of their hero. Crusoe remembers that he is writing an account of his own adventures in Siberia, and not a description of the Tartars.[5]

[5] *Robinson Crusoe*, II, p. 295.

Though deficient in the construction of plot, Defoe is a master of incident. He has an eye for action. Far-away places interested him, not as subjects for abstract speculation or description, but as possible ground for human adventure. The vast unexplored regions of Tartary and Muscovy and Africa, and the seas about Australia, challenged him to send his heroes through them.

For these travels suitable action must be invented. This action, however, nearly always has an element of truth at its base—a suggestion found in the source. The island story of Crusoe is founded upon fact. Its suggestions came from the experiences of Selkirk, Knox, and others. Even the incidents were appropriated from numerous authentic records. Crusoe's practice of keeping goats in pens and breeding his tame flocks has its origin in the genuine experience of Robert Knox; his growing of grain and other vegetables from seed brought from the ship is the amplification of an incident in the Leguat story; his methods of housebuilding and of constructing canoes are taken from Dampier.

The incident in the "Farther Adventures" of the purchase of a vessel with which a pirate crew had run away after the captain had been murdered by Malayans is, as we have seen, adapted with little change from Dampier's report of Captain Johnson's experiences. More characteristic is the account of Crusoe's adventures with the natives around Tonquin Bay. Dampier had stated that the people were addicted to the practice of enslaving seamen shipwrecked upon their coasts. With this suggestion Defoe invented a detailed account of how Crusoe and his men, having careened their vessel on the beach, avoided the attempt of the natives to enslave them. Similarly Crusoe's greasy Chinese don who rode in a "state of perfect quixotism" is a striking example of the way in which Defoe improved upon the impersonal descriptions in his sources. Le Comte told of the inordinate pride of even the meaner sort of Chinese magistrates and of their pretentious but tawdry dress. Defoe visualizes the situation, and portrays one of those petty lords in his slovenliness and his beggarly pride. So from Ides's account of the superstitious idol worship of the Tartars he invents an exciting episode in which Crusoe helps to destroy one of their filthy gods. Suggestions from Ides concerning the Kalmuck-Tartar brigands reappear in "Robinson Crusoe" in the form of desperate encounters with those brigands. Writers on Muscovy mentioned Tobolsk as the capital of Siberia whither the Russian state prisoners were exiled; Crusoe carries one of those exiled lords to freedom.

Defoe's procedure in "Captain Singleton" is exactly the same as in Crusoe's story. He read in Mandelslo that the people of Madagascar, valuing brass and tin above gold and silver, trade cattle and other commodities for brass trinkets; he read in Dampier of a cutler whose duty it was to keep the party supplied with scraps of metal for bartering with the natives; he read in the story of Leguat of a silversmith who was useful in making nails and other necessities of the sort. With these three suggestions he created Singleton's cutler or artist or silversmith (he calls him by all three titles) who contrived trinkets of many kinds and also (like Leguat's silversmith) made nails.

The geographies told of the ravenous beasts of Central Africa, and of the hybrids resulting from cross breeding at the watering places. Singleton is made to relate the desperate attempts of those beasts to force the palisades of his camp, and especially of a monster "which seemed to be of an ill-gendered kind, between a tiger and a leopard." The most exciting episode in the Singleton story is, perhaps, the hollow tree fight on the north coast of Tasmania. The treachery of the people of that region Dampier had described, dwelling upon their sullenness and their practice of killing indiscriminately any Europeans whom they could get in their power. These traits Defoe puts into action. To the hollow tree siege he brings all his interest in powder explosions and in heroic action, and his power of realizing a scene.

In the "Journal of the Plague Year" much of the illustrative material is thus invented or at least worked over to fit his purposes. The incident of Solomon Eagle, the Quaker fanatic who ran about the streets naked, prophesying all manner of calamity, is an example of this fact. No such character figures in Defoe's known sources, and the attempt of Dr. Nicholson to identify him with John Gibson[6] only serves to emphasize the fictitious nature of the episode. Unquestionably, as Dr. Nicholson asserts, Defoe had a prototype for Solomon Eagle;[7] but so did Shakespeare for Falstaff, and Thackeray for Becky Sharp.

The inventions in the "Journal" are naturally limited in great measure to incident. This is the case, likewise, in the Carleton story. The principal events are in the main authentic happenings; but Carleton's part in those happenings is fiction. The well-known fact that after the battle of Solebay the body of the Earl of Sandwich was found floating at sea becomes a nucleus for the fictitious statement that the discoverer was the master of a packet boat running between Harwich and the Brill, who later told Carleton of the circumstance. Though Carleton was at the battle of Seneffe, the account in the "Memoirs" of his flight over a hedge to a hill from which he watched the operations below, is Defoe's invention from

[6] Nicholson, p. 14ff.

[7] The name is suspiciously like that of the leading character in a seventeenth century play entitled *Sir Solomon Single*. This drama was performed as late as May 21, 1714. (Genest, II, p. 526.)

suggestions contained in the "Gazette's" reports of the fight. The versions of the sieges of Mastricht, Namur, and Barcelona, and of the taking of Lethindy Castle are on the whole truthful; but the exploits attributed to Carleton therein are fictitious.

This presence of fact in his narratives is important. It helps us to understand why they are convincing. They impress us as being authentic matter-of-fact records because they are to a large extent made up of actual occurrences, though these are transformed for purposes of fiction. Defoe's invention begins where history leaves off, embroidering fiction around the facts.   Over it all he extends the atmosphere of truth and actuality; and he may defy any one unacquainted with his source materials to determine when he passes the border line of truth into the field of fiction.   For the reader of the Carleton account of Seneffe and of the retreat from Arseel, truth is inextricably blended with fiction, though the presence of the latter has not been suspected by many readers—among them Dr. Johnson, Sir Walter Scott, and a number of military men.

With the background of his narratives Defoe works more carefully than is usually recognized. This is true especially of the geographical and physiographical features in his stories of travel and adventure in foreign lands. There, as we have observed in considering "Robinson Crusoe" and "Captain Singleton," he endeavors to secure the most accurate information available. The reason for this is not that he scrupled to deceive, but that he was jealous of his reputation for learning, and that he prided himself particularly upon having the world's geography at his fingers' ends. Accuracy in such external matters was, moreover, one of his methods of securing credence. He was not, we may be sure, the shrewd uncanny guesser, anticipating modern geographical discoveries at significant points, that Professor Minto and others thought him to be. Nor is there any indication that for his physiographical facts he used unpublished notes and maps of actual travellers to which the general public of his day did not have access. In places where the geographies were plainly inadequate, he occasionally ventures a solution of his own; but that solution is merely what appears to him to be most probable from the information given in the maps. Thus he has Singleton sail through the strait between Australia and Tasmania, though the map-makers of the time did not believe that any such strait was there. The maps, however, showed no coast line connecting the two islands, and Defoe rightly assumed that none existed. His more usual practice, however, is to adhere to facts as set forth by reputable geographers and map-makers.

To the matter of historical accuracy "Robinson Crusoe" and "Captain Singleton" are almost entirely indifferent. The former, as we have seen, mentions neither the civil war, which had not closed when in 1651 Crusoe ran away to sea, nor the revolution of 1688, which occurred about the time of his return to England at the end of Part I. Defoe ignores likewise the state of war existing at Salee throughout the time of Crusoe's period of slavery there. In the "Journal of the Plague Year" and the "Memoirs of Carleton" he is, of course, alert to historical facts; they replace in a manner the geographical element of "Robinson Crusoe" and "Captain Singleton."

In the use of that more intangible thing called atmosphere, Defoe is not uniformly successful. The account of Singleton as a pirate is almost as colorless as its models. Singleton and Quaker William are the only characters of whom the reader is aware; the seamen and the ships are shadowy objects necessary to the progress of the adventure but not essential to its interest. Though expert at handling dialogue between two characters, Defoe very seldom introduces more than two at once. General conversation of a group of characters he seems unable to manage. One or two individuals stand out; the others are indicated vaguely. On the other hand, the island story of Crusoe and the African journey of Singleton have discernible an appropriate and consistent tone or atmosphere. His best performance in that respect is, no doubt, the "Journal of the Plague Year," for, though part of the credit for the excellency of that feature of the "Journal" belongs to his sources, some of which Dr. Nicholson regards as superior to it, Defoe's accomplishment there is worthy of high admiration.

His characters are usually motivated satisfactorily. Crusoe's roving trait to a large extent determines the course of the action. It was this adventurous disposition that led him successively to London, Guinea, Salee, Brazil, and his island; that took him from his family back to the island; that kept him occupied for years trading in the Orient; and that at last induced him to return through the unexplored domains of Tartary and Muscovy. Singleton's career as a pirate is prepared for by a series of misfortunes which befell an otherwise promising youth and led him into bad associations. While very young he was kidnapped and passed about among professional criminals; later at sea his rescue from Barbary pirates threw him into the company of Portuguese seamen, from whom he "learned particularly to be an arrant thief and a bad sailor." With neither education nor principle to guide him, he drifted by stages into open piracy.

A little more unusual was the induction of Quaker William into the pirate calling. William obviously liked the excitement and profits of the trade, but was too prudent to run unnecessarily the risk of hanging. When, therefore, as a captive he accepted the opportunity of joining Singleton's crew, he insisted upon receiving a written statement certifying that he served under compulsion. By avoiding violence and by discouraging cruelty on the part of others whenever possible, he sought no doubt to ease his conscience; upon occasion, however, he was an intrepid fighter.

In the Carleton story there are good illustrations of how a writer of fiction may use his materials to motivate the action. Consider, for instance, the description of the siege of Mastricht. Defoe knew that Carleton was there, and that later he became an ensign, but did not know just what Carleton's actions were in that operation. How does he proceed? He attributes to Carleton an important share in the fighting and rewards him with a commission in Sir John Fenwick's regiment,—an organization of which Carleton was at no time a member. The reason for assigning him to Fenwick's is not hard to find. The prominent part played in the siege by that unit was mentioned in all the reports. Fenwick, moreover, was better known than the commanders of the other English regiments, especial attention having been called to him through his connection with the conspiracy of 1696, for which he was executed. Carleton's fictitious exploits at the capture of Lethindy Castle are offered in explanation of his promotion to a captaincy in Tiffin's. A more significant series of inventions, those having to do with the pretended services of Carleton at Namur (where he gained the attention of Lord Cutts) and in apprehending certain of the conspirators of 1696, paved the way for his elevation to Peterborough's staff in 1705.

We must not forget that Defoe's method of characterization, though it neglects some great possibilities which later novelists were to develop, was nevertheless very effective in certain respects. In addition to a group of lesser men (and women), it produced, in Robinson Crusoe, one of the great personages of fiction.

Though Defoe invariably lets his hero reveal his own character in the process of telling his own story, he is not content to withdraw himself and take a non-committal attitude. His ideas and interests are perpetually creeping into the narrative. One of his most noticeable characteristics is his restraint of sentiment. In his works there is little harrowing of the emotions. Terrifying situations there are; but that probing into the depths of the heart by which Richardson revealed character is almost entirely lacking in Defoe. Though he comments upon the motives and feelings of his men and women, his usual method of portraying character is through the use of incident. The natives along the bay of Tonquin, he says, are a barbarous people. But their barbarity is not abstractly analyzed; it is set forth only in action, principally in their attempt to enslave Crusoe's seamen.

Restraint of sentiment is welcome in the story of Crusoe's island loneliness, where a less skilful writer would have fairly ruined the narrative. Some critics have complained that Defoe is even heartless, citing the fact that he gives Crusoe's dog no name. But such an assumption is unwarranted. Many threads of his narrative are left at loose ends. He has Carleton say that when he became a Spanish prisoner he was given a daily allowance of mutton, so much for himself and so much for his man. This "man" has not been mentioned previously; he is not mentioned again. Defoe at that point suddenly bethought himself of giving to his captain hero a man servant, and having done so as speedily forgot about it.

Nature interested Defoe chiefly for its curious and instructive features, rather than for its sentiment. Anecdotes illustrating the unexplainable instincts of birds he liked; and powder explosions, storms, and earthquakes interested him deeply.

In spite of his lack of emotionalism, Defoe had a genuine concern about life. We may feel that he dissociated belief and conduct too much, but of the sincerity of his moralizing we can have no question. Though a religious element enters all his principal sources for "Robinson Crusoe," he goes much beyond them. Not only does he have Crusoe embrace Christianity in his island solitude, but he has him return later with a priest and convert the whole colony which had sprung up in his absence. There is no reason, furthermore, for believing that he was not honest in regarding the "Serious Reflections of Robinson Crusoe" as more important than its two precursors. An insincere man must have suspected that the ordinary reader would care little for it.

The day will come when the student of Defoe, like the modern student of Shakespeare or any other great author, will read the sources of Defoe in his endeavor to understand his author better. In that day the craftsmanship of Defoe will receive more appreciative recognition than formerly. The sources of Defoe are not literature; his best works are. We may concede that his plots as a whole lack unity and suspense; that his portrayal of character is frequently inadequate; and that his story is overloaded with moralizing. But when we pass from considering these shortcomings to view his performance in its larger aspects, we realize that he was a master of the narrative art. His sources are in the main forgotten by all but the historian and, in some cases, the man of letters. Defoe's novels, on the other hand, are receiving increasing attention. A half-dozen of them interest students of literature; several appeal to a large group of more general readers; and one belongs with those literary masterpieces cherished by the people of all nations.

BIBLIOGRAPHY

N. B.—Bibliographical details of passages bearing on minute aspects of Defoe's works are not given here, but are appended in foot notes in their proper places. The following are the most important works appertaining to the subject. The arrangement, however, unless otherwise stated, is chronological.

BIBLIOGRAPHIES OF DEFOE

William Lee, "Daniel Defoe," 1869, vol. i. (To be used with caution.)

Thomas Wright, "The Life of Daniel Defoe," 1894, Appendix D. (This list is based upon William Lee's.)

W. P. Trent, "Bibliographical Notes on Defoe," (in "The Nation," vol. lxxxiv, 1907-8).

"Cambridge History of English Literature," vol. ix (1913), bibliography of chapter 1.

COLLECTIONS CONTAINING HIS IMPORTANT NARRATIVES

"The Novels and Miscellaneous Works of Daniel Defoe," 1840-1, 20 vols. (Oxford).

"The Works of Daniel Defoe," 1840-3, 3 vols. (London).

"The Novels and Miscellaneous Works of Daniel Defoe," 1854-5, 6 vols. (London).

"The Romances and Narratives of Daniel Defoe," 1895-6, 16 vols. (London).

"The Works of Daniel Defoe," 1903, 16 vols. (London and New York).

BIOGRAPHIES AND CRITICISMS: GENERAL

George Chalmers, "The Life of Daniel Defoe," 1785.

Walter Wilson, "Memoirs of the Life and Times of Daniel Defoe," 1830, 3 vols.

William Chadwick, "The Life and Times of Daniel Defoe," 1859.

William Lee, "Daniel Defoe," 1869, 3 vols. (Only the first volume is biographical.)

Leslie Stephen, "Defoe's Novels," (in "Hours in a Library," vol. i, 1907; first printed in the "Cornhill Magazine" in 1871).

William Minto, "Defoe," 1895. (In "English Men of Letters," vol. viii. First published in 1879.)

Thomas Wright, "The Life of Daniel Defoe," 1894.

G. A. Aitken, General Introduction to "Romances and Narratives of Daniel Defoe," vol. i, 1895.

"Defoe's Library," (in the "Athenæum," 1 June, 1895).

W. P. Trent, "Defoe—the Newspaper and the Novel," (in "Cambridge History of English Literature," ix, 1913, chapter 1).

"Daniel Defoe: How to Know Him," 1916.

MATERIALS CONCERNING INDIVIDUAL NARRATIVES

"Robinson Crusoe": Studies bearing thereon.

"Catalogue of the Library of the Royal Geographical Society," 1895.

Arno Schneider, "Die Entwickelung Des Seeromans in England im 17. und 18. Jahrhundert, 1901. (Dissertation, Leipzig.)

Geoffroy Atkinson, "The Extraordinary Voyage in French Literature before 1700," 1920.

"The Extraordinary Voyage in French Literature from 1700 to 1720," 1922.
"A French Desert Island Novel of 1708,' (in "Publications of the Modern Language Association of America," vol. xxxvi).

Henry Kingsley, "Biographical Introduction to 'Robinson Crusoe,' " 1905. (Globe edition; printed first in 1867.)

E. E. Hale, "Daniel Defoe and Thomas Shepard," (in the "Atlantic Monthly," vol. lvi).

G. A. Aitken, Introduction to "Robinson Crusoe" in "Romances and Narratives of Daniel Defoe," vol. i, 1895.

Paul Geissler, "Defoes Theorie über Robinson Crusoe," 1896. (Dissertation, Leipzig; printed at Halle.)

Hermann Ullrich, "Robinson und Robinsonaden," 1898. ("Litterarhistorische-forschungen," hrsg. von J. Schick and M. v. Waldberg, vii heft.)

Max Günther, "Entstehungsgeschichte von Defoes Robinson Crusoe," 1909. (Dissertation, Greifswald.)

Friederich Wackwitz, "Entstehungsgeschichte von D. Defoes 'Robinson Crusoe,' " 1909. (Dissertation, Berlin.)

Léon Polak, "Vordefoesche Robinsonaden in den Niederlanden," (in "Germanisch Romanische Monatschrift," vol. vi).

W. P. Trent, Introduction to "Robinson Crusoe," 1916.

Albert Lüthi, "Daniel Defoe und seine Fortsetzungen zu 'Robinson Crusoe,' " 1920. (Dissertation, Zürich; printed at Stuttgart.)

"Robinson Crusoe": Sources.
(Arranged in order of importance)

Richard Hakluyt, "The Principal Navigations, Voyages, Traffiques, and Discoveries of the English Nation," 1903, 12 vols.

Samuel Purchas, "Hakluytus Posthumus, or Purchas his Pilgrimes," 1905, 20 vols.

Woodes Rogers (Capt.), "A Cruising Voyage round the World," 1712. (Second edition in 1718. Part pertaining to Selkirk reprinted by G. A. Aitken in "Romances and Narratives of Daniel Defoe," vol. iii, 1895, Appendix I; and in Wackwitz's "Entstehungsgeschichte von 'Robinson Crusoe.' ")

Edward Cooke (Capt.), "A Voyage to the South Sea and round the World," 1712. (Part pertaining to Selkirk reprinted in Wackwitz's "Entstehungsgeschichte.")

Richard Steele, an account of Alexander Selkirk, (in "The Englishman," December 1-3, 1713. Reprinted by Aitken in "Romances and Narratives of Daniel Defoe," vol. iii, 1895, Appendix II).

"Providence Displayed: or a very surprising Account of one Mr. Alexander Selkirk." (An anonymous contemporary pamphlet; reprinted in "The Harleian Miscellany," vol. v, 1810, and in Wackwitz's "Entstehungsgeschichte.")

Robert Knox, "An Historical Relation of Ceylon together with (heretofore unpublished autobiographical manuscripts) . . ." 1911. (The "Historical Relation" first appeared in 1681. An important part of it was reprinted by Edward Arber in "An English Garner," vol. i, 1887.)

William Dampier, "A New Voyage round the World," 1697-1709, 4 vols. (A good modern issue, edited by John Masefield, appeared in 1906; this two volume work was based upon the edition of 1717.)

Maximilien Misson, "The Voyage of François Leguat," 1891, 2 vols. (Transcribed from the first English edition and annotated by Captain Pasfield Oliver for the Hakluyt Society.)

Louis Le Comte, "Memoirs and Observations Made in a late Journey through the Empire of China," 1697. (Translated from the French.)

E. Ysbrants Ides, "Three Years Travels from Moscow overland to China," 1706. (Translated from the Dutch.)

Daniel Defoe, "The Storm," 1704.

Henry Pitman, "A relation of the great sufferings . . . of Henry Pitman," 1689. (Reprinted in Arber's "English Garner," vol. vii, 1895.)

Garcilaso de la Vega, "The Royal Commentaries of the Yncas," 1688. (This translation made by Sir Paul Rycaut has been superseded by the more careful one of C. R. Markham, printed for the Hakluyt Society in 1869.)

Henry Neville, "The Isle of Pines, or a late discovery of a fourth Island in Terra Australis, Incognita. . . . " 1668. (Reprinted in an essay by Worthington Chauncy Ford entitled "The Isle of Pines," 1920. Printed privately in Boston.)

Hans Jacob Christoph von Grimmelshausen, "The Adventurous Simplicissimus," 1912. (The first known English translation of this German work of 1669.)

Hendrik Smeeks, "The Narrative of the El-Ho," 1921. (An episode from Smeeks's "Description of the mighty Kingdom of Krinke Kesmes," Amsterdam, 1708; translated by L. L. Hubbard and compared with "Robinson Crusoe.")

John Ogilby, "Africa," 1670.

Adam Olearius, "Voyages and Travels of the Ambassadors," 1662. (Translated from the Dutch.)

"Captain Singleton": Studies bearing thereon.

N. B.—The "Catalogue of the Royal Geographical Society," and the studies by Schneider and Atkinson, listed in the corresponding subdivision under "Robinson Crusoe," pertain also to "Captain Singleton."

Captain Charles Johnson, "General History of the Pyrates," 1724.

William Minto, "Through the Dark Continent in 1720," (in "Macmillan's Magazine," vol. xxxviii).

G. A. Aitken, Introduction to "Captain Singleton" in "Romances and Narratives of Daniel Defoe," vol. vi.

Theodore Watts-Dunton, Introduction to "Captain Singleton," in the "World's Classics," 1906.

C. H. Haring, "The Buccaneers in the West Indies in the XVII Century," 1910.

"Captain Singleton": Sources.

(Arranged in order of importance)

N. B.—Hakluyt, Purchas, Dampier, Misson, Knox, and Ogilby, listed in the corresponding subdivision under "Robinson Crusoe," pertain also to "Captain Singleton."

Daniel Defoe, "The King of Pirates," 1719. (Dated 1720. Reprinted by Aitken in "Romances and Narratives of Daniel Defoe," vol. xvi.)

Adrian Van Broeck (?), "The Life and Adventures of Captain John Avery," 1709.

Charles Johnson, "The Successful Pyrate," 1712. (A drama.)

J. Albert de Mandelslo, "Voyages and Travels," 1662. (Part II of Olearius's "Voyages and Travels of the Ambassadors.")

A. O. Exquemelin, "The Bucaniers of America," 1771, 2 vols. (Fifth edition. The principal parts of the work were first printed in 1684 and 1685.)

Captain Charles Johnson, "Lives and Adventures of the most famous Highwaymen," 1734. (Lives of the highwaymen are reprinted from Captain Alexander Smith's "Highwaymen," 1714.)

Étienne de Flacourt, "Histoire de la grand isle Madagascar," 1661.

"Journal of the Plague Year."

G. A. Aitken, Introduction to the "Journal of the Plague Year" in "Romances and Narratives of Daniel Defoe," 1895.

Watson Nicholson, "The Historical Sources of Defoe's Journal of the Plague Year," 1919.

"The Memoirs of Captain Carleton": Studies bearing thereon.

P. A. Carleton, "The Memorials of the Carleton Family," 1869.

Arthur Parnell (Colonel), "The War of the Succession in Spain," 1888. (Appendix C treats of the "Memoirs.")

"Swift and the Memoirs of Captain Carleton," (in the "English Historical Review," vol. vi).

C. E. Doble, "The Memoirs of Captain Carleton: Swift or Defoe?" (in the "Academy," vol. xliii).

"The Memoirs of Captain Carleton": Sources.

(Arranged in order of importance)

Abel Boyer, "The History of King William III," 1702-3, 3 vols.

"The Life of her late Majesty Queen Anne," 1721, 2 vols.

John Freind, "An Account of the Earl of Peterborow's Conduct in Spain . . . to which is added the Campagne of Valencia," 1707.

Marie Catherine Jumelle de Bernville, Comtesse d'Aulnoy, "The Ingenious and Diverting Letters of the Lady's——Travels into Spain," 1708. (The seventh edition of this French work.)

"The London Gazette," 1672-1700.

"The Post Boy," 1695-6.

"The Flying Post," 1695-6.

INDEX

Africanus, *see* Leo Africanus.

Aitken, G. A., 9, 10, 14-8, 22-3, 25n, 26, 28n, 32, 42n, 54, 63, 77, 87, 90, 104n, 106, 113, 115, 117-8, 127n, 134-6, 140, 144, 161, 165n, 171-3, 206, 208, 211, 224, 231-2.

Alvarez, Sir Francis, 127, 213.

Apparition of Mrs. Veal, 10, 13, 14.

Applebee, John, 16, 116, 219.

Arber, Edward, 23, 90.

Atkinson, Geoffroy, 23n, 30n, 75n, 106, 123.

Augusta Triumphans, 164.

Avery, Captain John, 114-5, 139-145, 147, 231; *see also* Johnson, Charles, *and* Van Broeck.

Baker, D. E., 115n.

Baker, E. A., 172-3.

Barrington, Michael, 172-3.

Bass, Captain George, 154, 156.

Battell, Andrew, 132.

Bernbaum, Ernest, 12-5, 18.

Birdwood, Dr., 113n.

Blackmore, Sir Richard, 198.

Blaeu, Wilhelm, 130.

Boswell, James, 166n.

Boyer, Abel, 175n, 183, 187-190, 192, 194-201, 203, 210-1, 229.

Bucaniers of America, *see* Exquemelin, Ravenau, *and* Ringrose.

Burton, J. H., 168, 172.

Burton, Richard, 12.

Captain Singleton, 10, 12, 16, 17, 19, 28, 30 2, 39-40, 45n, 53, 56n, 58n, 60, 62, 69, 87, 92, 94, 99-100, 102, 106, 112-164, 208, 212, 214, 220, 224, 229-238.

Carleton, George, *see Memoirs of Captain Carleton*.

Carleton, Captain Percival, 167.

Chalmers, George, 206.

Chandler, F. W., 13, 15, 88, 109, 144.

Chatham, Earl of, 17.

Churchill, A., and J., *Voyages*, 118.

Coleridge, S. T., 25, 163.

Collected Writings, 221, 223n, 224n, 228n.

Colonel Jacque, 11, 12, 15, 100, 116, 142, 153, 158, 164, 172, 208, 209, 211.

Complete English Gentleman, 26n, 50, 84, 85, 116, 214n, 227.

Complete English Tradesman, 84, 208, 213-216, 223.

Conjugal Lewdness, 214.

Consolidator, 221

Continuation of the Letters of the Turkish Spy, 12, 16-17, 230.

Cooke, Captain, 110.

Counterfeit Lady, *see* Kirkman.

Covel, Dr. John, 170, 175n, 177, 185.

Craik, G. L., 167, 172.

Cross, W. L., 10, 12-13, 74, 85, 109, 111, 230.

Crossley, James, 168, 172.

Cruso, Timothy, 42n.

Curll, Edmund, 16.

D'Acugna, 103n.

Dalton, Charles, 171-2.

Dampier, William, 26, 28n, 31, 40n, 41, 46, 49-63, 64, 68n, 88, 94, 99n, 100-5, 107, 109-111, 114-5, 117-8, 125-6, 130, 133-4, 137, 140-1, 143, 145, 148, 149-154, 160-3, 212, 230-1, 234-5.

D'Armand, *Algiers*, 86.

D'Aulnoy, Countess, 169, 187, 199, 201-3. 208, 212, 221, 227, 231.

Dawson, W. J., 14.

De Flacourt, Étienne, 117-8, 123, 126n.

Defoe, Daniel; *see also titles of separate works.*

  Bibliography, 10, 17.

  Character, 9-10.

  Character portrayal, 11, 163-4, 237-8.

  Critical opinion concerning, 10-17.

  Debt to literature of travel, 19-20, 24-6, 109, 114, 148, 161, 230-1.

  Historical accuracy, 87-8, 108, 236-7.

  Invention, 22, 109-111, 162, 234-6.

  Materialism in *Captain Singleton*, 164.

  Narrative method, 10, 118, 161, 230ff.

  Picaresque influence upon, 12, 13, 17, 74ff., 163, 230.

  Plots, 162, 232-3.